Also by Michael Moran

The Union of Post Office Workers: a study in political sociology
The Politics of Industrial Relations
The Politics of Banking

Politics and Society in Britain

An Introduction

SECOND EDITION

Michael Moran

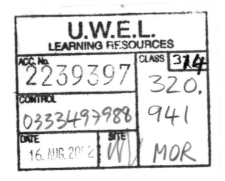

MACMILLAN

First published 1985 by
THE MACMILLAN PRESS LTD
Houndmills, Basingstoke, Hampshire RG21 2XS
and London
Companies and representatives
throughout the world

ISBN 0–333–49798–8 hardcover
ISBN 0–333–49799–6 paperback

A catalogue record for this book is available
from the British Library.

Printed in Hong Kong

Reprinted 1987
Second edition 1989
Reprinted 1990, 1992, 1993

For my mother and
in memory of my father

Contents

List of Tables and Figures   x

Acknowledgements   xi

Preface to the Second Edition   xii

Introduction   xiii

1 The Changing Social Structure   1

  Outline   1
  The First Industrial Nation   2
  Centralisation and the Rise of Class   7
  Equality and Inequality   12
  Economic Markets and Social Change   24
  Class: Persistence, Fragmentation or Realignment?   28
  Conclusion   32

2 Political Culture and Political Instability   33

  Outline   33
  Nature of Political Culture   34
  The Civility Model   35
  Objections to the Civility Model   36
  Alternatives to the Civility Model   39
  Northern Ireland: A Case Study of Instability   49
  Conclusion   57

3 Elections and Electors   59

  Outline   59
  Who Votes?   60

Class and the British Elector   63
The New Electorate   69
The Outcome of Elections   76
Explaining Electoral Change   81
Conclusion   86

4 The Political Parties   **87**

Outline   87
Parties: Organisation and Power   88
Parties and Their Ideologies   97
Parties, Members and Activists   103
Minor Parties   110
Parties in Decline   118
Conclusion   120

5 Pressure Group Politics   **121**

Outline   121
The Nature of Groups   121
Functional Groups: Capital, Labour, Professions   125
Preference Groups and Power   138
Understanding Pressure Group Politics   144
Conclusion   149

6 Rulers and Representatives   **150**

Outline   150
The Study of Elites   150
Political Elites   153
Administrative Elites   161
Economic Elites   167
Elites in Britain: Variety, Change and Stability   170
Power, Ceremony and Secrecy   175
Conclusion   180

7 The Decline of the British State?   **182**

Outline   182
The Decline of the British State   182
The New Economic Order   188
The End of Britain?   199

Recommended Reading   206
References   211
Index   222

List of Tables and Figures

Tables

1.1 English dominance in the United Kingdom, 1988   5
1.2 Regional and national inequality in Britain   9
1.3 Numbers employed in public and private sectors, 1961–86   11
1.4 Changes in housing tenure, United Kingdom, 1914–86   27
3.1 Popular votes and parliamentary representation, 1959 and 1983   80
6.1 Education and occupations of MPs, 1910–87   155
6.2 Education and class origins of Cabinet Ministers, 1916–84   159
6.3 Social and educational background of civil servants   163
6.4 Per cent of selected administrative elites educated at fee-paying schools, 1939–83   166
6.5 The financial elite, 1983   169

Figures

1.1 Trends in infant mortality rates for main occupational classes, 1930–80   16
1.2 Inequalities in earnings, 1913–78   17
1.3 Trends in the distribution of personal wealth, 1923–76   19
3.1 Class composition of Conservative and Labour Party support   65
3.2 Two-party share of vote, 1945–87   70
3.3 Where parties lose and gain votes between one election and the next   78
6.1 The variety of elites in Britain   173

Acknowledgements

I am grateful to David Howell, to Tim May and to three anonymous Macmillan referees for valuable comments on an earlier draft of this book. I learned a great deal from the experience of teaching British Politics with Tim May at Manchester Polytechnic and, latterly, from teaching the same subject with Lewis Minkin; to both I give warm thanks. Martin Burch and Bruce Wood advised me on important particular points. Steven Kennedy was a patient and encouraging editor. The considerable labour of typing successive drafts was done by Lynn Dignan, Karen Hall, Juliet Rodgers, Catherine Smith, Gillian Wooley and Joyce Wolfson: my thanks to them all.

Textbooks are shaped by the experience of teaching. My greatest debt is to the successive generations of students at Manchester Polytechnic and the University of Manchester who have taken my courses since 1970.

Victoria University of Manchester   Michael Moran

The author and publishers are grateful for permission to reproduce the following copyright material: Her Majesty's Stationery Office for permission to use extracts from tables in Cmnd. 7595 (1979–80), Cmnd. 7679 (1979–80), *Inequalities in Health* (1980), *1980 Mortality Statistics* (1983), *Social Trends* (1984); to the authors and to Cambridge University Press for permission to use part of Table 3.6, p. 90, of B. Särlvik and I. Crewe, *Decade of Dealignment* (1983). The quotations at the heads of chapters, and of section 6 of Chapter 2, are taken from the King James Bible.

Preface to the Second Edition

If 'a week is a long time in politics' – as Harold Wilson once memorably suggested – the closing years of the 1980s were an age. In revising this book – originally written in 1983–4 – I have been conscious of the extent of the change, and of the problems this creates. This edition is an interim revision; I have concentrated on bringing the factual discussion up-to-date. There is a case for recasting the whole account of the nature of British politics; but that is a different book.

I am grateful to the colleagues and students who pointed out omissions, mistakes and stupidities in the first edition. These I have tried to correct; doubtless many others still remain.

I am, yet again, indebted to Karen Hall, the most efficient of secretaries. I would also like to thank Steven Kennedy and Keith Povey for their editorial encouragement and guidance.

Victoria University of Manchester   Michael Moran

Introduction

This book is designed to give an introduction to the social fabric of British politics. Its range is therefore narrower but its intended penetration deeper than is usual with introductory texts. The ideal reader will already be studying Britain at an elementary level – for instance, on the early stages of a degree or in the later stages of 'A' level – and will thus know something of the bare institutional outlines of the British system of government. The book largely ignores these familiar outlines, concentrating instead on organisations and processes beyond the range of formal institutions. The work is conventionally organised to cover conventional topics. Chapter 2 examines the changing shape of popular political values in Britain, the connection between those values and political stability, and the particular problem of political stability in Northern Ireland. Chapter 3 examines the changing structure of the electorate, the changing influences shaping individual electoral choice, and the way individual choice, the composition of the electorate and electoral rules combine to produce election results. Chapter 4 describes organisation, ideology and membership of the main party institutions now dominant in Britain. Thumb-nail sketches are also offered of a range of minority parties. Chapter 5 offers a definition and classification of groups, describes how groups operate and estimates the power of different groups. Chapter 6 examines the social composition and political culture of elites in Britain. It begins by defining elites as small minorities occupying prominent positions in institutions, and then discusses the case for studying their social and educational origins. This is followed by an examination of the changing pattern of recruitment at the top of political parties, administrative institutions and elites in the economy.

These chapters form the political core of the book. But it is a truism that the politics of a country are deeply influenced by the social context in which they are conducted. The first and last chapters examine this context. States are surrounded by two very different social environments. The more immediate and noticeable is provided by domestic society. Chapter 1 examines the changing structure of British society. It looks at the historical development of the economy, the changing scale of organisation, the balance between equality and inequality, and the social impact of developing economic markets. But the British state operates not only in British society; it is also a member of a world society populated by other states and by international institutions. This second social context is often neglected in the study of British politics, yet the changing organisation of world society and Britain's altered place in it are central to the condition of our country today. Just over a century ago Britain dominated world society; now she has been relegated to a position of comparative insignificance. The decline of the British state in world society, and its domestic implications, are the concern of the last chapter.

Arguments about the relationship between politics and the wider social context raise some of the most intractable and abstract issues in the social sciences. To what degree, for instance, are political institutions shaped by economic structures? Do political ideas exercise an independent force on political action? Is political change determined by broad historical forces or by the decisive intervention of outstanding personalities? These issues are neglected in this book, not because they are unimportant but because they are too important to be tackled as a subsidiary part of a work whose main purpose is to provide a bread-and-butter summary of evidence about changing values and organisations. The book does not pretend, however, to be plainly descriptive. Although part of the purpose of studying politics is to encourage dispassionate assessment of evidence, 'facts' in politics rarely point decisively to particular conclusions. A body of evidence only begins to make sense when we try to fit it to alternative theories or models. One aim of the succeeding chapters is to describe some of the available alternative models: to ask, for instance, how far changing political values in Britain are the product of the rise of a 'post-affluent' or of a 'populist' culture; how far the 'class model' of British voting behaviour has been superseded; how far a 'corporatist' model makes sense of the changing organisation of pressure groups.

All these questions raise the issue of how far British politics has altered and continues to alter. This fascination with a change is the product of our present political condition. The extensive academic study of British politics dates only from the 1950s and 1960s. Most of those now teaching and writing either began work in those decades or were educated by people and books formed by the experience of that time. Tranquillity, continuity with the past, and decisive government were the most commonly noticed features of British politics in those innocent years. The succeeding decades have been dominated by images of violence, the decay of established institutions, and the multiplication of government failures. These are the images; the succeeding pages examine how far they fit reality.

1
The Changing Social Structure

> We looked for peace, but no good came; and for a time of health, and behold trouble.

> Jeremiah, 8.15

1 Outline

Politics is a social activity. The solitary occupant of a desert island can develop a simple economy, practise religion and produce art; but only the arrival of a Man (or Woman) Friday makes politics either possible or necessary. Because political activity has this special character, it is intimately affected by the way social life is organised: by the historical development of a community; by its economic organisation; by the relations of equality and inequality existing between its members.

This is true of the simplest societies and of ancient, complicated and economically advanced countries like Britain. Our account of Britain therefore begins by sketching the changing social surroundings of British politics. 'The first industrial nation' shows the significance for Britain of early industrialisation. 'Centralisation and the rise of class' shows how the early social impact of industrialisation was consolidated in the twentieth century. 'Equality and inequality' examines trends in class inequalities. 'Economic markets and social change' traces the significant alterations produced by developments in labour markets and in housing markets. 'Class: persistence, fragmentation or realignment' draws together the strands of the evidence to examine a general interpretation of the nature of change in the British social structure.

2 The First Industrial Nation

All countries experience a critical moment that fatally affects their history. Britain's critical moment came in the middle of the eighteenth century with the start of her Industrial Revolution. In the Industrial Revolution she pioneered the greatest economic transformation in world history, and in so doing profoundly altered her own economy and society. Any examination of modern Britain must begin by understanding that transformation and tracing its legacy.

The Industrial Revolution brought vast technical changes, and it greatly altered the landscape, but it was above all a social revolution. Before industrialism Britain was a country where wealth came largely from agriculture; where loyalties were mainly to local communities; and where power and privilege were largely in the hands of a small, hereditary aristocracy. The Industrial Revolution greatly disturbed this traditional social order. It magnified the scale of economic activity, created new wealth and brought into existence new social groups who produced and controlled that wealth. By the middle of the nineteenth century Britain was the first industrial nation in history. Though agriculture and domestic service were still the largest employers, manufacturing and mining were the most dynamic parts of the economy. Though most people still lived in the countryside or in small towns, it was the industrial cities that were growing fastest: between 1801 and 1861, for instance, Birmingham's population grew more than seven-fold, Manchester's by nearly the same magnitude. By the turn of the century Britain was 'the most urbanised country in the world' (Thompson, P., 1975, p. 38). Though government in 1900 was still dominated by a hereditary aristocracy, both the new industrial capitalists and the industrial workers were asserting themselves in politics. In short, industrial change was transforming the country both socially and politically.

The fact that Britain experienced an Industrial Revolution transformed society at home; the fact that she experienced it before any other country dramatically altered her place in the world. By the middle of the nineteenth century the country's international power was unmatched. She dominated the world economy, producing perhaps two-thirds of the world's coal and half its iron (Hobsbawm, 1969, p. 134). Her military power was also unparalleled, particularly at sea. She was in turn using this military power to create the largest empire in history. This empire secured raw materials for industry, protected trade routes and provided markets for her manufactured goods.

At home, the Industrial Revolution made society both more complicated and more simple. Industrial development increased the complexity of the social structure by multiplying new industries and new occupations. The division of labour created numerous groups distinguished from each other by their functions, skills and incomes. The new factory system also had its own finely graded internal hierarchies, stretching from owners and managers at the top to unskilled workers at the bottom.

But the factory system also contained the bones of a new social structure which, by growing over traditional social distinctions, simplified the lines of social division. Perkin has expressed the change succinctly: 'the most profound and far-reaching consequence of the Industrial Revolution was the birth of a new class society' (Perkin, 1969, p. 176). Two important features marked this birth. The first was the growth of occupational class, based on common organisations and perceptions of common economic interests between workers in different industries. The second was a corresponding decline in the ability of other social groupings to influence beliefs or to provide the basis for social organisation. Occupational class posed a particularly strong challenge to locality and to religion as signs of social location and as foundations for political alliances.

The distinctive character of local communities was the most obvious victim of industrialism. Before the Industrial Revolution communities were comparatively isolated and often virtually self-sufficient economically. Improved communications, the growth of markets on a national scale, the concentration of populations in large cities: all of these ended the isolation and reduced the distinctiveness of local life. By contrast, class organisation became more widespread both in the economy and in politics. In the late 1880s 'general unions' began to organise manual workers in different industries, and there occurred the first stirrings of an independent labour movement in politics. In the same decade employers also began to organise nationally to meet the unions' challenge in the workplace. In politics, the Conservative Party began to grow into a class party, dominated by an alliance between the controllers of financial institutions, manufacturing industry and landed wealth.

At the outbreak of the First World War in 1914 a 'new class society' had thus been born in Britain. But the infant's development was slow. The hesitant advance of class is well illustrated by the fact that it still only sporadically intruded into politics. In his famous study of crises in Edwardian Britain, Dangerfield (1966) identified only one – arising from industrial conflict – that had the unambiguous marks of class struggle. The others involved constitutional problems (votes for women, the power of the House of Lords) or chiefly arose from a mixture of national loyalties and religious beliefs (the Irish question). Class organisations were also still weak. Trade unions were usually parochial institutions, drawing their strength from particular industries and even from particular districts. Radical politics was dominated by a Liberal Party which represented, not a class, but a collection of economic, religious and territorial interests.

The underlying reasons for the slow advance of class before the First World War merit examination, because they make sense of much that came later. Three reasons are especially important: the uneven initial impact of industrialism; the way the continuing development of the British economy reinforced these initial variations; and the fact that such class divisions as were created by industrialism often corresponded to, and were influenced by, more traditional lines of social cleavage. Each are here examined in turn.

The impact of industrialism transformed British society, but the actual spread of industrial development was both complex and incomplete. In Ireland, industry touched only a small area around Belfast. In Wales and Scotland it was heavily concentrated in particular places and in particular sectors, characteristically in heavy industries like mineral extraction and shipbuilding. Much of English social and economic life was transformed by industrialism (Mathias, 1969). The result gave England an overwhelming dominance in the United Kingdom. Even by the beginning of the nineteenth century, she dominated the UK in both population and wealth. In the last one hundred and eighty years, as Table 1.1 shows, this domination has been consolidated. But even in England, the advance of industry opened up great territorial gaps: in the nineteenth century, for instance, the North of England was economically dynamic and industrial, much of the South stagnant and rural.

While economic change in Britain thus undoubtedly broke down the isolation and distinctiveness of small communities it by no means eliminated territorial divisions; on the contrary, by widening the gap between the economically advanced and the backward it

TABLE 1.1   *English dominance in the United Kingdom, 1988*

Territory	Population (millions)	Persons per square kilometre	% total UK Gross Domestic Product
England	47.3	362	85.4
Scotland	5.1	66	8.4
Wales	2.8	136	4.3
Northern Ireland	1.6	111	1.9

Source: Adapted from Birch (1977, p. 35), with revised figures from Central Statistical Office, 1988b, pp. 30, 123.

reinforced the significance of territorial variations. Even in England economic change varied greatly in its impact: though by 1911 agriculture had diminished to a position where it employed only 8 per cent of the workforce (the comparable figure was three times greater in 1831), rural culture and society were still powerfully distinctive (Thompson, P., 1975, p. 190).

The significance of territorial divisions was heightened by continuing economic development. At the start of the First World War Britain's industrial lead over her competitors had disappeared; her superiority now rested on domination of international finance and on a trading empire closely connected to the political empire. The industries on which the country's early economic power had rested were in a slow but unmistakable decline. They were located disproportionately in the North of England, in Scotland and in South Wales. By contrast, imperial power, and the financial and trading might which it supported, was disproportionately controlled from the South East. In a famous passage from his *Imperialism*, the radical journalist Hobson pointed critically to some of the social and political consequences. The South, he remarked, was 'richly sprinkled' with a class produced by the Empire,

> many of them wealthy, most of them endowed with leisure, men openly contemptuous of democracy, devoted to material luxury, social display and the shallower arts of intellectual life . . . men of local influence in politics and society whose character has been formed in our despotic Empire and whose incomes are chiefly derived from the maintenance and furtherance of despotic rule . . . Could the incomes expended in the Home Counties and other

large districts of Southern Britain be traced to their sources, it
would be found that they were in large measure wrung from the
enforced toil of black, brown or yellow natives. (quoted, Nairn,
1981, pp. 23–4).

The divide between a prosperous 'metropolis' in the South East,
heavily dependent on international finance and trade, and a less
prosperous 'hinterland' either untouched by industrialism or dependent on declining industries, helps explain why before 1914 the
politics of the 'new class society' were so often about issues other
than class. These issues reflected, notably, territorial divisions reinforced by different religious convictions. The electoral strengths of
the two major parties derived from different national and religious
groups: the Liberal Party was Celtic and Nonconformist, the
Conservative Party English and Anglican. Some of the most contentious questions – the place of churches in education, the position of
the established church in the different countries of the United
Kingdom – reflected this divide. Class conflict in the years immediately before the First World War was certainly often bitter, but
the only issue in British politics that could not be managed without
large-scale violence was 'the Irish question': that conflict between
Irish Catholic nationalism, Ulster Protestantism and the Westminster government which culminated in the separation of the Irish Free
State in 1921.

Even the organisations typifying the 'new class society' drew
much of their strength, and their characteristics, from the way they
organised along, rather than across, the territorial and religious
divides. Before the First World War the infant political wing of the
labour movement had many of the marks of a territorial and
religious party, rather than of a class organisation (though territorial
features in some degree mirrored variations in industrial development). Of the 1906 intake of Labour MPs (the first significant
Labour representation in Parliament) only five out of thirty came
from constituencies in London and the South. That same intake was
also more influenced in its philosophy by religion than by any
theories of class war: a survey of those returned to Parliament in
1906 showed that over 60 per cent had been brought up as
Nonconformists and that the Bible was one of the two most
common influences on their thought (cited, Alexander and Hobbs,
1966).

Conversely, the main party representing those with power and wealth in the community drew its electoral strength disproportionately from the South, and was closely allied to the Church of England. In the December 1910 General Election – the last before the outbreak of the First World War – the Conservative Party won 133 of its 272 seats in the South of England. The comparable figure for the Liberal Party was 75, and for Labour 6. These differences reflected striking territorial variations in political opinion: in that same election the Conservatives won over 56 per cent of the vote in South East England, but only 30 per cent in Wales (Pelling, 1967, p. 415).

The first industrial nation did indeed bring into existence a new class society. By the beginning of the twentieth century it was plain that class organisations based on occupation were becoming increasingly important in economic life and in politics. These organisations – trade unions and political parties – were moved by often fierce battles about the distribution of power and wealth. But the supremacy of class over other social groupings had yet fully to be established. Some of the old divisions of pre-industrial Britain remained alive. The uneven impact of industrialism had widened the old territorial dividing lines between the different nations in the United Kingdom. Class organisations, even when they developed, drew much of their strength from territorial and religious groupings. It was only during the first half of the twentieth century that the 'new class society' grew to maturity. The development is detailed in the next section.

3 Centralisation and the Rise of Class

In 1914 class was rivalled by religion and by territory as the basis of social organisation and political action. In the intervening seventy years religion has, with the important exception of Northern Ireland, declined into insignificance. This is not a matter of declining attachment to religious beliefs. On that the evidence is uncertain: some denominations – like the Congregationalists – have disappeared as separate groups, while immigration has swelled the ranks of Jews, Muslims and Hindus. Nor is it the case that churches have retreated from politics: on the contrary, Christian churches in particular have shown a growing tendency to intervene in a wide range of questions covering foreign policy, economic management and social policy. But the close links that existed in 1914 between religious institutions and political parties have disappeared. Nonconformist churches are no longer a distinctive influence on political radicalism; Anglicanism is no longer distinctively associated with the Conservative Party. The churches have ceased to be the bases of major political alignments and have become instead part of the array of pressure groups in the community.

The evolution of territorial divisions is more complex. The development of the economy since 1914 has widened the gap between the 'metropolis' and the 'hinterland'. The South East has been increasingly integrated into a prosperous multinational economy, as a key centre of finance and trade; South Wales, Northern England and Scotland – the old nineteenth-century centres of economic dynamism – have seen their traditional industries decay and die. Table 1.2 illustrates the size of the South East's 'lead' in the 1980s. On virtually every measure of prosperity it is ahead of other regions. On some measures the gap between the systematically privileged South East and the systematically deprived Northern Ireland is extraordinary.

Yet the persistence of important regional divisions has been accompanied by a sharp decline in the distinctiveness and autonomy of local communities, and by a corresponding growth of centralisation in both government and in the economy. Rural society is the most obvious victim of these developments. Before the First World War rural Britain, while of diminishing importance, retained its own social hierarchies and culture. In the 1980s this uniqueness has been lost. Rural culture has been replaced by a national culture transmitted by such institutions as the mass media. Improvements in transport have spread the suburban habit, blurred the division between town and country and attracted large numbers of urban workers to live in villages and small towns. Changes in agriculture have cut numbers working on the land from over 1,400,000 in 1911 to just 306,000 in 1987 (Routh, 1980, p. 42; Central Statistical Office, 1988a, p. 114). Only a minority of those living in the countryside now get a living from the land. Rural Britain is inhabited mainly by people who work in the urban economy.

This change is itself part of a more general decline in the distinctiveness and vitality of provincial life. The provincial press, one of the glories of Victorian culture, has been eclipsed by

TABLE 1.2 *Regional and national inequality in Britain*

	South East	West Midlands	East Anglia	South West	East Midlands	Wales	North West	Yorks & Humberside	North	Scotland	Northern Ireland
% of persons aged 16 and over in managerial/ professional occupations, 1986	**17.1**	13.2	13.7	13.2	12.6	11.1	11.8	11.5	10.8	12.3	**10.5**
Av. weekly income per head (£), 1985–6	**106.3**	77.4	87.5	90.1	82.1	77.7	80.0	76.3	74.9	81.7	**66.4**
% of UK total Gross Domestic Product	**35.7**	8.3	3.5	7.7	6.6	4.3	10.5	8.0	5.0	8.4	**1.9**
% households with deep freezer	**70.0**	58.0	71.0	70.0	65.0	63.0	60.0	56.0	57.0	51.0	**43.0**
Unemployment rate, %, 1987	**7.7**	12.1	7.6	9.3	9.9	14.3	14.0	12.7	15.3	14.5	**20.3**
Perinatal mortality rate, 1984–6*	**9.1**	11.6	8.8	9.3	9.5	10.4	9.9	10.8	10.3	10.3	**10.5**
Cars per 1000 population, 1986	**356.0**	323.0	359.0	366.0	303.0	298.0	282.0	272.0	249.0	243.0	**267.0**

Sources: Adapted from Sharpe (1982), with revisions from Central Statistical Office (1988b).
* Still births, and deaths of infants under one week of age, per 1000 live and still births.

newspapers and magazines produced in London. In education, the great civic universities like Manchester, Birmingham and Leeds, who once drew most of their students from their own communities, are now part of a national university hierarchy increasingly controlled from the centre. Even in leisure the same tendencies exist: professional football and county cricket, once dominated by clubs reflecting the character of their own localities, are now nationally organised industries.

Centralisation is particularly marked in politics and administration. Since 1914 local government has been stripped of responsibility for a wide range of services, losing to regional or central bodies control over hospitals, gas and water supply. The financial independence of local authorities has also declined substantially: just before the First World War nearly 80 per cent of local government spending was funded from local sources, notably from rates; by 1986 the contribution of rates was under a third (Peacock and Wiseman, 1967, p. 197; Central Statistical Office, 1988a, p. 276).

The root cause of this growing centralisation lies in the changing economic structure. Before the First World War Britain's economy was distinctive among those of capitalist nations. Monopolies and cartels were less common than in Germany or the United States, while locally owned small and medium sized firms were more significant. Giant firms certainly existed, but they rarely dominated: in 1909 less than a sixth of manufacturing production was accounted for by the 100 largest firms. The publicly owned part of the economy was small, and nationally organised public corporations were unknown: at the turn of the century under a sixth of the Gross National Product was accounted for by total government spending (Peacock and Wiseman, 1967, p. 37).

This dispersed, competitive economy has since been transformed by waves of mergers and public acquisitions. The first wave originated between 1914 and 1918, when the war economy demanded central control and large organisations. The second wave came in the great inter-war depression, through 'rationalisation', which merged many firms, especially in cotton and coal, in attempts to cut production and increase efficiency. The third wave came during the Second World War and immediately afterwards and was marked by expanded public ownership and control. A fourth wave began in the 1960s, involving large numbers of industrial mergers, the growing domination of the economy by a small number of giant firms, and an accelerated expansion of public employment. 'The giant firm', says Pollard, 'has ... become typical for manufacturing as a whole and predominant in some sectors' (1983, p. 302). Depending on the measure used, somewhere in excess of 40 per cent of manufacturing activity is now accounted for by the one hundred biggest private enterprises.

The biggest giant of all, the public sector, has also grown spectacularly, as Table 1.3 shows.

TABLE 1.3   *Numbers employed in public and private sectors, 1961–86, (millions)*

	Public Sector	Private Sector	Total
1961	5.9	18.6	24.5
1981	7.2	17.2	24.4
1986	6.5	18.0	24.5

Source: Central Statistical Office (1988c, p. 70).

Changes in the economy and in government since the First World War have therefore vastly increased the scale of social organisation and the degree of centralisation. These changes greatly assisted the rise of occupational class as an influence on industrial and political action. Britain before 1914 was a society of small-scale, locally controlled institutions; in the 1980s both economy and government are dominated by big organisations. Some changes in scale are extraordinary: the Home Office, for instance, employed less than 800 civil servants in 1914; by the end of the 1980s the figure exceeded 37,000.

The increasing scale and increasing concentration of industry weakened the 'rivals' to class, like local communities. More positively, big organisations and growing central control encouraged the spread of class-based institutions. Among workers the most obvious sign has been the spread of trade-union membership and the concentration of workers into an ever-smaller number of big unions: in 1921 the four largest unions accounted for just over a fifth of all union members; by 1983 the figure was nearly one-half. There has also been a long-term growth in the authority of the Trades Union Congress as the central voice of organised labour in the community, although this has been challenged in recent years. Less commonly noticed has been the continuing rise of class organisation among employers. Before the First World War businessmen had already begun to organise into trade associations and employers' associations – like the Shipping Federation and the Engineering Employers' Federation – in order to combat union power, to lobby government and to restrict competition in markets. During the war, institutions were founded which claimed to speak for wide sectors of the business community. The years since then have seen the consolidation of class organisation on the employers' side. Virtually every industry has developed associations to defend business interests, and there has been a steady growth in the authority of organisations claiming to speak for business as a whole.

If we compare contemporary Britain with the country before the First World War we therefore see a society more centralised, more dominated by giant organisations and more permeated by class organisation and class feeling. There exist great territorial inequalities in the United Kingdom, and religion remains a force in the life of the people; but class organisation and class feeling are more important in Britain than in almost any other economically advanced country.

One result is that arguments about the distribution of power and wealth between classes, and about how far this distribution is altering over time, have dominated the study of British society. The next section examines the evidence about trends in class inequality. Since any judgement about trends has to be made by comparison with some moment in the past, we begin with two questions: how far is Britain indeed marked off into distinct occupational classes? And how far have inequalities between the classes lessened over time? In the next section these questions are examined by sketching in the class structure of the country before the First World War and by using this sketch as a point of comparison with relations between classes in contemporary Britain.

4 Equality and Inequality

Social Structure Before 1914
The social structure of Edwardian Britain was immensely complicated. Many social groups survived from the society existing before

industrialisation; the revolution in economic organisation had added a rich variety of new occupations and groupings; continuing economic change was creating yet more social diversity.

This complex structure was nevertheless arranged in a marked hierarchy, albeit a hierarchy whose order was indistinct in places. The hierarchy is best pictured like the outline of a mountain with three separate zones. At the peak was an upper class, most easily identified as that 1 per cent of the population which, Paul Thompson has calculated, owned 67 per cent of the nation's capital (1975, p. 12). This wealth came from industry, from the finance and trade closely tied to the Empire, and from agriculture. In short, the upper class consisted of those who controlled the main forms of productive wealth in the community. The alliance between different parts of the upper class was often uneasy – for instance, industrialists and financiers were often in conflict – but it was supported by powerful agencies. The upper class inhabited the same social world: its members were educated at the same great public schools and at Oxford and Cambridge universities; were tied by bonds of marriage and by economic connections; and tended to converge on the social world of the rich in London high society. They were also disproportionately represented in the upper reaches of the established church, the armed forces, the civil service and in the two dominant political parties, Conservative and Liberal. The upper class, in other words, was distinguished by the great control it exercised over wealth, power and prestige in Britain.

In its lower regions this upper class 'peak' shaded into a much larger and more diverse range of social groups, usually labelled 'the middle classes' (King and Raynor, 1981). Within the middle classes three occupational groups dominated: owners of small and medium sized businesses; professionals like doctors and lawyers; and a growing army of routine clerical workers. Though in its lower regions the middle class shaded into the working class, its members were still distinguished from manual workers by greater market power and by the higher esteem given to non-manual over manual work. These differences were reflected in the higher pay and greater job security enjoyed by most non-manual workers.

The broad base of the social mountain was made up of a working class composed of manual workers and their families. This class was divided internally in numerous ways, but still shared many important characteristics. Its members were virtually propertyless. Their living depended almost wholly on the sale of labour in the market. They had the lowest incomes in the community and the greatest chance of being unemployed. They were most likely to have poor health, to see their children die in infancy and to suffer early death themselves. From their ranks came most of those – amounting by one estimate to nearly 30 per cent of the population – who could not eat well enough to preserve sound health (Thompson, P., 1975, p. 21).

The country before the First World War was thus divided into classes possessing very different amounts of wealth and power. But these classes were not sealed off from each other. A constantly changing economy allowed some to move up the social hierarchy, and relegated others. Most mobility seems, however, to have been modest, involving small movements across the lines between classes, or up the ladder within classes. The peak of the upper class was particularly difficult for outsiders to climb. The rules guarding property, the workings of the market and the exercise of political power all ensured that inheritance rather than achievement was the easiest way to ascend the peak of the social structure: less than an eighth of all millionaires who died in the first decade of the century could be classed as 'self-made' men (Rubinstein, 1974, p. 163).

Patterns of Inequality Since 1914
The simple sketch of the social structure of Edwardian Britain provides a standard by which to estimate the social changes that have since taken place. The very simplicity of the sketch nevertheless makes caution necessary. We know the broad outlines of the Edwardian social hierarchy; the fine details of income differences, wealth distribution and social mobility are less clear. In many cases key statistics do not go back to before the First World War, so it is only possible to measure change from some later date. To this must be added the fact that there exists considerable uncertainty about the extent of inequality in modern Britain. Plainly, any generalisations about these matters must be made cautiously.

Some alterations are nevertheless so striking that they are immediately plain. Before the First World War, poor food, bad housing and low incomes meant that manual workers and their families were generally clearly distinguishable by the way they looked and dressed. These distinctions have been greatly lessened by significant rises in real incomes; by improvements in diet, health care and in housing; and by the development of mass markets in consumer goods. The rate of infant deaths, always a sensitive measure of the basic material quality of life, measures the change: at the turn of the century about 15 per cent of those born in Britain did not survive beyond the first year of life; eighty years later the equivalent figure had been reduced to almost 1 per cent. Growing prosperity has greatly lessened immediately observable differences between classes. Now, only the very rich and the very poor can be immediately distinguished by the quality of their clothes and the pallor of their skins.

These changes, while significantly lessening the outward signs of inequality between classes, could plainly result from the general increase in national prosperity, independent of any redistribution of wealth or power. The evidence indeed shows that great inequalities persist; opinions differ about how far these inequalities have lessened compared with the past.

In examining the debate, it is appropriate to begin with what are sometimes called the 'life chances' of individuals in different classes: literally, their chances of staying alive, and of staying alive in reasonable health. Mortality and health statistics are particularly useful, because they are highly sensitive to the material conditions enjoyed by individuals. The evidence here is indisputable: on key health and mortality statistics significant class differences persist, with manual workers and their families suffering poorer health than others in the community. Figures for infant mortality in different classes are especially revealing, both because they dramatically measure chances of staying alive and because it is recognised that they reflect other conditions, such as the quality of health care, the health of mothers and the standard of diets. Figure 1.1 – based on the Black Report and supplemented by later figures – shows that there remain marked class differences. The infant death rate in the lower occupational groups is nearly twice that in the highest. Statistical evidence is rarely conclusive, however, and Figure 1.1 can be interpreted in two very different ways. One interpretation would stress the persistent gaps between classes, and would point out that the gap between the richest – class I – and the poorest – class V – has barely altered. An alternative view would emphasise the huge absolute improvements for all classes: the chances of survival of the babies of the very poor are greater than were the survival chances of the very rich before 1914. Simple inspection of the bar charts also

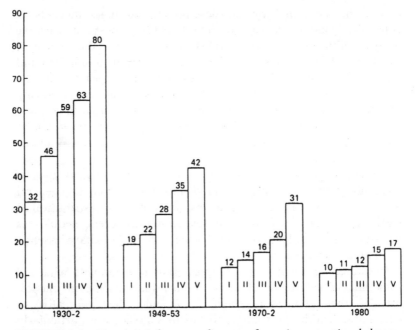

FIGURE 1.1   *Trends in infant mortality rates for main occupational classes, 1930–80 (deaths per 1000 legitimate live births, to nearest whole number)*

Sources: 1930–72, Black (1980) p. 75; 1980, Office of Population Censuses and Surveys (1983).

shows that the huge disparities between classes common in the past have been greatly reduced.

Evidence about the changing distribution of earned income shows that vast alterations have certainly taken place since the First World War. There have been great increases (exceeding 800 per cent in some cases) in money wages and less dramatic, but still substantial, rises in real incomes, when price rises are accounted for. This general progress conceals important deviations. Some middle-class occupations, like clergymen, have fallen dramatically in the incomes 'ladder' since the beginning of the First World War. These great changes have prompted a widespread belief that income differences between whole classes have greatly narrowed: during the high inflation of the 1970s, for instance, it was argued by commentators sympathetic to the middle class that militant trade unionism was using its power to narrow the income gap between manual and non-manual workers.

The most authoritative evidence does give some support to the view that differentials have indeed lessened. Some of the key figures, drawn from Royal Commission sources, and based on Routh's investigations, are given in Figure 1.2. The bar chart measures how much more or less than average pay for men was earned by important male occupational groups at selected periods. It shows, for instance, that while professionals earned nearly three-and-a-half times the average before the First World War, by the end of the 1970s they earned much less than twice the average. A growth in equality of incomes would show up as a 'flattening' of peaks and a lifting of 'troughs'; under full equality every group would record exactly one hundred per cent.

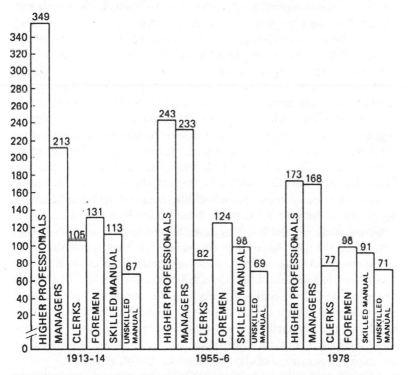

FIGURE 1.2   *Inequalities in earnings 1913–78 (average male earnings of different occupations as % of average earnings of all male employees)*
Source: Cmnd 7679, 1979–80, p. 81. Reproduced by permission.

Even a simple visual inspection shows that some 'flattening' has indeed occurred: professionals, who before the First World War earned three-and-a-half times the average, by the end of the 1970s earned only 73 per cent more than the average. Managers had also lost some of their lead, though not so dramatically. But the chart also shows that the poorest-paid, unskilled manual workers, made almost no advance: in 1913–14 they earned 67 per cent of the average; by 1978 the figure had risen to only 71 per cent. The most important changes in income inequality have occurred, as Routh has shown, not between classes but between the sexes: since before the First World War women of nearly all occupational classes have risen in the wages ladder, while men of nearly all occupational classes have descended (Routh, 1980, p. 125).

These measures of gross income differences of course take no account of the complicated system of taxation which has developed since before the First World War. Any examination of the effect of taxation on economic inequality is inseparable from discussion of changes in both the overall distribution of wealth and the economic benefits provided by government.

Measuring changes in the distribution of the stock of wealth – as distinct from changes in the flow of income – is exceptionally difficult. The very definition of wealth is unclear, because there is argument about how far should it extend to all property, including consumer goods and entitlements like pension rights. Much information, especially for the past, is simply missing or is unreliable. Many forms of wealth – such as company shares – have monetary values which are unstable. Some wealth, like great art treasures, may be 'priceless' because it has never been traded in a market.

Given these difficulties it is not surprising that experts differ, notably on the question of how far wealth has been redistributed in this century. Atkinson, in a series of authoritative studies, has concluded that while some modest redistribution has occurred since just after the First World War, much of this is due to the successful effort to avoid capital taxes by spreading wealth more widely within families. 'The redistribution of wealth over this century', he has concluded, 'has not been between rich and poor, but between successive generations of the same family' (1974, p. 23).

This judgement would be disputed by many, though the quality of available evidence leaves endless room for argument. Figure 1.3 collects the largest available run of figures for critical groups. It should be interpreted cautiously: figures to 1960 are for England and Wales, those for 1976 are for Great Britain. The data are thus most useful as a sign of broad trends. They suggest that there was a modest but steady advance by the poorest 80 per cent in the fifty years to the mid-1970s. As we will see in Chapter 7, however, some

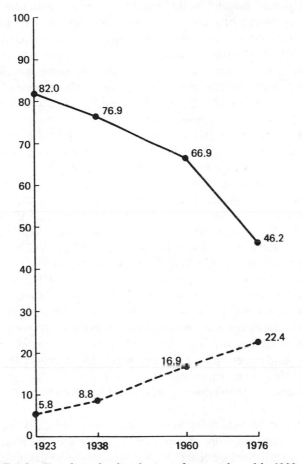

FIGURE 1.3   *Trends in the distribution of personal wealth, 1923–76*
Percentage of personal wealth owned by:
——— richest 5%   – – – – poorest 80%
Source: Cmnd 7595, 1979–80, pp. 93–5. Figures for 1923–60 for England and Wales were calculated by Royal Commission from Atkinson and Harrison (1978). Reproduced by permission.

of this gain has been lost through economic crisis and government action in the last decade.

The problem of estimating changes in the distribution of wealth has been further complicated in recent years by important alterations in the ownership of 'productive' wealth, notably shares in publicly quoted companies. Before the First World War, share ownership was largely in the hands of private individuals. The productive wealth of industry was disproportionately owned by a small 'rentier' class who lived off investments. Even as recently as the late 1950s the majority of shares were owned by private individuals. This has now changed: institutions – notably pension funds and insurance corporations – control more than half the value of shares, and the figure is still rising. The rentier living off income is apparently heading for extinction.

In one view, these changes in share ownership are immensely important, signalling the arrival of a people's capitalism. This argument asserts that ownership and control of productive resources have been transferred from private hands to those of corporate bodies serving the interests of millions of individuals, such as pensioners and insurance policy holders. A contrasting view is that institutions like investment trusts and insurance companies are elaborate means of perpetuating ownership and control by the very rich; that bodies like pension funds, while nominally serving the interests of their contributors, are still controlled by the traditional economic elite; and that the economic behaviour of financial institutions does not differ greatly from that of traditional capitalists. The argument continues unresolved, in part because it goes beyond economic arithmetic to more elusive judgements about power and motivation in the economy: to judgements, for instance, about who has power in pension funds and insurance companies and about how far their investing behaviour is dominated by profit motives (Minns, 1980).

Examining the effect of state intervention on class inequality likewise raises a mixture of arguments, only some of which can be settled by statistical evidence. Public institutions undeniably distribute goods, services and cash throughout the community; they equally undeniably fund much of this distribution through taxes. Since Edwardian times, and especially since the Second World War, a range of measures and institutions commonly labelled 'the Welfare State' has given to citizens a wide array of rights and benefits: rights to pensions in old age, to unemployment and child benefits, to free education and to health care free at the moment of treatment. One influential interpretation pictures the Welfare State as part of a long-term change in relations of status. This view, expressed by Marshall in a famous paper, asserts that the rights conferred by the Welfare State amount to 'social citizenship' akin to the right to vote (1963, pp. 67–127; Halscy, 1981, pp. 55–8). Since all these rights are conferred by law, the Welfare State can be conceived as working in contention with market forces, conferring rights on grounds other than those of market power and distributing benefits in ways that modify the inequalities of class.

The contrary view, that public services do not significantly modify the inequalities of class, rests on a variety of grounds, only some of which can be tested by looking at statistical evidence. Three main assertions are usually offered. The first is that transfers of resources in the Welfare State are more usually between members of the same class (between, for instance, those in work and those unemployed) than between classes. A second asserts that the principle of free services universally available as a right has never been fully implemented, and that recent cuts in services have made its realisation even more remote. Finally, it has been argued that patterns of service provision and use actually reinforce existing economic inequalities: that in health care and education, for instance, those already advantaged by the market are sufficiently powerful to extract superior services and to use those services more intensively (Le Grand, 1982, pp. 125–38).

Arguments about the impact of the Welfare State on the distribution of resources between classes can be referred to the statistical evidence, though the calculations required are so complex as to leave much room for continuing controversy. Some important critiques of the Welfare State, however, go beyond examining figures about its immediate impact on the distribution of wealth. Some Marxists argue that its institutions are the means by which a subordinate working class is controlled and the unequal institutions of capitalism maintained (Gough, 1979). Social citizenship, far from conferring status independent of the market, is in this view a servant of class inequality. Although these arguments rest partly on evidence about the distribution of resources they plainly go beyond economic arithmetic, to judgements about the nature of the wider forces shaping our society, about the historical forces that created the

Welfare State and to attempts to guess what pattern of inequality might have existed in the absence of the Welfare State. This recalls a theme already encountered: arguments about the changing nature of inequality cannot be settled by reference to statistics alone, because the issues transcend social arithmetic to encompass judgements about the influences shaping institutions and the historical forces bringing them into existence.

A similar elusiveness marks arguments about how far equality of opportunity has increased during this century, and how far any such change is reflected in the rate at which individuals can move up the class hierarchy by effort and ability. There is little doubt that, compared with Edwardian Britain, there is today much more stress in education, in the public services and even in the private sector on achievement as a criterion in recruitment and promotion. In education a variety of reforms – ranging from the provision of grants for students in higher education to the introduction of comprehensive schools – were partly inspired by the desire to give able working-class children increased opportunities to rise in the social scale.

Measuring how far these changes have promoted mobility is hampered by the complexity of the statistics and by gaps in the evidence. In particular, while it is fairly certain that social mobility in Edwardian Britain was very limited, the absence of any comprehensive studies of the Edwardian population make it impossible to estimate with any exactness the opportunities enjoyed by different groups to rise in the social hierarchy.

Whatever the precise pattern in the past, the evidence about contemporary Britain suggested until very recently that social mobility still occurred on only a modest scale. The first national study of mobility, conducted by Glass and others at the end of the 1940s, painted a picture of a society where the mobility achieved by individuals usually amounted to only a marginal movement across social boundaries, where few rose out of the families of manual workers and where few fell from families in the highest social groups. Subsequent, if more limited, studies confirmed this picture (Glass, 1954; Westergaard and Resler, 1976, pp. 297–313). Indeed, any increased upward mobility promoted by educational success (inter-generational mobility) seemed to be cancelled out by reduced chances of rising up the social hierarchy during a single adult working lifetime (intra-generational mobility).

Equality of opportunity seemed thus to reduce the chances of some groups achieving upward social mobility because, by emphasising formal educational qualifications as a criterion of recruitment and promotion, it excluded those who had not been successful in the education system. The evidence in turn suggested that educational success was closely tied to class origins. In higher education, the proportion of university students from the families of manual workers was no higher at the end of the 1970s than forty years before (Noble, 1981, p. 161). In the comprehensives, the common practice of streaming by expressed ability meant that schools tended to reproduce rather than modify the class inequalities of the wider society.

These pictures of social mobility were all either based on old evidence (such as the Glass study) or on studies with a limited scope. The results of studies by the Oxford Social Mobility Group, based on a national sample of 10,000 men interviewed in 1972, partly confirm but also substantially modify established pictures of mobility. There is, indeed, relatively little movement either out of the very highest social groups or into the very lowest. Downward social mobility has been comparatively rare (Heath, 1981). Upward social mobility has, however, been much greater than was commonly supposed, has involved much more than marginal movements up the social hierarchy and has created a social structure of unexpected fluidity. In every one of the seven class categories distinguished by the Oxford study, from higher professional and managerial at the top to unskilled manual at the bottom, only a minority of those in each class were born into that class. Indeed, nearly 30 per cent of those in the top class had made the long social ascent from the homes of manual workers, classes VI and VII (Goldthorpe *et al.*, 1980). Analysis of data for the 1980s (Goldthorpe and Payne, 1986) indicates the persistence of this social fluidity.

Greater equality of opportunity through the education system appears to have contributed little to this spasm of mobility. The most important causes lie in the labour market and in the long period of economic growth which, by the 1970s, had reduced the proportions in manual occupations and expanded the numbers in professional and other non-manual jobs. The demand for non-manual workers greatly exceeded the supply provided by the families of workers already in those occupations; hence the extensive recruitment from further down the social hierarchy.

There is dispute about the implications of large-scale social mobility for the future of class organisation and for the role of class in politics. The nature of this dispute is examined later. It is undeniable, however, that social mobility has been affected by more than changing legal rights and educational provisions. Economic change shaped by changing market conditions has been a critical influence. Changes in markets, especially those for labour and housing, have also had other great social consequences. The next section describes these alterations.

5 Economic Markets and Social Change

Labour Markets
The changing labour market in this century has involved striking alterations in the numbers employed in different jobs, in the geography of work and in the individual characteristics of workers. Each of these is here examined in turn.

Estimating historical changes in the proportional importance of different industries and occupations is very difficult. There exist numerous problems in devising satisfactory schemes of classification, in accurately assigning particular jobs and industries to appropriate categories and in assembling satisfactory historical evidence. Nevertheless, some changes are so great that they clearly stand out in this tangle.

The single most important alteration is the decline in the proportion of the workforce employed in manufacturing industry, especially in the traditional 'heavy' industries like mining, steel-working and shipbuilding. This change is part of a tendency universal in developed economies, but in Britain's case it also reflects the end of her dominating position as a world economic power and the decay of many of the manufacturing industries which gave her that dominance. The mirror image of the decline of manufacturing industry as a source of employment has been the rising proportion of the workforce engaged in 'service' occupations like banking, insurance and public administration.

The rise of the service sector is associated with a key long-term change which we earlier encountered in passing. At the turn of the century 5 per cent of all workers were in public employment; by 1986, even after seven years of Thatcherism, the figure was nearly a quarter.

Declining numbers in manufacturing, the expansion of service jobs and the long-term growth of public sector employment: these trends have been long recognised. Less commonly noted are changes in the geography of work, and in the geographical distribution of classes. A glance back to the first row in Table 1.2 illustrates the point, showing as it does the marked regional disparities in the numbers working at managerial occupations.

The decline of manufacturing industry in turn helps explain the great long-term changes which have occurred in the numbers in different occupational classes. Routh's figures show that just before the First World War the overwhelming majority of employees – over 80 per cent – were 'workers': that is, were manual employees or foremen. Clerks accounted for under 5 per cent of the workforce, while professionals and similar groups accounted for under 15 per cent (Routh, 1980, p. 5). By the 1980s, clerks and similar workers accounted for over 15 per cent of the workforce, while the professional and managerial category contained over a quarter. Most striking of all, the 'working class' – manual employees – now accounts for less than half of the workforce, for probably the first time in one hundred and fifty years (Office of Population Censuses, 1982, p. 17).

Some of the preceding developments are plainly connected to changes in the individual characteristics of workers. The most noticeable of these are the rising proportions of women and of non-whites in the labour market. As recently as 1951 only 29 per cent of those in work were women; now the figure is over 40 per cent. The most striking change involves the entry of married women into paid work, with significant consequences for both political attitudes and the structure of family life: just after the First World War only 4 per cent of married women were in paid jobs; in 1982 the figure was 58 per cent (Central Statistical Office, 1984c, p. 61). Most of these women have entered routine non-manual jobs; women have made little advance in the most highly paid and prestigious occupations.

The growth in numbers of non-whites has happened even more swiftly. In the last thirty years large numbers of non-white immigrants and their children have come on to the labour market. This significant new social group is a legacy of Empire, owing its settlement in Britain to the rights of citizenship given to all Commonwealth members under the 1948 Nationality Act. Since the early 1960s the attempts to limit rights to settle, and to deal with the social consequences of settlement, have been among the most controversial issues in British politics. Non-white immigrants and their descendants share several key characteristics, other than their colour. They live for the most part in the inner areas of large cities. They suffer from the economic decline of those cities. It has been estimated that unemployment rates among non-white men are twice as high as the comparable figure for whites (Central Statistical Office, 1988c, p. 69). The vast majority of non-whites in employment are working in low-grade manual jobs. Even among Asians, popularly caricatured as concentrated in small businesses, only about 8 per cent are self-employed (Miles and Phizacklea, 1977).

This simple sketch of the changing labour market reveals several important features. The complex occupational hierarchy created by the early stages of industrialism has been further refined by economic and social change. The pattern classically associated with industrialism – numerical domination by a class of manual workers – has passed away. The ranks of traditional manual workers have been depleted, and non-manual workers are the fastest-growing group in the workforce. Women have entered the labour market in increasing numbers. Public sector employment has expanded greatly. A significant minority of non-whites has joined the labour market.

Housing Markets

The transformation of housing markets in this century is even more striking. Before the First World War most housing in Britain was privately rented. Only a small minority, mostly the very rich, were owner occupiers. Hardly any housing was owned by local or central government. The most significant economic consequence of this state of affairs was that, while the quality of housing occupied by different social groups varied greatly, the majority of the population was alike in not having substantial economic assets in the housing market.

The scale of change since then is summarised in Table 1.4. The most important alterations are plain: the sharp decline in the proportions of dwellings rented from private landlords, the rise of owner occupation and the construction of substantial numbers of dwellings rented by local authorities. The simple table only hints at some other important changes. The divisions between people in different kinds of housing also mark other divisions. The unem-

TABLE 1.4   *Changes in housing tenure, United Kingdom, 1914–1986**

%	Owner occupation	Local Authority rented	Privately rented
1914	10.0	1.0	80.0
1939	31.0	14.0	46.0
1986	63.0	27.0	10.0

Sources: For 1914 and 1939, Cook and Stevenson (1983); for 1986, Central Statistical Office (1988c).
* Percentages do not sum to 100.

ployed, for instance, are also disproportionately concentrated in rented local authority housing. But the publicly rented sector is itself highly diverse, great differences existing in the cost and popularity of different kinds of public dwellings. There are also significant geographical variations in the proportion of the housing stock accounted for by the public sector: for instance, whereas in the UK as a whole 63 per cent of dwellings are owner occupied, the figure in Scotland is only 42 per cent.

The social characteristics of owner occupiers are also changing significantly. In the 1930s home ownership spread widely among non-manual workers; by the 1980s it was increasingly common among more prosperous and younger manual workers. The rise of the owner occupier has been helped by the Thatcher Administration's legislation on the sale of council houses: over 750,000 local authority dwellings were transferred to private hands in the first half of the 1980s (McMahon, 1987).

The changing housing market has immense implications for class structure and class organisation. The spread of owner occupation among manual workers has given them, for the first time, a substantial economic asset. It is now easier for most people to accumulate capital by home ownership than by saving out of income. The cost of buying a house is heavily affected by public policy, especially by taxation and interest rate policies. These facts give owner occupiers common interests and common grounds for intervention in politics. In the rented sector clear differences also exist, notably between council tenants, who live in accommodation receiving considerable public subsidies, and those who rent from private landlords. In short, the possibility exists that changes in

housing markets may significantly modify the kind of class groupings traditionally created by an industrial economy.

With this possibility we come to the various interpretations of our
changing class structure which have been advanced in recent years.
These interpretations also expose some of the varying political
implications of a changing society.

6 Class: Persistence, Fragmentation or Realignment?

The Industrial Revolution had by the beginning of this century
created a society where occupational class inequality was marked
and where class organisation was of growing importance. The social
changes that have taken place since then are, as the preceding pages
have shown, varied and complicated. Not surprisingly, the attempt
to make sense of these changes has provoked very different accounts. It is a serviceable simplification to arrange these accounts
under three broad headings: theories of persistence, theories of
fragmentation, and theories of realignment. The three offer very
different interpretations of the detailed changes in class structure
and of the political implications of those changes. Advocates of the
class-persistence thesis argue that neither occupational class inequality, nor occupational class organisation, has been seriously modified by social change. Those who argue for class fragmentation rest
their case on the belief that social change has indeed lessened
important inequalities. By so doing it has fragmented the internal
coherence of classes and reduced their significance as a foundation
for political action. Theories of realignment are diverse, but they
share a common view that, while social change is indeed undermin-
ing traditional occupational class alignments, the result is not
fragmentation but the creation of new social divisions or the
resurrection of old ones. Different writers identify different new
groups: some have pointed to divisions in the housing market as
evidence of the existence of housing classes; for others, the crucial
new groupings are to be found in the labour market in, for instance,
the divide between those employed in the public and private sectors.

One of the most powerful and popular statements of the view that
social change has not seriously modified established class inequalities is contained in Westergaard and Resler's *Class in a Capitalist
Society* (1976). After a detailed analysis of three scales of inequality

– 'condition and security', 'power', and 'opportunity' – they conclude that no significant long-term movement to a more equal society has taken place in this century. Trends in inequality of 'condition and security' – notably of income, of welfare provision and of property ownership – show, they suggest, a stubborn resistance to any efforts seriously to diminish class gaps. Inequality of power, they argue, has been substantially unaffected by either the rise of professional managers in industry or by the extension of state control over the economy. Class-based inequality of opportunity, they assert, has not been seriously changed by the pattern of social mobility. Two lines of division in British society remain crucial: that line separating off a small elite of owners of productive property from the rest; and that line dividing manual and non-manual workers. Westergaard and Resler examine other social divides – between, for instance, different races or regions – and conclude that none of these seriously diminishes the importance of occupational class divisions.

The strength of the 'class persistence' model, of which Westergaard and Resler's is the most trenchant and well-documented statement, is obvious: there is impressive statistical evidence that economic inequalities have indeed persisted, and have shown a stubborn immunity to treatment by a variety of public policy measures. Some important developments since the mid-1970s, when Westergaard and Resler finished gathering their evidence, reinforce their argument. Since the great economic crisis of 1976, and the rise of monetarism, economic inequality has increased: there has been a four-fold increase in the numbers of workers without a job since 1974; taxation has become even less progressive in its impact; and welfare services have in many cases been cut. (These points are elaborated in Chapter 7.) Nor need the evidence of the Oxford Mobility study – not available when Westergaard and Resler were writing – seriously modify this picture. Though upward social mobility is shown by the study to have been both more common and more dramatic than had been believed, two very stable features remain: entry into the privileged elite of substantial property owners is still difficult to accomplish except by the good fortune of birth; and the absence of much downward mobility has actually increased the homogeneity of the groups at the bottom of society.

Goldthorpe has indeed argued that social mobility has increased the prospects for effective working-class organisation (Goldthorpe

et al., 1980, pp. 268–71). For the first time in history most workers
are second or third generation members of their class, while there is
little dilution of class purity by the downwardly mobile. On the
British mainland, religion, once a significant rival to occupational
class as a foundation for political action, has ceased to have any
such significance.

The case for the class persistence thesis is, however, powerfully
contradicted by the class fragmentation interpretation. Four pieces
of evidence strikingly support the belief that the class structures
produced by industrialism are being fragmented. The first is the
general increase in affluence which has reduced the external signs of
differences between classes. The statistics show that great class-
related inequalities persist; but improvements in diet and dress,
better housing facilities, the spread of home ownership down the
social scale, the growth of mass markets in consumer goods and
services, have all reduced the visible signs of inequality which once
distinguished manual workers and their families from the rest of the
community. The second piece of striking evidence concerns economic change, notably in the structure of occupations. The group
most commonly associated with class action – manual workers – is
now outnumbered by a diversity of non-manual workers. More
generally, economic change has increased the complexity of the
occupational structure, by multiplying new occupations, creating
new skills and sources of esteem, and changing the relative rewards
of different occupations. Likewise, the growth of new industries, the
expansion of the public sector and the changing balance between
different parts of private enterprise have all contributed to fragmentation.

The third piece of evidence concerns the consequences of social
mobility. Though mobility down into manual work or up into the
ranks of the very rich is rare, the fastest-growing section of the
workforce – non-manual employees – is drawn from diverse social
origins. The most rapidly growing occupational sector does, then,
show a pattern of fragmentation. Fourth and finally, there is some
evidence that the traditional occupational classes are becoming less
distinctive in their attitudes. Roberts and his colleagues, in their
study of *The Fragmentary Class Structure* (1977), found that the
traditional line dividing manual and non-manual workers seemed no
longer to be significant in accounting for many social attitudes. This
evidence chimes with the observation that political action seems to

be organised to a growing extent along non-class lines. As we shall see, this is increasingly the case both with voting behaviour and with pressure group organisation.

Theories of class fragmentation assert that the old class alignments are in decline and that they are not being replaced by new alignments of comparable significance. By contrast, a variety of observers, while agreeing that occupational class is of declining importance, have claimed to see new patterns emerging which are more significant and stable than mere fragmentation. One of the most influential accounts derives from Rex and Moore's study of the sociology of depressed inner-city areas of Birmingham. They argue that 'there is a class struggle over the use of houses and . . . this class struggle is the central process of the city as a social unit' (Rex and Moore, 1967, p. 273). The notion of housing classes has been refined by Saunders, who suggests that three different groups can be distinguished by their place in the housing market: those who build and develop housing; owner occupiers; and those who rent in either the public or private sectors. He has also argued that these groups have different economic interests and that they are capable of mobilising politically to defend those interests (Saunders, 1980, pp. 93–102).

Efforts have also been made to assimilate the theory of housing classes to a more general model based on the notion that different forms of consumption distinguish the economic interests of different groups, shape different attitudes and stimulate political conflicts (Dunleavy, 1979). The crucial divide is held to be between groups which disproportionately consume collective goods and services (like public housing and public transport) and those disproportionately consuming goods and services produced by market mechanisms. Dunleavy has also argued for the significance of production sectors, groups systematically divided from each other by their place in the production process. He suggests that the conventional dividing line between manual and non-manual work – on the importance of which Westergaard and Resler insist – is now of doubtful analytical value (Dunleavy, 1980a, 1980b, 1980c). Drawing on the work of neo-Marxist theorists like O'Connor (1973), he argues that the critical dividing lines run between groupings such as the public sector, corporate big business, smaller businesses, and 'state dependent' groups like pensioners and the unemployed.

Yet another suggested line of division is territorial. Nairn's *The Break-Up of Britain* (1981) is only the most influential of a number of studies which, observing the gap in economic development between the 'metropolitan' South East and the 'hinterland' of Britain, have argued that the divide between metropolis and hinterland is a significant line of political cleavage.

It is clear that the accounts summarised here under the label of 'realignment' do indeed refer to significant groupings. There are important ties of common interest uniting owner occupiers, and dividing them from groups in other housing markets. Differences likewise separate employees in the public and private sectors, and those in work and those dependent on state benefits. It is plain that these differing groups do organise, and come into conflict, in defence of interests. All this, however, is compatible with the 'fragmentation' thesis, with its picture of society dissolving into competing sectional groups. It is not yet clear that housing markets, consumption processes, production sectors or territorial divisions can construct social groupings possessing the solidarity and capacity for political action still demonstrated by occupational classes.

7 Conclusion

This brief account of the different interpretations that have been placed on social and economic change shows that important connections exist between the wider society and the political system; but it also shows that the nature of those connections is the subject of continuous argument. Understanding social change, and pinpointing the political implications of social change, involves reference to both statistical evidence and to less-tangible intellectual judgements. No simple mechanical connection exists between what happens in the wider society and what happens in politics. Part of the reason for the subtlety of the connection is that changes in objective structures are filtered through a set of beliefs, rituals and patterns of behaviour; in short, through a culture. The nature of the political culture is the subject of the next chapter.

2

Political Culture and Political Instability

The fathers have eaten sour grapes, and the children's teeth are set on edge.

Ezekiel, 18.2

1 Outline

In 1963 two American political scientists published the first systematic comparison of popular attitudes to political authority in Britain and in other Western democracies (Almond and Verba, 1963). The British, they concluded, had a uniquely balanced attitude to authority – neither too rebellious nor too acquiescent – which promoted stable democracy. They nevertheless sounded a mild note of warning, remarking, on Britain, 'it is possible that deference to political elites can go too far'. If the British had a fault, in other words, it was that they were a little too ready to respect authority in general and government authority in particular.

Since that warning was uttered, the country that was in danger of deferring too readily to authority has had the following experiences: over 2300 people have been killed in a civil war in Northern Ireland; pitched battles have been fought on union picket lines between police and trade unionists; powerful institutions have defied the law; fiercely destructive riots have swept parts of London and other big cities; and public figures have been the object of bomb attacks, by an assortment of nationalists and left-wing revolutionaries.

Almond and Verba's picture of the British was itself only the most systematic and influential academic statement of a widely held view. Understanding the British political culture involves making sense of the gap between this view and the often violent reality of contemporary Britain. That is the task of this chapter. Section 2 examines what we mean by 'political culture'. Section 3 elaborates the most commonly accepted model of the political culture. Section 4 examines objections to that model, while section 5 considers some alternative accounts. Section 6 stands on its own. Few will deny that the most significant recent challenge to the prevailing political order has been mounted in Northern Ireland. Section 6 therefore examines the Irish case.

2 Nature of Political Culture

'Political culture' is an elusive notion. When in the 1950s sample surveys of public opinion first began to be widely used in Britain by political scientists, the political culture was often equated with the general attitudes towards political authority voiced by the people. Thus the most famous of all studies, Almond and Verba's *The Civic Culture*, analysed answers to a lengthy questionnaire presented to representative samples of the population. But 'culture' is more than what people believe, let alone what they tell of their beliefs to opinion pollsters. The root of the word – which describes the rites and ceremonies of religious worship – is instructive. A religion is distinguished not only by its doctrines but also by its forms of worship, its rituals and its ceremonials. A political culture likewise consists of more than attitudes to political authority or beliefs about the purpose of government; it encompasses the political practices and ceremonials of a community.

While survey evidence about popular attitudes is therefore invaluable in describing the political culture, it is only one part of an appropriate range of evidence. But once we go beyond the statistics of opinion surveys to wider descriptions of political rituals and practices we enter uncertain territory. The seminal writings on political culture are impressionistic accounts of aspects of the national character produced by literary geniuses with little direct experience of popular life. Thus, the notion that the lower classes 'worship rank' – are especially deferential to their social superiors – was most famously expressed by Walter Bagehot, an upper-class nineteenth-century banker and journalist (1867, 1964). The most famous modern statement of the view that the English have a special respect for the law came from George Orwell, an eccentric genius whose formative years were spent at Eton College and in the Burmese police (Orwell, 1941). The concept of political culture is, in short, contested and ambiguous, and its description allows the extensive use of intuition and imagination.

It is therefore not surprising that there are significant arguments about the character of the British political culture – and even about whether a single culture can be said to exist. There can be no doubt, however, that there existed until recently one dominant account, best called the 'civility model'. This we now examine.

3 The Civility Model

The civility model is most famously associated with the work of Almond and Verba, but the appeal of their account was due in part to the way it systematised a conventional wisdom about the British political culture. Three key components of the model are especially noteworthy: homogeneity, consensus, and deference.

Homogeneity
Similar political values, the model asserts, are widely distributed throughout the population. Though the community is divided in a variety of obvious ways – by class, religion, region, gender, age – there are no divisions to match in intensity or depth those found in many other countries (Pulzer, 1967). This cultural homogeneity is in part founded on social homogeneity (Blondel, 1963). The British experienced no foreign conquest in recent history, while industrialisation eliminated the peasantry and created a relatively simple class structure.

Consensus
The second part of the civility model looks beyond values and social structure to practices. It argues that the last violent political conflict of any scope was the English Civil War in the 1640s. Since then, it suggests, the dominant way of settling disagreements and arriving at decisions has been peaceful (Beer and Ulam, 1962, pp. 73–101). Movements like Fascism, which use violent language and reject peaceful argument, receive little sympathy. There is, in this view, widespread support for peaceful political action, for Parliament as

the appropriate forum for settling political differences, and for the laws passed by Parliament.

Consensus about procedures is bound up with agreement on the substantive purposes of government. This part of the model points out that – by contrast with most countries on the continent of Europe – political movements supporting revolutionary social and political change have attracted hardly any popular support: both Fascism and Revolutionary Marxism have proved unattractive to most Britons. The two parties dominant in modern British politics – Labour and Conservative – have for most of the last sixty years shared important assumptions about how government should be conducted and about what policies should be pursued.

This part of the civility model suggests, therefore, that the British political culture is marked by a consensus about the rules of political argument and about the purposes of government.

Deference

This is the most famous – and also the most disputed – element in the civility model. It takes a variety of forms, but usually asserts that there is a connection between deference and political stability. The most influential version – originating in Bagehot's phrase that the lower classes 'worship rank in their hearts' – argues that there exists a popular predisposition to defer to political leaders of high-born (preferably aristocratic) origins. A more general claim – it lies at the heart of Almond and Verba's account of Britain – is that the British are especially law-abiding because they defer to and trust civic authority, whether represented by the village policeman or the Prime Minister. A third version of the deference thesis pictures the British as exhibiting a tendency to defer in the face of social and economic inequalities (Jessop, 1971). The deference component of the civility model can therefore take three quite different forms: it may assert that the British defer to the high born, defer to all figures in public authority, or defer to social and economic hierarchies.

4 Objections to the Civility Model

Homogeneity, consensus and deference are parts of a model – in other words, parts of a simplified representation of reality. It is natural, therefore, that aspects of the British political culture are omitted or distorted. Some criticisms of the model are comprehensive; others only object to particular components; but the burden of criticism is that the model simplifies political history, is unconvincing in its account of the present and cannot make sense of trends indicative of the future. We can illustrate these points by looking in turn at each of the components identified above.

The Limits to Homogeneity

By comparison with the United States – a land of many races and nationalities – Britain is socially homogenous; by comparison with many European countries it has escaped the worst splintering effects of territory and religion. Britain is nevertheless still a remarkably diverse community, and is becoming more so. Britain is 'a multinational state' in which the national communities are strikingly different in their political behaviour, religious loyalties, economic circumstances and styles of life (Rose, 1982, pp. 10–65). Even within the dominant nation, England, there exist, as we saw in Chapter 1, significant regional differences. Waves of immigrants in this century – East European Jews, Black West Indians, Asians – have brought added ethnic and religious variety.

The civility model, in short, neglects the sheer social diversity possible in a state of fifty-six million people. It particularly neglects territorial divisions: even Almond and Verba's highly systematic study of *British* attitudes excluded the population of Northern Ireland from those sampled.

The Limits to Consensus

The civility model of British political culture was first systematised by academics in the late 1950s and early 1960s. This was an unusual period in British history, when full employment and growing prosperity seemed to be dissolving social tensions.

When we look back beyond the 1950s, or forward into the 1960s and 1970s, the extent of consensus over rules and policies seems much more limited. The historical creation of the British state was not the result of the growth of consensus but was the product of military conquest and economic sanctions. Alternative loyalties were also weakened by using state power to, for instance, discourage the teaching of languages other than English. The peasantry, a potentially disruptive class, was largely eliminated by state-sponsored 'clearances' in Scotland and by the state-supported 'enclosure' of common land by landlords elsewhere. Nor were the class tensions created by industrialism coped with simply by accommodation and compromise. It has proved necessary persistently to use the law – in other words, coercion legitimately embodied – to restrain trade-union behaviour. At particularly critical historical moments substantial public sanctions have been needed to maintain the existing social order: at the beginning of the nineteenth century, says Briggs (1960, p. 182), a larger army was employed in England against machine-breakers than in Iberia against Napoleon; and in 1984 there were more police involved in keeping the peace on coal-miners' picket lines than there were soldiers engaged in keeping the peace in Northern Ireland.

The historical past is thus less marked by consensus than the civility model suggests. More recent experiences – in Northern Ireland, on trade-union picket lines, in the inner-city disturbances of the 1980s – suggest that Britain today is also a far-from-consensual community.

The Limits to Deference

The notion that the British are especially deferential has been the most disputed part of the civility model. Critics have argued that the very notion itself is vague. In his seminal article on the subject, Kavanagh identified four different senses of the word and five ways in which investigators had attempted to identify its existence (Kavanagh, 1971). Even when meaning is narrowed to the senses identified earlier – deference to high-born political leaders, deference to public authority, deference in the face of social and economic hierarchies – difficulties remain. The most apparently unambiguous evidence – that revealed by responses in sample surveys – turns out on close inspection to show surprisingly variable, and often low, levels of deferential attitudes (Kavanagh, 1971).

When we look beyond the surveys, there is a gap between the image of the British as deferential and the reality of everyday behaviour. In particular, marked respect for authority is difficult to reconcile with civil insurrection in Northern Ireland, mass violence on picket lines, riots in cities, not to mention less politically overt law-breaking like tax evasion and the spontaneous hooliganism of football supporters.

5 Alternatives to the Civility Model

All models select and distort; that is how they make sense of an otherwise incomprehensibly complex reality. It is not enough, therefore, to show that the civility model omits and distorts; it is also necessary to show that there exists a more suitable alternative. Here we examine four possibilities. The first two focus on recent changes; the third and fourth involve more fundamental departures from the civility model.

Alternative 1: A Post-Affluence Model
The post-affluence model is derived from the comparative work of Inglehart, notably *The Silent Revolution* (1977), a study largely based on a survey of political attitudes in the countries of the European Economic Community, carried out in 1973. Inglehart argued that the development of rich Western economies with affluent populations had fundamentally changed popular expectations about government. In the past, most people lived near the level of physical survival, and their lives – and hence their politics – were dominated by that fact. Politics were primarily about economic issues, notably the allocation of scarce resources between individuals and classes. But with the rise of mass affluence these preoccupations changed. For the first time in human history large populations in advanced economies were lifted above mere physical existence. Economic abundance meant that the old materialistic politics faded. This did not, however, lead to political stability. Affluent populations turned instead to demands for radical changes in the quality of life and to an interest in non-economic issues. The speed of economic growth also created a divide in the population between the young, who had known nothing but affluence, and the old, who remembered, and expressed, the materialistic politics of the past.

These ideas have influenced interpretations of British politics offered in recent years by Marsh (1977) and by Barnes and Kaase (1979). They produced survey evidence showing marked generational differences in attitudes, with the young displaying more willingness than their elders to contemplate forms of protest involving breaking the law. Other developments also fit the post-affluence model. There has in recent years been a rapid growth in membership of groups – like the Campaign for Nuclear Disarmament – which make radical demands on non-economic issues and draw' their support disproportionately from the young. Much radical protest in Britain does indeed reflect the values of a post-affluent society.

The explanatory power of the post-affluence model is nevertheless limited in three key ways. First, Inglehart himself recognised that the proportion of the whole population avoiding vulgar economic issues in favour of non-materialist demands was small, and was concentrated among the well-educated, young middle class. The influence of post-affluent politics was especially weak in Britain because the country's economic growth was slower than elsewhere. Thus even in Inglehart's survey the differences in attitudes between young and old were less marked in Britain than elsewhere in Western Europe. Second, the great economic boom that produced affluence has been over for many years. Inglehart's evidence was largely confined to the period up to 1973. Since then we have experienced mass unemployment and low growth. Even the highly educated young are now greatly interested in the traditional political issue of unemployment.

The third and most serious defect of the 'post-affluence' theory as an account of what is happening to the British political culture is that, while it makes sense of some values and some points of stress, it makes no sense of the greatest points of tension in the system. The most serious challenges to authority have come not from the most privileged, but from the most deprived. The riots in Brixton and Toxteth in 1981 were an outburst from the very poor. The fiercest street fighting in Northern Ireland has been concentrated in working-class Belfast and Derry, two of the poorest cities in Europe. Whatever the problems of Brixton or the Bogside they are not the problems of affluence.

Alternative 2: Populism and the Collapse of Deference
The 'populism' model of the political culture has been most influentially outlined by Beer, from whom the label is taken. Writing at the start of the 1980s, he argued that in the preceding two decades there had occurred in Britain a decline in traditional restraints on social behaviour, a growing disrespect for authority, and rising popular demands on government. Beer connected this to what he called 'the romantic revolt' of the 1960s, an outburst in youth culture and popular entertainment against traditional disciplines (1982). One of the most striking features of this argument is that it does not stand alone. It is part of a long-established and still-influential interpre-

tation of the impact of economic change under capitalism on traditional values and restraints. According to this view the culture of capitalism – rational, calculating and innovative – destroys traditional values and hierarchies. The rational spirit of capitalism is especially corrosive of religion and of the supposedly non-rational restraints on behaviour produced by religion (Brittan, 1975).

The notion that changes in the political values of the British people are due to the decay of traditional constraints echoes a very old view. Nineteenth-century critics of industrialism and democracy likewise believed that economic change destroyed the traditional moral foundations of the social order. If capitalism truly is destroying the old political culture, traditional values have evidently been a long time dying.

Attempts to assess how far there has indeed occurred a 'collapse of deference', to use Beer's phrase, illustrate once again how difficult and uncertain is the task of identifying the characteristics of a culture. Some observers have, for instance, questioned the very relevance of Beer's evidence, especially his use of examples from popular music to illustrate his case (Norton, 1984, p. 357). It might be thought that with survey data Beer would be on surer ground. In the most careful existing review of survey evidence about popular attitudes towards government between the 1940s and the 1970s, Kavanagh certainly offered the judgement that there had been a 'decline' of deference (Kavanagh, 1980, p. 156). But his discussion also showed that the evidence was fragmentary, inconsistent, and rarely allowed the systematic comparison of trends over recent decades.

Indeed, two pieces of evidence show the striking stability of popular attitudes. They both come from the mid-1970s, when bombings, strikes and street violence seemed to indicate a crisis in British attitudes to authority. The first dates from 1974, when a national survey showed that almost exactly the same proportions were optimistic about the possibility of influencing government as had expressed optimism in Almond and Verba's survey in 1959 (Barnes and Kaase, 1979, p. 141).

The second piece of evidence concerns willingness to acquiesce in the face of inequality. In the 1960s Runciman had used survey evidence to show how inequality was accepted because the poor typically compared their lot with those close to them in the social hierarchy, rather than with the rich. In sociologists' language, their reference groups were narrow and their sense of relative deprivation mild (Runciman, 1966, pp. 179–288). In the mid-1970s Daniel replicated parts of the study, at a time when high wage demands and strikes seemed to many to indicate a sharp increase in working-class expectations. His evidence actually suggested that reference groups and tolerance of inequality had not significantly altered since Runciman's original findings (Daniel, 1975).

Changes in industrial relations were nevertheless the most import-ant reason for a feeling common in the 1970s that established values and hierarchies were under attack. Strikes seemed to involve both a new level of economic demands and a newly assertive attitude to authority in the workplace. Both trade-union membership and the readiness to strike were spreading to previously acquiescent workers. The evidence of a collapse of deference in industrial relations is nevertheless unconvincing, because there is no sign of a long-term rise in militancy. Strikes in Britain have come, not in an ever-rising tide, but in periodic waves: before and immediately after the First World War, in the late 1960s and in the early 1970s. They seem to reflect particular political and economic conditions rather than any long-term collapse of respect for the prevailing social order.

The particular evidence of industrial relations illustrates a more general point: when we push beyond survey evidence, and go back beyond the 1950s, the claim that there has been a long-term collapse of deference looks highly dubious. Claims about changes over time obviously depend crucially on the point from which change is measured. The large-scale academic study of British politics began in the 1950s, and it is natural to measure change from then. But the 1950s were an unusual decade, perhaps the only one in British history to combine full employment with economic growth and the rapid spread of consumer goods throughout almost the whole population. That decade now seems a short-lived golden age. The wonder is not that dissatisfaction has risen in the intervening years, but that popular attitudes seem to have altered so little.

If we go beyond the brief golden age of the 1950s, into the more distant historical past, the notion that there has been a long-term collapse of deference looks especially dubious. By comparison with the seventeenth century, Britain is now a calm and well-ordered society. In the seventeenth century the British Isles were one of the most unstable parts of Europe, plagued by civil wars, coups, guerrilla insurrections and murderous religious strife. In the eighteenth century the English were, according to one social historian, 'one of the most aggressive, brutal, rowdy, outspoken, riotous, cruel and bloodthirsty nations in the world' (Perkin, 1969, p. 280). Maintaining the social order in the early years of the nineteenth century demanded savage public sanctions. In this century, the years before the First World War saw fierce strikes, a series of constitutional crises and parts of the country on the brink of insurrection over the Irish question. After 1916 Britain was engaged not only in a war against Germany but in a civil war in Ireland, ended only by the negotiated secession of an Irish Free State in 1921.

Of course these historical crises must not obscure that fact that by comparison with many other countries Britain's has been a stable and peaceful political history. But they do show that the conflicts and tensions of recent years are not an historical aberration. They also suggest that peace and stability in Britain were in the past guaranteed not by some inherent deference and genius for compromise, but by the determined use of physical and economic sanctions against those who challenged the existing social order.

Deference, Bagehot rightly said, is in the heart. We can never be sure if there has been a long-term collapse of deference, because we can never now know what was felt in the hearts of past generations. The available evidence nevertheless suggests the following tentative conclusions.

There really does not seem to have occurred any dramatic long-term changes in what we earlier called deference to public authority. In other words, although in recent years there probably has been some increase in readiness to break the law and to defy authority, riotous and unlawful acts are still much less common than at many periods in the past.

Changes in readiness to defer in the face of social and economic hierarchies are difficult to estimate because such a wide and often elusive range of behaviour is involved. The only systematic historical study – Hart's examination of the ideas expressed by political activists in Birmingham in the 1880s – concluded with a suggestion of some change: in the 1880s, political argument was 'couched within a very modest and traditional framework characterised by both low substantive and low normative expectations of government', whereas 'by the 1970s the substantive expectations had become more extensive' (Hart, 1978, p. 196). This, though, is evidence of a subtle shift rather than of a collapse in deference.

When we look at the evidence for the third kind of deference – readiness to support high-born political leaders on the grounds that good breeding is itself a qualification for office – the evidence for once does indeed seem clear. Three signs suggest a significant decline in its incidence. First, surveys show this sort of deference to be much commoner among the old than among the young (McKenzie and Silver, 1968). Unless we make the unlikely assumption that deference grows with age we must conclude that it is, literally, dying out. Second, the evidence suggests that deference is commonest among workers whose numbers are in decline – for instance, among those employed in agriculture and in small firms. The major study of the new working class – Goldthorpe and Lockwood's survey (1968) of 'affluent' workers – found that deference had been replaced by 'instrumental' attitudes which coolly appraised political leadership and political institutions in the light of their operational effectiveness. Finally, the evidence of broad swings in voting behaviour in recent decades suggests a growing tendency to appraise governments by their short-term ability to manage the economy.

The strengths of the 'populism' model of the political culture are that it correctly identifies some key points of stress in contemporary British politics and rightly highlights a sharp decline in deference to the high born. But the model overstates the extent to which other kinds of deference have declined and is historically short-sighted in concentrating on the events of the last couple of decades.

The 'post-affluence' and 'populism' models of the political culture share this feature: they both assume that 'civility' once did best describe the British political culture, but that civility has recently declined. By contrast, a Marxist model denies that civility ever did best describe the British case.

Alternative 3: A Marxist Model
There is no single Marxist model of the political culture, because there is no agreed Marxist account of the British political system. Indeed, the role of culture has long been a point of argument between Marxists, because Marxism contains a theoretical tradition which emphasises the primacy of objective economic forces over cultural factors. Nevertheless, there does exist a distinctive Marxist view of the political culture. It is heavily influenced by the ideas of the Italian thinker, Gramsci, who elaborated the concept of

'hegemony' (Gramsci, 1972; Anderson, 1964). Where other political scientists would speak of a dominant political culture, Marxists speak of a hegemonic, dominant or central value system.

The function of this value system is social control. It produces patterns of behaviour – obedience to the state, acquiescence in the disciplines of work – which ensure that the interests of the dominant class of property owners are served. Much of the evidence used to support the 'civility' model – of deference and of consensus, for instance – is also consistent with a Marxist account. But Marxists believe these values to have been imposed by a small number of powerful institutions. In the civility model the culture reflects a fundamental unity in the community; in the Marxist model, deference and consensus are values serving the interests of a small capitalist class in a community deeply divided on class lines (Leys, 1983, pp. 280–309). The dominant value system is propagated and inculcated by a range of powerful institutions, notably through the socialising effects of schooling and through the values conveyed by the mass media.

One of the great strengths of the Marxist model of the political culture is that it makes sense of much that is either ignored or just incomprehensible in the models already discussed. It is apparent, for instance, that the 'civility' model depends on a reading of British political history which neglects the often violent conflicts experienced in the making of the political culture. But a Marxist account can recognise the existence of values like deference, while also recognising that the creation of the culture involved the often violent imposition of one group's values on the rest of society. Likewise, Marxists can make sense of what in the civility model only appears to be inconsistency or bloodymindedness. It is well known, for instance, that many workers give 'civil' answers to questions about strikes (deploring 'unconstitutional' disputes) but then themselves take part in such disputes. This is perfectly comprehensible if popular attitudes are viewed as reflecting an imposed value system, while actual behaviour reflects the realities of workers' positions in the labour market. Marxist models also have a distinct advantage over the 'post-affluent' and 'populist' versions, because they do not have to assume a golden age of 'civility' from which Britain has declined.

A Marxist model of the political culture nevertheless faces three serious difficulties. The first is that, while the model could have predicted the tensions and conflicts of the last two decades, it has difficulty making sense of the form taken by those tensions. Some of the most serious disturbances to the political order have not been over class, but over nationality, religion and race. The significance of non-class issues like nationalism has long been a recognised problem in Marxist theory: 'the theory of nationalism represents Marxism's greatest historical failure' (Nairn, 1981, p. 329).

A second difficulty concerns the question of whether a dominant value system does indeed exist. It cannot be doubted that there exist values 'dominant' in the sense of being held by the overwhelming majority of the population; indeed the absence of such agreed values would make social life very fragile. That these fundamental values are stressed by important institutions also cannot be doubted; it would be odd if the most powerful institutions in Britain did not reflect widely held beliefs. But the notion of a dominant value *system* implies that institutions like the mass media and schools propagate a coherent and consistent set of values. It has undoubtedly been established that in certain parts of the mass media there exist biases: national newspapers overwhelmingly support the Conservative Party; studies by the Glasgow Media Group have shown that nominally neutral television news broadcasts often given unfavourable portraits of trade unionists, strikers and radicals (1976, 1980). But demonstrating that there is propagated a dominant value system requires more than evidence of such biases. The values expressed through the mass media are not only contained in overtly political reporting; they are reflected in the whole range of plays, films, popular music and other entertainment. It is not at all clear that the values thus conveyed form a system. For example, in one of the most influential attempts to specify the contents of the dominant value system Parkin (1967) included support for the Established Church as one of its components. Yet it is very doubtful that either popular music or popular entertainment reflect the values embodied in Anglicanism: the enquiring reader will find little evidence of Christian values in the *Sun* newspaper. There are numerous, often conflicting, biases in the content of the mass media: suspicion of radicals but obsession with the novel and dramatic; support for the virtues of discipline and work, but celebration of the idle and hedonistic.

A third difficulty with the Marxist model is posed by the attempt to show that the values propagated by the mass media and the education system actually shape popular beliefs. A number of studies have attempted to isolate the effect of the mass media on attitudes, and they all essentially come to the same conclusion: exposure to the media reinforces previously held values, but it rarely creates new ones. Most individuals selectively perceive communications, filtering out information and views which challenge their existing beliefs (Klapper, 1960; Blumler and McQuail, 1968; though for a different view see Dunleavy, 1985).

It can be objected that the evidence of existing studies is inconclusive, since they commonly investigate only short-term effects, typically during election campaigns. Those who propose the 'dominant value system theory'.argue, by contrast, that it is the long-term effect of repetitive bias which is important. It has not yet proved possible satisfactorily to test this notion. Any study conducted over a number of years faces the great methodological problem of disentangling the effect of media bias from the impact of the whole range of other experiences to which individuals are subject.

Doubts also exist about the shaping influence of political socialisation – learning political facts and values – in schools. It was once widely believed that such experiences were crucial, on the apparently sensible assumption that what we learn in childhood is indelibly imprinted on us for life. Those who have looked in detail at the political effects of schooling have, however, been sceptical of its long term political consequences, and even of the ability of schools significantly to affect political values in childhood (McQuail, 1968; Marsh, 1971). The notion that official institutions like schools imprint a dominant value system seems an excessively determinist view of the way political learning takes place: it understates the impact of unofficial influences, like family and friends, and it understates the human capacity to reject or ignore doctrines which do not correspond to daily experiences.

In brief, a Marxist model of the political culture performs much better than its competitors in revealing points of stress in the political system, but its account of the content of values, and of how they are created, is difficult to verify.

Alternative 4: The Conflict Model

Models of the political culture are themselves cultural creations. The concept of a political culture is so broad, and the principles by which we select appropriate evidence so uncertain, that any description will be the product of intuition and instinctive political preferences. The 'civility' model was precisely such a creation. In its original literary form it was a view of British history and of the British people from the top, usually from the vantage point of London. Even its more radical exponents stressed the unity of the British experience: George Orwell, after reviewing the inequalities in Britain and the great variations in class cultures, nevertheless concluded that 'the nation is bound together by an invisible chain' (Orwell, 1941).

These literary accounts were systematised academically in the 1950s and early 1960s, a most unusual period of peace and prosperity in British history. Even the academic studies reflected the biases of the literary originals: not only did Almond and Verba's original sample omit Northern Ireland but, as Kavanagh points out, it included only fifty-eight Welsh residents, and ninety-four from Scotland, in a total sample of 963 (Kavanagh, 1980, p. 131).

From the troubled vantage point of today we are beginning to see that it is more fruitful to stress conflict and sanctions, rather than civility, in the evolution of the political culture. This recognition is in part due to the work of historians who have examined the past in terms of the victims of historical change. Their studies highlight the importance of violence in suppressing some alternatives and facilitating others. Moore has described British political history in terms of 'the contribution of violence to gradualism', stressing how the evolution of a democratic political system depended on the extensive use of violence and other sanctions to suppress dissenting groups and to manage social tensions (Moore, 1969). E. P. Thompson (1963, 1975) has excavated hidden areas of the popular experience: the struggles between an authoritarian state and an emerging working class in the early decades of the nineteenth century; the brutality with which property rights were enforced in the eighteenth century. Studies of working life reveal that the 'deference' of the British worker was, in so far as it was forthcoming, a deference exacted by economic power and its associated institutions, not freely given in recognition of social superiority (Foster, 1979; Joyce, 1980).

In short, the political culture of Britain now looks less like an area of life where the British display their 'civility', and more like a focus for the conflicts of British society. The tensions of the 1970s and 1980s are not of course simply an extrapolation of the past; they reflect the particular circumstances of Britain's present historical position. But the fact of conflict is not at all novel. The 'civility' model reflected and celebrated a particular political settlement which was at its peak in the 1950s. This settlement involved the dominance of English nationalism over the other nationalisms in the United Kingdom; the organisation of most of the working class into a single labour movement; and the integration of that labour movement into Parliamentary and Whitehall politics. That settlement has been disturbed in recent decades, and this disturbance has given the civility model an air of unreality.

When the British reached the plateau of the affluent society in the 1950s, it seemed, looking back, as if the long journey to peace and prosperity had followed a distinctive pattern. It had been a long and arduous journey and many sacrifices had been demanded, but all classes and groups in the community had been engaged in the same upward progress and all had gained from the struggle. Moreover, the crises along the way had, it seemed, produced a united people with a shared history.

In the 1970s and 1980s, when that plateau gave way to rougher terrain, the journey from the past took on a different aspect. We remembered that not all wanted to make the trek: it had been necessary to eliminate peasants and Luddites, coerce laggards and allow the Irish to go their own way. The continuing journey had involved murder, robbery and the destruction of minority cultures. The British were indeed united by some historical experiences, but they were bitterly divided by the memory of others. After 1969, in particular, an old and terrible tragedy came back to life. Ireland once again became a central issue in British politics.

6 Northern Ireland: A Case Study of Instability

> Tribulation worketh patience; and patience, experience; and experience, hope.
>
> Romans, 5.3

The most serious challenge to the stability of British politics has occurred in Northern Ireland. The violent deaths caused by the troubles since the late 1960s are ample evidence of the British authorities' failure to maintain public security, the most elementary measure of effective government. Since Northern Irish politics are intimately shaped by a sense of the past this discussion begins with a brief historical review, ending with the imposition of direct rule in

1972. This is followed by an examination of the crux of the matter, the reasons for the breakdown of public security in the late 1960s. Finally, some important developments since 1972 are briefly summarised.

Historical Background

The history of Ireland is the history of foreign failures to conquer that country. For over four centuries after the first Norman/English landing in 1169 the province of Ulster proved especially troublesome. At the beginning of the seventeenth century the English government therefore 'planted' on the best land in the province 170,000 settlers, mostly Scottish Presbyterians, at the expense of the native Catholic population. This ambitious social experiment began a history of violent conflict between the two religious communities (Arthur, 1980). These differences did not initially involve conflict of national identities; Ulster Protestantism for long proved as troublesome a source of Irish separatism as was Catholic nationalism. Protestant unionism – support for unity with mainland Britain, under the English crown – was the product of nineteenth-century economic change. Belfast and the surrounding part of North East Ulster experienced an industrial revolution based on shipbuilding and textile production. The remainder of – largely Catholic – Ireland was almost untouched by economic development. 'Unionism' in its modern form was a response to the integration of industrial Ulster into the economy of mainland Britain, and to the threat to that integration posed by the prospect of political separation (Budge and O'Leary, 1973, pp. 101–27).

These economic differences shaped the settlement ending the Irish Nationalist uprising (1916–21). Twenty-six Southern Counties – Catholic and economically backward – were given Home Rule. Six northern counties, carved out of the historic province of Ulster so as to leave Protestants in a majority, remained in the United Kingdom. Key government powers – notably those concerning education, the maintenance of public order, the control of local government and the administration of justice – were devolved to a Parliament eventually established at Stormont, just outside Belfast.

For the whole of its life this Parliament was controlled by the Protestant majority organised in the Unionist Party. The political history of the new Province was from the beginning dominated by the divide between the Protestant majority and the Catholic minority. Religion was the chief influence on party allegiance, and national loyalties the chief ground of political differences: Protestants overwhelmingly supported, and Catholics opposed, the link with Britain.

This Catholic opposition was quite ineffective. Within a decade of Irish independence all major political groups in the South had given up everything but symbolic opposition to partition. In the North, Unionism remained perpetually dominant, sustained by a popular majority and by control over the instruments of state power. By the 1960s it seemed that the impulse behind Catholic resistance to the link with Britain was exhausted. The Irish Republican Army abandoned violence in favour of agitation based on a programme of revolutionary socialism designed to appeal across the religious divide. In Stormont, the leader of the Nationalists signalled partial acceptance of the constitution by adopting the title of 'Leader of the Opposition'. The foundation of the Northern Ireland Civil Rights Association in 1967, to campaign for social and constitutional reform, seemed a further sign that Catholics were turning from the national question to the reform of existing policies and institutions.

On the Unionist side, too, there were changes. The Unionist Premier, Captain O'Neill, held a highly conciliatory meeting in 1965 with the Irish Taoiseach. O'Neill also prompted mild measures of reform in the North and made mild gestures of sympathy towards Catholics. These changes, coming as they did after over two decades of modestly growing prosperity in the Province, seemed a sign that time and social change were healing the wounds of partition.

This optimism was destroyed in the last two years of the 1960s. Catholic demands for reforms — especially in the allocation of public housing and in the workings of local government – were increasingly voiced in popular protests, marches and other demonstrations. The Protestant majority was divided over how to respond. The leadership, while Captain O'Neill was Prime Minister, favoured compromise; lower-middle-class and working-class Protestants, especially those in the security forces, reacted with hostility. A series of street battles culminated in violence between the two communities in Derry and Belfast in 1969. The intensity of violence forced the British government to send troops into the Province.

This act began a process which within three years destroyed the constitutional arrangements established in 1921. Control over the security forces gradually passed from the hands of Unionist politicians into the control of the British authorities. Hostility between troops and Catholics grew as the army began to try to police Catholic communities. In 1970 the Provisional IRA was founded. In early 1971 the first British soldier was killed. There began a prolonged phase of sectarian murders in both communities, indiscriminate bombings by Irish Nationalists and shootings of civilians by the army. The growing security crisis destroyed the civilian apparatus of law enforcement. Internment without trial was introduced in August 1971 and jury trials were suspended for many offences in 1973. In March 1972 the British Government abolished the Stormont Parliament, imposing direct rule under a Secretary of State appointed from Westminster. Thus was abandoned the attempt to preserve the political settlement established by partition in 1921. The British Government now began a long, unsuccessful, search for an alternative set of enduring political arrangements. The imposition of direct rule marks an appropriate moment at which to turn from narrative to analysis.

Explaining the Crisis

Any satisfactory account of the breakdown of order in Northern Ireland at the end of the 1960s has to distinguish the long-term social setting from the more immediate causes of crisis. The setting was a society divided by religious and national loyalties. The division between Catholic and Protestant communities was reinforced by segregation in schools, housing, and even in leisure. It is well established that conflicts of religious and national loyalties are more difficult to reconcile than are the conflicts between classes which are characteristic of mainland Britain (Rose, 1971, pp. 397–414). But religious conflict and segregation cannot by themselves explain the breakdown of order, for the Province had been divided, yet stable, since partition. Some new and unsettling elements must have been added by the 1960s. Three elements have been identified by observers; they each correspond to a different image of the origins of the troubles.

The first element is the Catholic community's sense of grievance about discrimination by the Protestant majority. This sense of grievance certainly fuelled the political campaigns of the late 1960s. The single most important issue, for instance, concerned the way public housing was allocated between Catholics and Protestants. Rose's survey of opinion in Ulster in 1968 – the most authoritative picture of the public mood on the eve of the troubles – found a widespread belief among Catholics that they were the victims of discrimination (Rose, 1971, p. 272). There is indeed evidence that Catholics are more deprived than Protestants. The most striking sign of this is the higher unemployment rates among Catholics, especially among Catholic manual workers compared with similar groups of Protestants. Those who have examined the evidence in detail have concluded, however, that economic inequalities between the two communities are not due to discrimination (Rose, 1971, pp. 293–8). The practice of allocating jobs, houses and political office by religious affiliation rather than merit was widespread among all groups in the Province; Catholics and Protestants suffered at each other's hands. The Protestant economic advantage was largely due to other factors, notably to a history of economic development which favoured the Protestant north east at the expense of the Catholic west. Inequality was thus not mainly the result of conscious discrimination but had its roots in the economic history of the Province.

These facts have led some to stress a second element in the Ulster crisis. On this view, the breakdown of order reflected, not a response to discrimination, but a new mood of aggressive nationalism among Catholics. Supporters of this view point to the improved electoral performance of nationalists in the period before the troubles began and to evidence of nationalist support for the civil rights movement (Hewitt, 1981, disputed, O'Hearn, 1983). That there was indeed widespread Catholic rejection of the constitution is demonstrated by the evidence of Rose's survey: only one-third of Catholics expressed approval of the Northern Ireland Constitution and 40 per cent thought it acceptable for Republican groups to hold meetings or parades in defiance of the law (Rose, 1971, pp. 189–94). There is also evidence of a new political confidence among Catholics in the late 1960s. The agitation for 'civil rights' in jobs, housing and elections is evidence of the new mood.

This new confidence was itself a product of social change. By the 1960s the education system was producing significant numbers of young Catholic university graduates, who gravitated towards political activity and towards work in the expanding public sector. This public sector middle class provided many of the leaders of political agitation.

Yet it is too simple to label this new political mood nationalist. Indeed, in the second half of the 1960s there occurred, as we have already seen, a shift away from the tactics and aims traditionally associated with nationalism. Agitation for civil rights, though it posed grave problems for the Protestant majority, was a sign that Catholics were neglecting the fundamental demands of nationalism for less ambitious efforts to secure economic and political reforms.

That these more modest demands nevertheless led to the breakdown of order owed much to a third, often neglected, element in the crisis: the response of the Protestant community. The most momentous act in the crisis – the use of British troops in Derry in August 1969 – was caused by the violent Protestant response to Catholic demonstrations and, in particular, by the breakdown of discipline among the Protestant-dominated security forces. This violent response occurred in spite of the Unionist leadership which, under Captain O'Neill in particular, pursued a policy of conciliation and piecemeal reform. To understand why the Unionist leadership was unable to control its followers it is necessary to understand the character of Protestant unionism.

It is common to speak of the existence of two religious communities in the Province. This is useful shorthand, but it obscures important differences between the Catholic minority and the Protestant majority. Catholics are indeed a community: they are united doctrinally, belong to a disciplined religious hierarchy, are part of a large and influential worldwide movement and are among the most faithful church attenders on earth. Ulster Protestantism lacks this cohesion. Church attendance, though high by British standards, is lower than among Catholics. Protestant Unionism, it has often been noted, tries to create an alliance between different classes. It is less commonly noticed that Unionism also tries to ally groups with different religious beliefs and forms of worship. There are over fifty Protestant denominations in Ulster, ranging from the sophisticated latitudinarianism of the Church of Ireland to the charismatic fundamentalism of small Presbyterian sects (Moxon-Browne, 1983, pp. 81–100). Unionism has thus always been an uneasy alliance between different classes and between different religious groups. These divisions, furthermore, coincide: the traditional leadership of the Unionist party was predominantly upper class and belonged to the Church of Ireland; the mass following contained a large group that was working class and Presbyterian.

The tensions in this uneasy alliance were made more acute by economic circumstances at the end of the 1960s and by the content of Catholic demands. Unemployment, always higher in Ulster than elsewhere in the United Kingdom, rose with the general UK rise in the numbers without jobs after 1966. The housing stock was one of the poorest in Western Europe, and the level of working-class home ownership among the lowest in the regions of the UK. Catholic demands for jobs and for a larger share of public housing were thus a direct threat to the hard-pressed Protestant working class. It is small wonder that there occurred a revolt against the reforms offered by the Unionist leadership.

Developments Since Direct Rule
Developments since the early 1970s mark the working-out of many of the tensions that created the original crisis. Violence has occurred in varying waves and has taken different forms. Hostility between Catholics and Protestants, and within the two communities, has defeated numerous initiatives by the Westminster authorities. The terrorist campaigns and the more orthodox political initiatives make the recent history of Ulster complicated, but beneath the flux of everyday politics three important developments should be noted.

The first is the collapse of Ulster's industrial economy, the original economic foundation of Unionism. Between 1970 and 1979 industrial production in the Province rose by only 2 per cent; the comparable figure for the rest of Ireland was 56 per cent (Rowthorn, 1981). Between 1979 and 1982 industrial production in the Province actually fell. Registered unemployment in 1975 was, at 7 per cent, high by UK standards; for many years now the figure has exceeded 20 per cent. Even these figures understate the magnitude of decline because some significant industrial employers continue in existence only because of British government subsidies. These economic difficulties reflect partly the troubled condition of the Province and partly the fact that Ulster is the weakest part of a weak UK economy. Were the present political problems to be solved, the task of producing economic recovery would still be daunting.

The second important long-term change concerns the movement of opinion in the Province. The violence of the last fifteen years might be expected to have caused growing bitterness between Catholics and Protestants, but an equally plausible alternative expectation is that exhaustion with violence might lead to a desire for reconciliation. Impressionistic evidence can be found to support both expectations: on the one hand, there is apparently growing

electoral support in both communities for those opposed to conciliation; on the other, there have occurred periodic surges of sympathy
for those who advocate reconciliation. The most striking illustration
of the latter was the rapid growth of support for the 'Peace People'
after some especially horrific killings in 1976.

Moxon-Browne's survey of public opinion in the Province, carried out after a decade of the troubles, suggests that neither of these
expectations has been fulfilled. Comparing his findings with those
reported by Rose a decade earlier, Moxon-Browne suggests that
opinions, and notably differences between the communities, have
'crystallised' over the years, but that the evidence does not support
the common caricature of a society rent asunder (1983, p. 167). The
clearest sign of crystallisation is the change in perceptions of
national identity compared with the perceptions uncovered by Rose.
In the late 1960s 32 per cent of Protestants were ready to use the
label 'Ulster' to describe their national identity, and a small minority
of Catholics were ready to do the same. The notion of an Ulster
nation has subsequently often been canvassed as a compromise
between Unionism and Irish Catholic nationalism. Moxon-
Browne's findings suggest that such a compromise is now unlikely.
There has been no significant rise in the proportion of Catholics
prepared to identify with Ulster, while large numbers of Protestants
have deserted Ulster nationalism in favour of a firm identification
with Britain. In 1968, 39 per cent of Protestants said they were
British; ten years later the figure was 67 per cent (Moxon-Browne,
1983, p. 6).

These shifts in national identity were the product of a decade of
trauma for Protestants. This trauma shattered the old Unionist
Party. The realignment of the political forces previously organised
under the single banner of Unionism is the third major long-term
change since the beginning of the troubles. For a time in the 1970s it
seemed that Protestantism would become almost as fragmented
politically as it is theologically. It now appears, however, that two
broad groupings have formed: the Official Unionists, the heirs of the
traditional Unionist Party; and the Reverend Ian Paisley's Democratic Unionist Party (DUP), the voice of those Presbyterians who
rebelled against the conciliatory policies of the Unionist leadership
in the 1960s. The DUP is weakest among Church of Ireland
members and among those of high socio-economic status; conversely, it is strongest among Presbyterians and especially among
skilled and semi-skilled manual workers. Demographic change is

firmly on its side: Moxon-Browne found that whereas just over 55 per cent of its supporters were under forty-five years of age, the same was true of only 40 per cent of Official Unionist supporters (1983, p. 97).

Much writing about Northern Ireland is apocalyptic in tone. Many events since 1968 justify that tone. It is nevertheless worth empha-sising, in closing this brief review of the politics of the Province, that Northern Ireland is in many ways a stable and successful part of the United Kingdom. The major surveys of opinion show a high level of satisfaction with life in the Province. In Rose's survey, for instance, the second most disliked feature of life in Northern Ireland was that trivial perennial, the weather. This satisfaction is partly due to the marginal place occupied by politics and the discontents of politics in most people's lives; and partly to the well-documented capacity of human beings to adapt to odd and stressful circumstances.

But the sense of popular satisfaction also rests on solid social achievements. Family life is more stable in the Province than anywhere else in the United Kingdom: the divorce rate and the rate at which children are taken into care are both the lowest in the UK. Perhaps in consequence, educational standards are remarkably high. Measured by standard tests, and by success in public examinations, Ulster children achieve results which are above average for the United Kingdom. This is striking when we recall that most features usually associated with educational failure – unemployment, low income, poor housing – are commoner in Ulster than on mainland Britain. Northern Ireland is also a remarkably peaceful Province. This statement is less odd than it sounds. Before the troubles began, the rate for deaths by violence was among the lowest in the Western world. In 1982, rates of sexual offences were the lowest in any region of the UK and the incidence of violence against the person was lower than in England. On most other measures of criminality Northern Ireland is also low in the UK scale (Central Statistical Office, 1988b). The breakdown of a particular political order has not led to a more general collapse of social stability.

7 Conclusion

The future, we know, is always unpredictable; studying the British political culture reminds us that the past can also be unpredictable.

Our view of the political culture is influenced by our understanding of our country's history, but the British experience is too rich and contradictory to form a single shape. Our view of the past is governed by our own instinctive preconceptions and by the particular historical vantage point which we occupy. Models of the political culture – notably the civility model – portray particular and partial images of the past. They have to be treated as cultural creations, not as straightforward factual representations. The British political culture is a baffling and contradictory phenomenon not, as is sometimes implied, an immediately obvious and coherent system of values. Culture constrains both the forms of popular political participation and the content of mass political demands. The most popular kind of mass participation is voting – the subject of Chapter 3.

3

Elections and Electors

> The race is not to the swift, nor the battle to the strong, neither yet bread to the wise, nor riches to men of understanding, nor yet favour to men of skill; but time and chance happeneth to them all.

> Ecclesiastes, 9.11

1 Outline

Few people in Britain participate in party politics. Less than 5 per cent of the electorate subscribe to a political party and only about three in every thousand hold some party office (Butler and Stokes, 1974, p. 21). One partisan political act is nevertheless widespread. On thirteen occasions since the Second World War over 70 per cent of adults on the electoral register have cast their vote in favour of a political party in a General Election. The fact that voting is such a common political act gives it a special interest. This interest is heightened by the consequences of elections. The votes cast in a General Election influence – though in an arithmetically complicated way – both the composition of the House of Commons and the partisan control of government.

This chapter therefore examines the voting behaviour of the British people. It begins by answering the most elementary questions: who votes? And how has the composition of the electorate changed over time? Section 3 examines the role of class, traditionally seen as the greatest influence on voting loyalties. The preferences of electors have altered greatly in recent years; section 4 examines these changes. Section 5 describes how individual choices are converted into winning combinations in British elections. The final section of the chapter looks back to changes in individual behaviour, examining the major general interpretations of the forces creating a new electorate in Britain.

2 Who Votes?

Since the United Kingdom is conventionally pictured as operating a system of universal adult suffrage it might be imagined that voters are simply identical with the adult population. This is not so. 'Universality' is limited by the rules governing eligibility to register as an elector, by the practicalities of registration and by the obstacles that registered electors face in casting a vote. The effect of each separate obstacle is small; cumulatively they help explain why in elections held under 'universal' suffrage between 20 and 30 per cent of adults do not vote.

Legal prohibitions disqualify a wide range of groups from voting. Some – such as peers of the realm – are minute in number. Others are much larger: they include aliens, most inmates of mental hospitals, and the 36,000 convicted inmates of prisons. To these should be added many thousands of vagrants and itinerants who, having no fixed address, cannot register as voters.

Those adults who can claim a vote (the vast majority) must do so by registering as electors. Since 1918, registration has been simple, with most of the work being done by public officials. Nevertheless, filling in the appropriate forms is a voluntary act which is the responsibility of the head of each household. It is estimated that 4 per cent of those eligible are not registered. The excluded are drawn disproportionately from young, poor, and non-white citizens: in 1970, for instance, only about 70 per cent of the newly enfranchised 18–21-year-olds were on the register, while survey evidence for the late 1970s suggests that a fifth of eligible non-white citizens are not registered (Butler and Stokes, 1974, p. 228; Crewe, 1983b, p. 269).

Casting a ballot is such a simple task that it might be thought that no interested elector would find difficulty in doing so. A variety of limitations nevertheless creates obstacles for a sizeable minority. Voters must normally cast their ballot in person at a particular polling station near their home on a single working day. The appropriate polling station for an elector is fixed by home address when registration takes place each October. These rules make it difficult or impossible for many to vote. Every year nearly a million electors move house a significant distance from their registered polling station (Electoral Register Working Party, 1978). Though postal votes can be cast, they have to be independently applied for and are given only under restrictive conditions. Population change means that throughout the year of its life the annually compiled Electoral Register becomes increasingly inaccurate as a guide to who can vote. In addition to the effects of removals, it is estimated that each month fifteen voters in every thousand are lost by death.

These mundane facts have important consequences. They mean, for instance, that 'measured' turnout in an election is not an accurate indicator of the proportion of electors capable of voting who actually do so. When a register is 'old', measured turnout significantly understates the true proportion of those voting. This in turn can affect important interpretations of British politics. In the mid-1970s, for instance, many commentators pointed to apparently declining turnout as evidence of disillusionment among voters: in 1951, for example, turnout was over 82 per cent, while in October 1974 the figure was 72.5 per cent. But when the latter figure is adjusted for the age of the register (based as it was on voters registered in October 1973) real turnout in 1974 rises to nearly 79 per cent. The 'disillusion' of voters thus turns out to be a statistical quirk (Särlvik and Crewe, 1983, p. 364).

The obstacles adults face in casting a vote also help explain an important feature of non-voting. It was conventionally thought that non-voters formed a distinct group drawn from the poorest and least well educated. The best survey evidence now contradicts this view: only a minute proportion (about 1 per cent of national samples) never vote; most non-voters abstain in a single election and turn out in the next; and abstainers are not distinguished from voters by any of the usual signs of class or education (Crewe *et al.*, 1977, pp. 47–63).

It will be obvious even from this sketch that the identity of those who vote in any particular election is influenced by many factors, including the laws governing the right to claim a vote, the way registration is organised and the conditions under which elections are actually held. These conditions have in the past modified the extent to which the electorate accurately mirrored important characteristics of the wider population.

The most important long-term trends in the composition of the electorate are its growing size and its growing statistical representativeness. The two developments are connected. In 1831 there were just over half-a-million voters in the United Kingdom; by 1900 the figure had grown to just over six and a half million; in the mid-1960s it was over thirty-one million; now it exceeds forty-three million. Part of this long-term growth was due to population increase: between 1900 and 1981, for instance, the population over the age of 21 nearly doubled. The most dramatic increases have, however, been caused by changes in electoral law. A succession of Reform Acts (in 1832, 1867 and 1884–85) progressively moderated the property qualifications needed by adult men to claim a vote, and in so doing increased both the size of the electorate and the range of social groups which it contained. The biggest changes came under the Representation of the People Act, 1918. This Act made the electorate more demographically representative by enfranchising women aged 30 and more. It also made voters more socially representative by greatly simplifying the registration laws so as to allow almost all men over 21 to register as voters. Under the laws previously in force about 40 per cent of men – mostly from the poor and the young – had in effect been prevented from registering by contentious and cumbersome procedures (Blewett, 1965). Later changes have made the electorate more representative in terms of gender (by enfranchising women of 21 and over, in 1928) and more representative in terms of age (by lowering the qualifying age to 18, in 1969).

Electoral laws have thus decisively changed the size and composition of the electorate in the past. The scope for further dramatic change is probably limited. Future alterations in size and structure will reflect the slower agencies of social change. The century-and-a-half-long expansion in the size of the electorate will soon be halted by the sharp fall in birth rates of the last two decades. Three important changes in social character are occurring: the electorate is becoming more suburban, more ethnically diverse, and more middle class occupationally. Each are here examined in turn.

Electoral reforms in the nineteenth century were as much influenced by the need to give representatives to territorial units – the new industrial cities – as to enfranchise social classes. Modern electoral law is guided by the principle (not always observed) that voters should be grouped in constituencies of equal proportions. Shifting populations therefore eventually cause shifts in constituency boundaries. The most noticeable effect has come with the decline of the population of inner cities and the migration of electors to suburbs and, to a lesser extent, to small towns and villages.

The growth in ethnic diversity is long established. Since before the First World War Catholic and Jewish immigrants have formed significant blocks of voters. Non-white immigrants and their descendants are now adding to diversity. The importance of ethnic voters exceeds their size because ethnic groups tend to be concentrated in particular constituencies: ethnic minorities make up more than 25 per cent of the population in sixteen constituencies and are numerous enough to decisively influence the vote in perhaps thirty more, though this influence is far from being fully realised because minorities rarely vote as a united block.

Changing class composition is plain whether we use the indicators of occupational or of housing classes. After 1832 successive reforms broadened the class base of the electorate; this culminated in the reforms of 1918 which put manual workers and their families into a clear majority. The social and economic changes noted in Chapter 1 have since then been reducing the size of that majority: even in the relatively short span between the mid-1960s and the end of the 1970s the proportion of the electorate made up of workers declined from 64 to 56 per cent. The transformation in housing tenure during the century has had equally important effects: by the late 1970s, 40 per cent of the 'occupational' working class lived in their own homes, and by the late 1980s the figure was well over a half (Crewe, 1982, 1987).

Changes in class composition are important because of the key part played by class in shaping British voting behaviour. Section 3 examines our understanding of the role of class before the upheavals in voting that occurred in the last decade.

3 Class and the British Elector

The Shape of Class Voting
In an often quoted judgement delivered in the 1960s Pulzer summed up our understanding at that time of the forces shaping electoral loyalties in Britain. 'Class', he wrote, 'is the basis of British party politics; all else is embellishment and detail' (1967, p. 98). Class did indeed shape the structure of party loyalty in the electorate; but the embellishment and detail were often so rich as to hide that basic structure. These embellishments were in part a historical legacy, but even in the 1960s the influence of class was also being modified by new social conditions. Two decades later social change has seriously damaged important parts of the structure of class politics.

The shape of class-based voting before it was seriously damaged by social change can be established by looking at the electorate in the mid-1960s. At that time the most economical way of making sense of British voting behaviour was to picture the electorate as divided into two broad occupational classes, non-manual and manual workers and their families, who overwhelmingly supported the Conservative and Labour Parties respectively. For instance, in the 1966 General Election – the last before the structure began to suffer serious damage – Conservative and Labour between them attracted 89.8 per cent of all votes cast. The most reliable survey evidence of the time also indicated that 80 per cent of the electorate pictured themselves as supporters of (as distinct from mere voters for) one or other of the two main parties. In their social profiles, the same survey evidence suggested, the parties were almost mirror images of each other. In 1963, of those who identified with a major party, 75 per cent of non-manual workers described themselves as Conservatives while 72 per cent of manual workers said they were Labour supporters (Butler and Stokes, 1974, p. 203).

These figures show the importance of class on voting at the time, but they also reveal its limits: over a quarter of all voters crossed social and political boundaries to desert the party supported by a majority of their own class. These limits become even clearer when we examine, not the proportions in each class supporting particular parties, but the contribution to the Conservative and Labour vote made by those different classes. Figure 3.1 contains figures, derived from the major surveys, of the class composition of party support after 1959. The figures show that the two big parties have long differed in the extent to which they rely for electoral support on a single class. Labour emerges as the quintessential class party in the three general elections between 1959 and 1966. Survey evidence indicates that in this period non-manual workers accounted for less than a fifth of its total vote. By contrast, in the same three elections the manual worker vote never accounted for less than two-fifths of Conservative support. These differences largely resulted from the majority enjoyed by manual workers and their families in the population, rather than from differences in the ability of the two parties to draw voters across class boundaries. In 1966, for instance, Labour attracted 26 per cent of non-manual workers' votes but this only yielded 19 per cent of the Party's total vote; the Conservatives attracted a quarter of the larger manual workers' votes and this yielded 40 per cent of the Party's total support. (The increased contribution made by non-manual workers and their families to Labour's total vote in the 1970s, evident in Figure 3.1, is examined in the next section.)

The greater importance of a single class to the Labour vote than to the Conservative is emphasised by an additional fact. The survey evidence shows that not only has Labour drawn its support overwhelmingly from one class, but that Labour voters are more likely

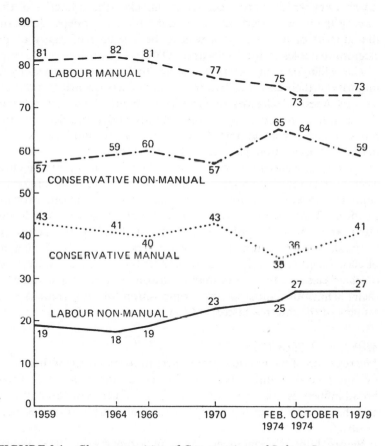

FIGURE 3.1 *Class composition of Conservative and Labour Party support* (% of total vote for each party accounted for by manual and non-manual electors)

Source: Särlvik and Crewe (1983) p. 90, table 3.6; data from successive British Election Studies. Reproduced with permission.

than are Conservatives to be moved by a sense of class consciousness. Surveys taken at different times over nearly two decades show Labour voters as more ready to see society divided between classes, to picture politics as the expression of class conflict, and to justify party loyalty on grounds of class interest (Butler and Stokes, 1974, p. 91; Särlvik and Crewe, 1983, pp. 137–40).

In the 1960s – the first decade for which we have satisfactory evidence – class was thus the key to British electoral behaviour, but it was a key which more successfully unlocked the mysteries of the Labour than the Conservative vote. Labour's greater dependence on the support of a single class was to be a source of many of its electoral troubles in the 1970s and 1980s.

The willingness of voters to desert the party supported by a majority of their class has had important effects on British politics. The readiness of electors in families of manual workers to vote Conservative created both an opportunity and a problem for the Party: without such support the Conservatives would have been in permanent opposition; gaining that support forced Conservatives to adopt some policies not readily approved by the bulk of middle-class electors. Conversely, Labour's failure to attract full working-class support compelled it to appeal to middle-class voters in order to win elections. That necessity created a continuing argument inside the Party about how far policy should be modified to the perceived demands of the middle class. Those electors who, even at the height of class-based voting, declined to support the party chosen by most of 'their' class are thus more than a curiosity of electoral arithmetic; their behaviour coloured the composition of government and influenced the internal history of the two major parties.

Modifiers of Class Voting
The rejection of the political preferences of the majority of their class by this crucial group is best understood as the product of three broad influences: the legacy of history, the influence of sub-cultures, and the impact of economic change. Each of these is examined here in turn.

Before Labour's emergence as a major party in 1918, voting loyalties were deeply influenced by religion, region and tradition. Labour's rise was accomplished not only by converting older voters from their past habits, but also by attracting disproportionate support among successive generations of new working-class voters.

Butler and Stokes found that, as late as 1970, the percentage of working-class Conservative voters among those who were old enough to have voted before 1918, was nearly double that of those who were first able to vote in 1945 (1974, p. 186).

Higher levels of Conservative voting among the old has sometimes been ascribed to the process of ageing itself, on the grounds that advancing years bring hostility to change. Survey evidence refutes this apparently common sense notion. There are distinct generations of voters. Their views are deeply influenced by the historical epoch in which they came to political maturity. Electors who matured up to 1918 did so in a society where influences other than class were powerful and where Labour was an insignificant force. Voters who matured up to 1945 did so under the influence of depression and war, when Labour was a major political force. Historical experience, not the mere process of ageing, is what lodged so many older working-class Conservative voters in the electorate in the 1960s.

Influences from the past also explain why levels of Conservative voting in all classes were until recently higher among women than among men in the same class. This was not due to some innate feminine Conservatism but to the fact that older voters included a majority of women. Women live longer than men on average, and – among the generation reaching adulthood before 1918 – fewer were killed in the First World War. Time has now almost obliterated political differences between the sexes: among younger women the Conservative lead has disappeared (Hills, 1981, p. 17; Crewe, 1987).

The influence of the past on voting behaviour partly operates through sub-cultures, some of which are shaped by traditional institutions and values. A sub-culture is a set of beliefs, distinct from those common in the wider society, formed by a particular group united by some common characteristic such as territory, religion or occupation. In a diverse society such as exists in Britain, individuals will often be pulled in a variety of directions by membership of different groups. Some sub-cultures actually increase the tendency to vote on class lines: that seems the best interpretation of the especially high proportions of manual workers who vote Labour in traditional working-class communities, and likewise of the especially high level of support among non-manual workers for the Conservative Party in localities where there exists a dominant middle-class population and its institutions (Butler and Stokes, 1974, pp. 130–2).

These very influences, however, also seem able to draw voters away from the party supported by a majority of their class. In Wales, for instance, where the Conservatives have always been in a minority, middle-class support for Labour has been strikingly higher than the average for the whole of Britain; in the 1960s it was more than double the average for the rest of Britain, while the standard study of the Welsh electorate in the 1979 election demonstrated that the Conservative weakness still persists. A significant amount of this support has been shown to derive from a sense of being Welsh, and from a rejection of the Conservatives as too 'English' a party (Butler and Stokes, 1974, pp. 126–7; Balsom *et al.*, 1983).

Middle-class Conservatism has also been weaker than average among certain religious groups: middle-class Catholics, Jews and Nonconformists have all been more likely than the more secularly minded of their class to desert the Conservatives, usually for the Labour Party. Middle-class Labour voting – indeed middle-class support for all kinds of radical political action – is also especially strong in certain occupations, such as university lecturing and social work. The explanation for this seems to be twofold: some jobs are disproportionately attractive to middle-class Labour sympathisers; and in those occupations the dominant set of values is consequently hostile to many of the beliefs associated with the Conservative Party.

The importance of sub-cultures also makes sense of much working-class Conservatism. It has been shown in repeated surveys that working-class support for the Party is disproportionately high in localities where Conservatism is already dominant – like the seaside resorts of the South Coast and in dockyard towns. There has in the past also been some connection between active membership of the Church of England and working-class Conservatism. Likewise, certain groups of manual workers – notably those in small enterprises where unions are weak and where there exists personal contact with employers – have been especially likely to vote Conservative.

The decline of some sub-cultures and the creation of others is plainly connected to economic change, the third broad modifier of class voting. Even before the electoral upheavals of the 1970s and 1980s it was plain that economic change was altering electoral loyalties. The Labour Party's defeat in the 1959 General Election – its third successive failure – produced a highly influential theory that, with affluence, 'embourgeoisement' was spreading middle-class ideas and voting habits into sections of the working class previously loyal to Labour (Abrams *et al.*,1960). This simple theory of embourgeoisement was false. Labour's victories in the two General Elections held in the 1960s, and a detailed study of the attitudes of 'affluent' workers (Goldthorpe and Lockwood, 1968) disproved the notion that affluence inevitably inclined workers away from the Party. There is nevertheless convincing evidence that by the 1960s economic change was altering the way electors, especially working-class electors, viewed the political parties. Manual workers prepared to vote Conservative on the grounds of deference to its high-born leaders were declining in number, to be replaced by working-class voters who gave support on a narrower estimate of the Party's ability to run the economy (McKenzie and Silver, 1968). A similar growth of what came to be called 'instrumental' voting was observable among working-class Labour voters. In Butler and Stokes's monumental survey, the working-class generation which first voted in 1945 was more marked than either its predecessors or its successors by a readiness both to vote Labour and to picture politics as turning on class conflict. By contrast, younger working-class voters, when they supported Labour, tended to do so more often on grounds of individual economic calculation rather than because the Party was viewed as promoting working-class interests (Butler and Stokes, 1974, pp. 193–208).

Change was also altering the political outlook of the middle class. Labour's chances of tempting middle-class voters were raised by a number of social trends, notably the rise of a substantial group of non-manual workers who were upwardly mobile from the working class, and the expansion of public sector occupations more sympathetic to Labour than was usual among non-manual workers in the private sector.

In short, even at the height of class-based voting, changes were already creating a new British electorate.

4 The New Electorate

Since the late 1960s great changes have occurred in the outlook and behaviour of electors in Britain. Some very complicated developments can be reduced to three broad trends: a decline in support for the two parties who have dominated British politics since shortly after the First World War; a decline in the significance of occupational class, the major influence on voting since the First World War; and a growing fragmentation in the electorate.

Declining Support for the Two Major Parties

Electoral support for the Labour and Conservative Parties has fallen in two ways: they attract fewer votes; and the commitment felt by their remaining supporters has weakened. Figure 3.2 illustrates the magnitude of the change in the first of these. Up to and including 1970 the overwhelming proportion of votes cast favoured the two major parties; the sharp fall since then culminated in their receiving a smaller combined share of the votes cast in 1983 than at any General Election held in the last sixty years, and while the 1987 figure shows some reversal of this trend, the historical decline is still

FIGURE 3.2   *Two-party share of vote, 1945–87 (% of votes cast)*

clear. The decline is even more striking when we trace changes in the proportion of all electors prepared to turn out for Conservative or Labour: figures show that the parties' hold over the electorate began declining after 1964 and reached a post-war low in 1983.

This simple summary conveys some of the important changes that have occurred, but in two important ways it misleads: by magnifying the rate at which voters have rejected the two parties, and by concealing the differences in misfortune experienced by Labour and Conservatives. Much of the variation in the two-party share of the vote was due to the changing fortunes of the Liberal Party. Changes in the Liberal vote were heavily influenced by the number of Liberal candidates fielded. In 1979, for instance, the Party's share of the vote was nearly five times greater than in 1951. This improvement was, however, almost all due to the fact that whereas in 1979 Liberals fought 523 seats, in 1951 they fought only 109. The average share of the vote per Liberal candidate actually only rose 0.2 per cent in the intervening twenty-eight years. Of course the very readiness of third parties to fight more seats is a sign of the growing challenge to Labour and the Conservatives; but the resulting fall in the two-party share of the vote exaggerates the severity of decline. The drop in the popularity of the two main parties, while significant, is therefore not as great as the simplest measures suggest.

Decline has also affected the two big parties unequally. Great care has to be taken in interpreting trends in popularity, because the result in any single election is affected by transitory influences. Despite the uncertainties of interpretation it does, however, seem safe to conclude from Figure 3.2 that the Conservative decline has been less steep and less continuous than has that of the Labour Party. By 1983 Labour was less popular with the electorate than at any time since 1918. The Conservative decline, though marked, has been more erratic in its progress and less precipitous.

Election results give us a simple and important measure of the support enjoyed by parties, but they tell us nothing about the way voters view those parties. Surveys have shown that most electors in Britain not only vote periodically, but also think of themselves as supporters of a particular political party, even though they may desert that party in the polling booth. Voters are also prepared to say how strongly they identify with, or support, a party, discriminating between 'very strong', 'fairly strong' and 'not very strong' support. 'Very strong' supporters are a critical group. The survey evidence shows, not surprisingly, that they are most likely to vote for their party in successive elections. They are therefore a bedrock who can be rested on in good times and bad. The experience of recent elections would lead us to expect a decline in the extent and intensity of identification with the two main parties. The evidence only partly bears out this expectation. Reliable survey evidence goes back to the mid-1960s. It shows that between 1964 and 1979 the percentage of the electorate who identified with one of the two main parties fell from 81 to 74 per cent. However, 6 per cent of this fall was in the Labour Party's share, and even this is of no great significance given the margins of error within which surveys work. By contrast, the proportion of supporters prepared to identify 'very strongly' with one of the main parties has shown a catastrophic fall. In 1964, 48 per cent of Conservative and 51 per cent of Labour supporters identified 'very strongly' with their respective parties; by 1979 the figures had fallen to 24 and 29 per cent respectively. In both parties the sharpest falls occurred between 1970 and 1974 (Särlvik and Crewe, 1983, pp. 333–8).

This erosion of the foundations of party support has some connection with the way the class base of voting has altered.

Declining Influence of Occupational Class
Occupational class is still a key influence on voting in Britain, but the significance of the divide between manual and non-manual workers is declining. The single most important change – and the reason for the Labour Party's decline – is Labour's growing inability to attract the votes of manual workers. The most instructive comparison is between 1959 and 1983, both occasions when the Conservatives won 'landslide' Parliamentary majorities. Labour's humiliation in 1959 – a defeat which provoked a widespread feeling that the Party was out of touch with a newly affluent working class – nevertheless saw it attract the support of 62 per cent of manual workers and their families. By 1983, Crewe has calculated, only 38 per cent of the same class voted Labour. Even in the very lowest socio-economic groups of semi-skilled and unskilled workers, traditionally the core of Labour's support, the Party got less than half of the vote (Crewe, 1983a).

As recently as the 1960s those manual workers and their families who declined to vote Labour were an interesting minority whose departure from the political loyalties of their class required special explanation; by the 1980s it was the minority loyal to Labour among the working class who were the statistical curiosity. The collapse of Labour strength is the more remarkable when we recall that many of the factors that drew the working class away from the Party as late as the 1960s had by the 1980s declined to insignificance: voters who inherited pre-Labour loyalties are now almost all dead; the special Conservative sympathies of women have likewise died away; and the tradition of working-class Tory Anglicanism has withered.

The declining political unity of the working class has been accompanied by a fall, though of lesser proportions, in the political unity of the middle classes. The Conservatives apparently attracted a slightly lower percentage of the non-manual vote in 1983 (when they achieved a great Parliamentary victory) than they attracted in 1966, when they were the victims of a Labour Parliamentary landslide. Labour has been a beneficiary of this trend, though only in a modest way. While its support among manual workers was being eaten away, the proportion in the non-manual categories voting Labour held steady, at least until the disaster of 1983. Indeed, among the very top groups Labour advanced: in the social categories A/B (professional and managerial) the Party's share of the vote rose from 9 per cent in 1964 to 23 per cent in 1979 (Harrop, 1982). Even in the 1983 election this figure, survey evidence indicates, was still higher (at 12 per cent) than in Labour's much more successful campaign nineteen years before (Crewe, 1983a).

The result of this change, coupled with the increasing proportion of the electorate drawn from the families of non-manual workers, is that the percentage of the Labour vote accounted for by the occupational groups conventionally labelled 'middle class' has risen in the last twenty years. Labour's reliance on the votes of a single class – its most distinctive electoral feature in the 1960s – has therefore lessened. This change is due in part to the Party's declining attraction to working-class electors. That is the gloomy side of the tale from Labour's point of view. But the gloomy conclusion for the Conservatives is that their traditionally firm hold on the middle-class vote is weakening, and that the middle class are finding their principal rival increasingly attractive.

Fragmentation of the Electorate
The declining level of strong identification with the two main parties, and the weakening hold of occupational class on voters, has reduced

the strength of two powerful anchors of stability in the electorate. It is commonly believed that the result has made voters more volatile in their behaviour. Some striking evidence supports this view. Over the post-war years the results of by-elections have increasingly failed to confirm the result in the preceding General Election, particularly when that original result was in favour of the governing party: in the ten years after the end of the Second World War the Government lost only one seat in a by-election; in the decade after 1970 governing parties lost twelve by-elections. (In some degree, however, this is a reversion to a pre-1945 pattern.) Opinion polls have also shown some extraordinary swings in levels of popular support for particular parties. Before the formation of the Social Democratic Party in 1981, for example, the popular support for the Liberal Party was only 15 per cent of those questioned in national surveys. Within two months over 43 per cent of voters were expressing a readiness to vote for an Alliance between Liberals and the SDP; within another year, after the Falklands war, support had dropped to below 20 per cent; in the election of 1983 just over a quarter of those voting actually gave the Alliance their support; and in 1987 the figure fell to 22 per cent. Oscillations of this magnitude reflect the fact that support for third parties is exceptionally unstable. The Liberals and their allies again provide the best-documented case: nearly half who voted Liberal in February 1974 did not do so in the General Election of the following October; even of those who stayed, only half voted Liberal in May 1979 (Rasmussen, 1981). It seems from all this that the British elector is growing increasingly fickle.

The best evidence does not support such a view. It suggests, not that the rate of change in loyalties among electors has grown, but that the electorate has become much more fragmented in its loyalties than was the case when two big parties virtually monopolised voter choice. The 'stability' of electoral loyalties in the past was largely a statistical illusion produced by inspection of aggregate results. Superficial inspection of the results of the 1959 and 1964 General Elections would suggest, for instance, that the electorate was largely divided into two great blocks of Conservative and Labour voters, and that Labour overtook the Conservatives between the two elections by detaching a small number of Conservative voters from their Party. Thus in 1959 Labour lost the Parliamentary battle with 43.8 per cent of the vote and in 1964 won with 44.1 per cent. This apparent stability actually hid hectic change. We discover the way individual voters alter their loyalties by asking them in surveys to recollect their past voting behaviour and by conducting 'panel' surveys which interview the same voters at different times. Butler and Stokes found – using both these methods – that between 1959 and 1964 only 54 per cent of their representative samples were supporters of the same party on both occasions. Labour's apparently stable block of support was made up not only of those who supported it in 1959, but also of first-time voters, those who had abstained in 1959, and converts from other parties. A similar flux was observable in the body of Conservative support (Butler and Stokes, 1974, p. 269). Thus even in the great age of the two-party system the superficially stable levels of support for the parties hid largely self-cancelling transfers of voters between the parties, and into and out of voting. Särlvik and Crewe's authoritative surveys of voters in the 1970s, using similar methods to trace changes in the loyalties of individual voters, found no marked alteration in the rate at which this kind of flux occurred (1983, p. 66). There has evidently been no increase in the rate at which voters desert parties from whom they previously voted. (It is possible, however, that increased campaigning in highly publicised by-elections is encouraging voters to abandon established loyalties on those occasions.)

Electors are not, therefore, more volatile than in the recent past; but the electorate as a whole is more fragmented in the choices it makes. The result is that changes are less likely than in the past to 'cancel out', leaving parties with stable overall levels of support. As recently as twenty years ago the overwhelming majority of voters, if they deserted a party, only opted for one of two choices: abstention or support for the other major party. In the 1980s a third choice – the 'Alliance' – was selected by a sizeable minority, while in Wales and Scotland a smaller but still significant group opted to support Nationalists.

The fragmentation of partisan choice has been compounded by a growing territorial fragmentation of the electorate. Although there have always been great variations in the strength of different parties in different regions, in the great age of class-based voting 'swings' in the two-party vote (the net percentage shift in the strength of the two parties between two elections) were remarkably uniform throughout Britain. In other words, the electorate deserted or moved to a party at much the same rate throughout the country. This uniformity is disappearing. Curtice and Steed's detailed examination of the statistics now shows that since the mid-1950s there has been a systematic cumulative variation in swing between North and South Britain and between urban and rural areas. The Conservatives have fared better in swings in the South and in rural areas, their opponents better in the North and in inner cities. The consequence has been an increase in the extent to which class division in the electorate is overlain by geographical division (Curtice and Steed, 1982 and 1986). Survey evidence for the two General Elections of the 1980s indicates a growing gap between the working class in the South (where the Conservatives are the main attraction) and the North, where Labour retains its traditional lead (Crewe, 1983a and 1987).

The electoral system has greatly magnified this territorial fragmentation at the Parliamentary level. The way in which popular votes are converted into Parliamentary seats is described in the next section.

5 The Outcome of Elections

The literature on electoral behaviour is largely concerned with how individual voters make choices. For most parties, however, winning the support of individual electors is only a means to other ends. Candidates 'win' Parliamentary elections in Britain by securing more votes than any single rival in a contest fought in a territorial constituency; parties 'win' elections when a sufficient number of their candidates are elected to allow the Party a majority of seats in the House of Commons. Analysing the outcome of elections thus involves examining how two quantities are fixed: the popular vote secured by a party, and the number of Parliamentary seats which it can claim as a result of that popular vote. A party's share of the popular vote is rarely the same as its share of Parliamentary seats. The determination of the two different quantities is here examined in turn.

We already know that support for all political parties is in a constant state of flux. The make-up of a party's popular vote is the outcome of a complicated sum balancing out those whose support has been retained from a previous election, those who for various reasons have ceased to vote for the party, and those who have been newly attracted to its ranks.

Aggregate voting statistics, especially measures of 'swings' in the popular share of the vote between the parties, convey the impression that a party's popular vote is overwhelmingly composed of those who voted for it in the past. Survey evidence shows, however, that the proportion of voters retained from the previous General Election varies greatly between different parties and at different times. Even the biggest parties with the most stable bodies of support typically only retain around three-quarters of their support between elections; smaller parties, with more volatile support, can lose more than half of their voters.

Parties lose voters between elections for a variety of reasons. A small minority leave the register by emigrating, though no particular party seems to suffer disproportionately through these losses. A much larger group leaves the electorate through the graveyard and the crematorium. In a typical five-year period – the legal limit of a Parliament's life – nearly 8 per cent of the electorate die. This inevitable loss, mostly among the old, means that a party's fortunes from one election to another can be critically affected by its relative popularity among different generations of electors. Losses through voters leaving the register are a major drain on a party's vote between one election and the next. A second major loss comes from supporters who fail to turn out on election day: parties typically lose between 5 and 10 per cent of their support between two elections through such abstentions. A third loss is sustained by the conversion of past supporters to active voting for other parties. The language of 'swings' in support between parties implies that conversion is the main determinant of the changing share of the vote between parties. The evidence is that straight conversions between supporters of the two main parties are rare: even in the Conservatives' great victory of 1983 only 7 per cent of Labour's voters from four years before had moved into the Tory camp (Crewe, 1983a). The most significant loss through conversion occurs through desertions to third parties.

All parties, even those enjoying great electoral success, therefore suffer a constant drain of support. A small minority are lost to emigration; a much larger group to the undertakers; significant numbers abstain from voting or switch to rivals.

A party which failed to make up these losses would soon be reduced to insignificance. The most important source of new recruits comes from the young voters who join the electorate each year. In the legal life of a Parliament nearly 10 per cent of the electorate will usually be created in this way. The loyalties of this group – which are in any case more fickle than those of older voters – are critical to electoral change. Labour did well in Parliamentary contests in the decade from 1964 – when it won more seats than did the Conservatives in four of the five General Elections – because it was more attractive to each successive generation of new voters. New parties which emerge as significant powers – Labour after 1918, the Nationalists in the 1960s, the SDP/Liberal Alliance in the 1980s – have typically drawn support disproportionately from the newest voters.

A second important source of new support for a party lies in those who failed to vote at the previous election. This group is important because, as we now realise, few citizens persistently abstain from voting over several elections. Most non-voters are therefore available for mobilisation: between one-tenth and one-fifth of a party's support in any particular election will usually come from those who failed to turn out last time. A small but often strategically placed injection of new voters has also periodically resulted from immigration into the country. Labour has been a particular beneficiary from waves of Irish Catholics, East European Jews, and Asians. Finally, parties gain – in very different amounts at different times – by converting those who last time voted for their rivals. Figure 3.3 tabulates the elements in the 'profit and loss' account of votes, listing the elements in their order of quantitative importance. The standard surveys of voting behaviour, by Butler and Stokes (1974) and Särlvik and Crewe (1983), estimate more exactly the figures involved at different moments in recent electoral history.

The total vote received by a party in any particular election is

Losses	Gains
1. Deaths	1. New voters attaining qualifying age
2. Abstentions	2. Previous abstainers
3. Conversions to a small rival party	3. Converts from smaller rivals
4. Conversions to a major rival	4. Converts from a major rival
5. Emigration	5. Immigration

FIGURE 3.3   *Where parties lose and gain votes between one election and the next (in order of importance)*

therefore the result of a complicated sum, whose elements are influenced both by changes in the structure of the electorate and by swings of opinion among voters. The outcome is the result of a balance struck between voters retained between elections, those lost (by death, emigration, abstention, conversion to rivals), and those newly attracted from among first-time voters, previous non-voters and those who previously voted for rivals.

In British elections the total popular vote of a party is only a means to the end of securing the largest possible representation in Parliament. The distribution of the popular vote affects, but does not determine, Parliamentary majorities, because two other influences intervene: the territorial organisation of constituencies, and the way 'victory' is decided in those constituencies. As is well known, the Member of Parliament for each of the country's 650 constituencies is that candidate who in the Parliamentary election secures the largest number of votes cast. This 'first past the post' system means that no provision is made for proportional Parliamentary representation for parties who attract votes without securing the largest vote in any (or many) constituencies.

It is commonly said that such an electoral system automatically favours bigger parties who, by winning the largest vote in many separate constituencies, end up with Parliamentary representation greatly in excess of their relative support in the electorate at large. Conversely, the system is usually held to discriminate against small parties who, attracting a small but significant minority of the popular vote, fail to 'win' a proportional number of constituencies.

These conventional beliefs are not accurate. The electoral system does indeed favour the best-supported parties, but in different ways at different times, and it only discriminates against some minority parties. Because of the territorial fragmentation which we identified in the last section it is also beginning to play unexpected tricks on the big parties.

The changing relationship between popular votes and Parliamentary representation is illustrated in Table 3.1, which compares outcomes in 1959 and 1983. The two elections, separated by nearly a quarter of a century, make a striking comparison, because they both produced Conservative Parliamentary landslide victories.

The table immediately shows that the disproportion between the popular vote and the share of Parliamentary seats varies over time and between parties. In 1959 the Conservatives did markedly better in terms of Parliamentary seats than in terms of the popular vote, an advantage well known to accrue to the biggest party under our electoral system. By 1983, however, what had once been a modest disproportion was greatly magnified: though in the intervening twenty-four years the Party's share of the vote fell nearly 6 per cent, its share of seats actually rose. The chief victims of this change were the Liberals and their allies.

The reasons for change can be found in our earlier discussion of long-term alterations in electoral loyalties in different regions. The division of the electorate into territorial constituencies, combined with the first-past-the-post system, means that parties are favoured in the contest for Parliamentary seats if their vote is concentrated in particular areas. Conversely, they suffer disproportionately if their support is widely dispersed. The Conservatives have benefited from the way in which their vote is increasingly concentrated in Southern Britain; the Liberals, and later the Alliance, suffered from a wider geographical dispersion of support.

Similar processes explain why not all small parties suffer in the Liberals' manner. Where support is packed into a small area, the existing method of calculating winners, combined with division into territorial constituencies, can actually raise a party's Parliamentary strength above its proportional support in the whole population:

TABLE 3.1   *Popular votes and parliamentary representation, 1959 and 1983*

	1959		1983	
	% Total British voters	% Parliamentary seats	% Total British voters	% Parliamentary seats
Conservatives	49.4	57.9	43.5	61.1
Labour	43.8	41.0	28.3	32.1
Liberal/Alliance	5.9	1.0	26.1	3.5
Plaid Cymru	0.2	0	0.4	0.3
Scottish National Party	0.07	0	1.0	0.3
Official Unionist	n.d.	n.d.	0.8	1.7
Democratic Unionist	n.d.	n.d.	0.5	0.4
Social Dem. and Labour Party	n.d.	0	0.4	0.1

Source: Calculated from Butler and Sloman (1980); *Times* Books (1983).
Note: n.d. = no data.

Table 3.1 shows that this happened to the Official Unionists in Ulster in 1983.

Third parties in Britain do not therefore automatically secure a smaller proportion of Parliamentary seats than of popular votes because they are small parties; they suffer such a disproportion if their support is geographically dispersed. The Alliance suffered because its geographical appeal was wide. Minority parties with geographically concentrated support either do not suffer markedly or – as in the case of the Unionists – actually benefit.

Nor does the electoral system work so unambiguously to the advantage of the two main parties as is commonly assumed. Though, in aggregate, Conservative and Labour have long secured a higher proportion of Parliamentary seats than popular votes, the electoral system has played tricks on both in particular regions. The reasons have been documented by Curtice and Steed (1986). The growing concentration of each party's vote in particular territories, when coupled with the 'first past the post system', means that each party is underrepresented to an increasing extent in those territories where it is weak. In 1983, for instance, the Conservatives failed to win a single seat in either Liverpool or Glasgow, despite receiving a combined vote in the two cities of over 311,000; Labour secured over one million votes in constituencies below the line joining Cornwall and Kent, yet managed to return only one MP in that area.

The way in which the electoral system works in the future will not therefore be determined only by the formal rules for calculating how candidates win; as much will depend on the level of support for different groupings and on the changing geographical distribution of that support. In the preceding pages we have summarised some of the most important changes in electoral loyalties that have occurred in recent years. But understanding electoral behaviour involves more than summarising electoral arithmetic; it also involves making general theoretical sense of the forces working on electors. The next section examines some of the main theoretical accounts of change presently on offer.

6 Explaining Electoral Change

The changes summarised in the preceding section have been explained in many ways. Four accounts are examined here, because they have all enjoyed some popularity and because, while none provides a complete explanation, each has some illumination to offer.

The most obvious explanation for the decline of the two main parties is that they are being punished for failures in government. This explanation is the one most commonly offered in everyday argument. The decline in the two-party share of the vote certainly coincided with growing difficulties of economic management faced by both Conservative and Labour Governments. The sharpest fall in the proportion of Conservative supporters who identified with their Party 'very strongly' – a fall from which the Conservatives have never fully recovered – also occurred during the difficult years of the Heath Government, 1970–74.

But a simple 'punishment' theory only explains some of the change. Both big parties have had long periods in office since the mid-1960s, but both have not suffered to the same degree. Indeed between 1979 and 1983 – when a Conservative Government presided over a stagnant economy and rising unemployment – the Conservatives actually made gains at the expense of Labour. Some more fundamental social causes must be at work.

A second explanation looks to these causes, by arguing that the class foundations of two-party politics are crumbling. Non-manual workers no longer give such automatic support to the Conservative Party; manual workers no longer so readily look to Labour. The political groupings who have challenged the two main parties in recent years – the Liberals and latterly the Liberal/Social Democratic Party Alliance throughout Britain, the Nationalists in Wales and Scotland – have all had a much more even spread of support across the occupational classes than the spread achieved by Conservative or Labour. Every index of class voting shows a progressive decline over time in the association between occupational class and electoral loyalty.

The causes of the decline of class voting are numerous. Upward social mobility has injected the middle class with large numbers of voters of working-class origins; such people are known to be more likely to vote Labour than are those born into middle-class families. Labour has lost, conversely, through a wide range of other changes. The spread of home ownership among manual workers has created a rift between that group and a Labour Party traditionally committed to public housing. The rising proportion of working-class incomes taken in taxes has hardened working-class opinion against much public spending, and has harmed Labour as the Party associated with high spending, especially on welfare. Change in the occupational structure has reduced the size of traditional heavy industries, where Labour's vote was strongest, and has blurred the divide between manual and non-manual workers.

The thesis that electoral change is due to the declining hold of occupational class is more powerfully convincing than is the 'punishment' theory, because it can make sense of both the general decline in support for the two major parties and of the particularly severe decline of the Labour Party.

It was an account which dominated our understanding of the nature of electoral change for the 1970s (Särlvik and Crewe, 1983). It has, however, been challenged by the authors of the most detailed subsequent studies of voting behaviour (Heath *et al.*, 1985, 1987).

Heath and his colleagues picture the social changes of recent decades not as a fragmentation of the working class, but as reduction in its size. Labour has not significantly lost its capacity to appeal to its traditional class vote; but changes like the decline in the proportion of manual workers in the population mean that there are fewer Labour voters about. The Party, according to this view, is not markedly less skilled than in the past at angling for votes; there are just fewer fish in the pool to be attracted by Labour's bait. Disastrous Labour results, like 1983, are the consequence of this long-term social change and of 'trendless fluctuation' – transient circumstances particular to a single election. The dispute about how best to make sense of the changing electorate (Crewe, 1986; Heath *et al.*, 1987) is in part a disagreement about social imagery – about how far social change should be pictured as involving the contraction or the fragmentation of the working class. One observation can, however, be made with certainty: regardless of whether its class base is fragmenting or contracting, the news is still bad for the Labour Party.

A third influential account of the causes of electoral change echoes themes discussed at the end of Chapter 1. It recognises that the established occupational classes – based on manual and non-manual workers – are of declining importance in influencing votes. It suggests, however, that electors are not simply fragmenting into many competing sectional interests, but are regrouping into cohesive sectors or classes. The important divisions include those between tax-payers on the one side, and the state-dependent population like pensioners, the jobless and the unemployed on the other; between workers in the public sector and those in private industry; between those who depend heavily on the public sector for key services like housing and transport, and those who consume those services privately by buying cars and houses in the marketplace (Dunleavy, 1979, 1980a, 1980b, 1980c; Dunleavy and Husbands, 1985).

The notion that traditional occupational classes are being superseded by groups based on 'production sectors' or 'consumption classes' has been especially popular with neo-Marxist scholars. The groups distinguished by these scholars do identify important divisions in the population, but the extent to which such divisions shape voting loyalties has been the subject of argument, much of it involving complicated statistical analysis. The appropriate verdict at the moment seems to be, not that 'sectoral' theories are false, but that they are 'not proven'. Särlvik and Crewe's analysis of the 1979 election found some 'sectoral' effects: for instance, workers in the public sector were, when compared with like occupational groups in the private sector, more ready to vote Labour. The effects of public sector employment were nevertheless modest, and were outweighed by the effect of the traditional manual and non-manual divide (1983, pp. 93–103).

A fourth and final interpretation of the causes of change in the electorate also recalls themes examined at the close of Chapter 1. This interpretation focuses, not on class or sectoral divisions on the vote, but on its territorial distribution. This account enjoyed most influence in the mid and late 1970s when the sudden emergence of popularly strong Nationalist movements in Wales and Scotland seemed to portend, in the title of a widely read book of the time, 'the breakup of Britain' (Nairn, 1981). Scottish Nationalism was for a time a particularly vigorous movement. Between 1966 and 1974 its share of the vote in Scotland rose from 5 per cent to 30 per cent; its membership grew more rapidly than that of any other Scottish political movement; it made inroads into traditionally Labour strongholds; and its voters were young and were drawn from across the whole spectrum of occupational class (Miller, 1981, pp. 153–216). Support for Plaid Cymru, the Welsh Nationalist Party, though more limited geographically and socially, also grew impressively, raising the per cent share of the national vote from just over 4 per cent in 1966 to nearly three times that level four years later. The advance of two nationalist parties, coupled with the existence of a fierce conflict of national identities in Ulster, seemed for a time to suggest that territorial loyalties would increasingly determine the behaviour of electors, to the point where the United Kingdom might disintegrate.

Subsequent developments have confirmed part, and refuted part, of the thesis stressing the importance of territorial divisions. As we saw earlier, electors in different parts of the country are indeed behaving in increasingly different ways. The result has been to give the two biggest parties geographically distinct bases: the Conservatives are increasingly the Party of the metropolitan, relatively prosperous South and of suburbia; and Labour the Party of the declining industrial North and the inner cities.

In other respects, however, the tide of electoral support for 'the break-up of Britain' has ebbed away. Many electors – especially in Scotland – vote Nationalist without supporting the Nationalists' demand for independence; the peak of Nationalist voting overstated the strength of separatist opinion (Rose, 1982, p. 75). The referenda on the Labour Government's devolution proposals in 1979 showed support for even restricted devolution to be weak in Wales and limited in Scotland: only 11.9 per cent of Welsh electors supported the measures while in Scotland the figure was 32.9 per cent. The elections since then have exposed the popular weakness of Plaid Cymru in particular. Though it now looks to be an enduring institution with a respectable level of support, the level of that support is seriously limited by the Party's inability to break out of those areas of Wales where Welsh language and traditional Welsh culture are strong (Balsom *et al.*, 1983). The performance of Nationalist parties in General Elections in the 1980s suggests that on mainland Britain separatist sentiment is well rooted, but that the roots are narrowly confined: in Scotland Nationalists seem to be able to rely on a little more than a tenth, and in Wales a little less than a tenth, of the national vote. In one part of Great Britain, indeed, the support for a national identity other than 'British' has declined: as we saw in Chapter 2, there occurred during the 1970s a substantial decline in the proportion of the Northern Ireland population choosing an 'Ulster' rather than a 'British' nationality. While territorial fragmentation of the electorate has grown, the separatist dangers of this fragmentation have decreased.

7 Conclusion

Elections are the most important form of mass political participation in Britain. Yet voting itself is both an individual and a secret act. Indeed, for most electors, casting a vote is not so much a form of public participation in government as an act of approval or disapproval of particular political parties. Parties are our next subject.

4

The Political Parties

They have sown the wind and they shall reap the whirlwind.

Hosea, 8.7

1 Outline

Political parties as we now know them are a modern invention. Only
in this century has it become usual for a party to try to develop a
large membership and to offer a wide programme of policies to
electors. Yet these relatively novel institutions are now central to
political life. British government is party government. Parties control ministries, and therefore determine who become ministers and
what policies ministers try to carry out. To understand the political
system it is therefore necessary to understand how parties are
organised and controlled; what beliefs they stand for; and what kind
of people they recruit to political activity. This chapter examines
each of these matters in turn.

Three groups have dominated party politics in Britain. Since 1918
the Conservative and Labour Parties have alternated in government.
The Liberal Party, which until the First World War was the
Conservatives' main rival, persisted as a minor influence into the
1980s. However, for a brief period in that decade it seemed that an
'Alliance' of the Liberals and a new Social Democratic Party might
emerge as a third major force, or even displace the Labour Party as
the Conservatives' chief opponent.

After the 1987 General Election – which disappointed Alliance
hopes – the grouping broke up, the Liberal Party disappeared and a
new party, the Social and Liberal Democrats, was founded. The
causes and consequences of these events are described in section 5 of
this chapter.

But there are also numerous other parties. In the 1983 General Election, for instance, candidates fought under more than sixty different banners, ranging from the most general (Workers' Revolutionary Party) to the most parochial (Put Southport back in Lancashire Party). Most of these parties are transitory but a few have endured sufficient time to merit examination. Some are significant because – like the Nationalists in Wales and Scotland – their support has been considerable in particular areas of the United Kingdom. The Communists, by contrast, have never attracted substantial popular support but claim attention because they have been part of a powerful wider international movement. Others still – like the Fascists – are significant because they challenge the prevailing political order. The minority parties are examined in section 5. Section 6 summarises the main trends in the recent development of parties in Britain.

2 Parties: Organisation and Power

Political parties, like all complex organisations, have their own institutions, rules and hierarchies. The way a party is organised is affected by two influences: the common political environment in which all parties operate; and the particular traditions and outlook unique to each party. The most important influence from the wider political environment is well known. With the appearance of a mass electorate (following the 1867 Reform Act) and of voting by secret ballot (after 1872) parties could only win office by arousing popular support and by converting that support into votes. These necessities transformed party organisation: before 1867 parties were mainly loose alliances inside Parliament; after 1867 they gradually became nationwide institutions with mass memberships. National organisation was needed to convert electors, to deliver them at the polls and to help fund campaigns.

The development of complex national institutions faced parties with common questions: what was to be the division of labour between national and local bodies? How much power over policy could be allowed to those local bodies? What was to be the relationship between the party in Parliament and the party in the country? Parties evolved different answers to these questions depending on their traditions and outlook.

The Conservative Party: Organisation and Power

The organisation of the Conservative Party is, it has often been noted, constructed from three pillars: the Party in the country, the professional organisation controlled from Central Office in London, and the Party in Parliament. Of these three, the last has always been the most powerful.

The Party in the country is largely made up of separate Conservative associations in the Parliamentary constituencies, joined in the National Union of Conservative and Unionist Associations. The National Union originated from an initiative of the Parliamentary leadership in 1867 to create an organisation which would, in the words of a founder, make 'Conservative principles affective among the masses' (quoted in McKenzie, 1963, p. 191). Three years later the Parliamentary leadership set up Conservative Central Office to provide the professional services needed to fight elections among the growing mass of voters.

The fact that the Conservative Party in Parliament preceded and sponsored both the National Union and Central Office has given it a position of great influence. The formal organisation of the Party in Parliament is nevertheless comparatively recent. The main organisation of backbench Conservatives, the 1922 Committee, dates from a meeting in October of that year at the Carlton Club, when backbench MPs and peers rebelled against the Conservatives' continued presence in the coalition government led by Lloyd George. The '1922' now organises a wide range of committees for Conservative backbenchers, covering most of the usual subjects of political debate; has an executive committee composed of senior backbenchers; and has a chairman who exercises considerable influence especially at times of crisis in the Party (Norton and Aughey, 1981, pp. 193–201).

Formal rules for choosing the Party leader also developed late. Until 1965 Conservative leaders 'emerged' after private bargaining between the most senior figures in the Party. This method reflected the old domination of the Party by a small upper-class group of leaders in Parliament, but it produced some odd consequences by the 1950s, when the Conservatives had a mass membership and were successfully fighting elections under a democratic franchise. In 1957, Mr Macmillan unexpectedly 'emerged' as Party leader ahead of the favourite, Mr Butler. In 1963, Lord Home – an aristocrat who was not even at the time a member of the House of Commons –

'emerged' as the even more unexpected successor to Mr Macmillan, after an extraordinary series of public scrambles for the leadership in full view of the mass media at the Party's Annual Conference (Churchill, 1964). By then it was apparent to even the most devout Conservative that some better way of choosing the leader was needed.

New rules were introduced in 1965, requiring that the successful candidate win a secret ballot of Conservative MPs. In 1975, an additional provision was introduced allowing the Leader to be challenged in an annual contest. The change was designed to help oust Mr Edward Heath from the head of the Party. Since his removal no contest has taken place.

The modern structure of the Conservative Party is the product of the piecemeal adaptation of an aristocratic Parliamentary faction to the demands of modern democratic politics. The structure of the Party still bears the imprint of these elitist origins. The preference for hierarchy is vividly illustrated by the great formal powers vested in the single figure of the Leader. Three sources of Mrs Thatcher's powers are particularly striking: the considerable bureaucratic resources of Central Office are formally under her control; she has the final say over Party policy, especially as expressed in election manifestos; and she independently selects the Cabinet (and, in opposition, the Shadow Cabinet). The rituals of the Annual Conference of the National Union also emphasise the supremacy of the Parliamentary Party in general and of the Leader in particular. Every year over four thousand representatives gather, formally to discuss policy but in reality to provide carefully stage-managed demonstrations of public enthusiasm for the Conservative cause.

These formal arrangements and public rituals help explain why the Conservative Party has a reputation as the least internally democratic of all major British political parties. This reputation is not wholly deserved. The supposedly autocratic powers of the Leader are in practice limited by well-documented restrictions. The history of the Party shows that Central Office is not just an instrument of the Leader's will: it is a powerful bureaucracy with many of the independent resources and capacities possessed by all bureaucracies (Pinto-Duschinsky, 1972). Nor is it possible for a Conservative leader to determine policy in an autocratic way: even a determined and assertive figure like Mrs Thatcher has often had to abandon preferences and suffer defeats at the hands of her senior colleagues. In choosing Cabinets and Shadow Cabinets Leaders are also limited. They have to reward allies, conciliate opponents and balance different interests in the Party. Failure to observe these limits endangers their own position: one of the contributory causes of Mr Heath's removal from the leadership in 1975 was the belief among Conservative backbenchers that he too readily excluded from office those with whom he disagreed.

It is particularly misleading to picture constituency associations as subservient. It is true that rank-and-file Conservatives have rarely tried to intervene in national policy-making, but it is also true that there exists in the Party a long tradition of local autonomy. Local independence is reinforced by the fact that many local associations are rich and well organised so that the national leadership relies heavily on them for financial subsidies. The best sign of local independence is that though there exists a central register of Parliamentary candidates the choice between individuals is still largely in the hands of local associations.

The modern Conservative Party has thus never been as hierarchical as formal arrangements might suggest. Furthermore, over the last twenty-five years it has become more difficult still for a small circle to control decisions. Three factors have contributed to the change. First the election of leaders, though on a narrow franchise, has made the contest for supreme office in the Party a more open affair. A second factor has been the changed scale and style of policy-making. The Conservative manifesto in the General Election of 1900, for instance, contained three promises; the manifesto issued in 1979 contained seventy-four (Finer, 1980, p. 122). The change was accompanied by a growth in the formality of decision-making: the promises given in 1979 were ground out of over sixty separate policy groups. A leader could realistically hope to determine the simple manifesto produced in 1900; the modern scale of policy-making is beyond the control of even the most determined individual. The shift to more open forms of argument has even affected the Party Conference. This traditionally docile gathering has altered in recent years. It is now much less a social event than was formerly the case and has become more overtly political in its concerns. Speakers from the floor are less respectful to the platform than was usual in the past. The idea of a Conference 'fringe' of unofficial meetings has been borrowed from other parties, providing Conservative dissenters with a public platform for their views.

The third source of change concerns the way debate is conducted. The Conservatives were traditionally a party of 'tendencies' rather than of 'factions': that is, while there existed broad divisions of opinion it was rare for Conservatives holding similar views to try to advance these views by forming pressure groups inside the Party (Rose, 1964). In recent decades, however, organised factions have become increasingly common. Almost all the best-known groups in the Party – like the Monday Club, the Selsdon Group and the Tory Reform Group – have been founded within the last twenty-five years (Seyd, 1980).

We can sum up the changing structure of power in the Conservative Party as follows. The history of the Party gave a special predominance to the Parliamentary leadership. This predominance, however, was nowhere as great as formal organisation suggested. The Leader in particular was circumscribed by important restrictions. In recent years traditional hierarchies have been further modified by changes in methods of leadership selection, by the growing complexity of policy-making and by the spread of factions.

Even these alterations have, however, been mild compared with the convulsions gripping the Labour Party.

The Labour Party: Organisation and Power
If the clue to the Conservative organisation lies in the fact that the Parliamentary leadership preceded and sponsored the Party outside Westminster, the clue to understanding Labour lies in the way substantial Parliamentary representation came after the emergence of a wider national movement. Williams has expressed the point thus:

> the Labour Party was built up from below in protest against a Parliament unresponsive to working-class concerns . . . it took the form of an elaborately structured federal coalition, on which the Parliamentary Party, born in 1906, had to be awkwardly grafted. (Williams, 1979, p. 291.)

The movement therefore was, and it remains, a set of uneasy alliances. The Party's organisation reflects the fact. Labour is a federation, the chief parts of which are the trade unions, the parties in the constituencies and a numerically insignificant motley of organisations collectively labelled the 'socialist societies'.

These very different institutions are united by the mechanism of affiliation. The mechanism has been crucial to the nature of the Party, especially to the role of trade unions. The affiliating organisations have always differed greatly in wealth and size, the unions being the richest and best supported. The machinery of affiliation reflects these inequalities. Affiliating bodies join the federation that is the Labour Party by paying a fixed annual subscription per head for every individual member they wish to affiliate. The bulk of this affiliated membership comes from unions. Affiliation is linked in turn to one of the Party's most distinctive features, the practice of 'block voting' at Labour's Annual Conference. The 'block vote' assigns to organisations in the Party a voting strength proportional to their affiliated membership. The casting of block votes is popularly identified with the unions, but it has a more general significance. Labour was from its beginning at the start of this century a federation of institutions of very different sizes. Voting rules in the Party reflected these disparities. At Annual Conference the convention has been to measure voting strength by numbers of affiliated members. Thus all the affiliated bodies – unions, constituency parties and socialist societies – have block votes. The identification of the system with unions is due to two facts: since the early days of the Party it has been conventional for each individual union to cast its votes as a single block, without reflecting differences within its own ranks; and the affiliated membership (and thus the voting strength) of unions has in recent years outweighed the votes of all other affiliated bodies by a factor of at least ten to one. In 1982, for instance, there were more than 6,280,000 affiliated union members, while constituency parties affiliated only 602,000 members. (Even the latter figure was, we shall see, more than twice the true individual membership of the Party.)

Block voting is an attempt to reflect the differing strengths of the institutions federated in the Labour Party. It is, though, a system open to endless argument, about the very principle of block allocations, about the methods used to calculate voting strength and about internal decision-making inside the big union blocks. Arguments about the block vote have focused on its role at the Party's Annual Conference, where it is the usual method of calculating majorities. The Party's own supporters often picture Conference as 'a parliament of the movement' (Attlee, 1937, p. 93). Indeed it is, but not in the sense of being the sovereign source of Party decisions. It is a 'parliament' because it is a forum of the main interests – the affiliated organisations – who make up the federation that is the Labour Party. Block voting is the institutional expression of that federated character.

The Party's federal nature is also reflected in the arrangements by which Conference elects the National Executive Committee, the formally supreme executive organ of the Party. The NEC is composed of twelve members elected by affiliated unions, seven elected by the constituency delegates, and one elected separately by the Young Socialists. Six other members – five women delegates and the Treasurer – are elected by the whole Conference, thus giving the unions a decisive say in the choice. Finally, the leader and deputy leader of the Party sit ex-officio.

Note an odd and significant omission in all this: there is no formal mechanism of representation for the Parliamentary Labour Party on the NEC. The emergence of Labour as a party of government obviously gave Labour Parliamentarians great prestige and influence; yet one legacy of the Party's origins as an extra-Parliamentary movement was that institutional links between the PLP and the rest of the federation making up the Labour Party have been poor. Labour MPs had no voting rights at Party Conference unless attending as delegates of other institutions in the Party. Before Mr Kinnock's selection as leader in 1983, under the new electoral arrangements, the figure conventionally called the 'Party Leader' was only the choice of MPs. The Parliamentary leadership itself had only limited control over the Party's headquarters' staff and over its national organisation.

The divide between the Parliamentary Labour Party and the rest of the Party was always a potential source of conflict. For much of the Party's history this potential was suppressed by a variety of mechanisms. As early as 1907 a 'time and method' formula gave to Conference the power to instruct the PLP on policy, but gave the PLP the right to decide the timing and method of action (Minkin, 1980, pp. 5–6). More informally, Parliamentarians always had a good voice on the NEC, both because the Leader and Deputy Leader were ex-officio members and because MPs usually won contests to sit on the 'constituency' section of the NEC. The Parliamentary leadership could also usually claim a moral authority by its success in elections among voters at large, and it could buttress this authority by tactical alliances with powerful unions.

Labour was therefore never an internally democratic party. For most of its history the loose federation was held together by a small group of leaders in Parliament, supported by the wealth and the block votes of the big unions.

The convulsions in the organisation of the Party in recent years are due to the decline of that alliance. The difficulties of Labour Governments between 1964–70 and 1974–79 diminished the authority exercised by the Parliamentary leadership over the rest of the Party and ruptured the alliance between the PLP leadership and powerful unions. There occurred a period of intense argument over organisation and power, focusing on three issues: control of the manifesto on which the Party fights elections; the relations between MPs and their constituency parties; and the method of selecting the Leader. Each of these are here examined briefly.

There was always a tension in the Party's method of deciding its programme. On the one hand, official Party policy was produced by bargaining and manipulation *at* Annual Conference between the NEC and Conference delegates, and *between* Conference by the complicated workings of the committees and sub-committees of the NEC. On the other hand, periodic manifestos were produced on which the Parliamentary leadership had to fight General Elections. The tension between the two could be contained by the ascendancy of the Parliamentary leadership, by machinery for consultation, by compromise over differences and by occasionally obscuring or ignoring the differences. The breakdown of these mechanisms culminated in an acrimonious argument over the manifesto for the 1979 General Election, when critics alleged that the Parliamentary leadership, especially the Prime Minister, vetoed key commitments supported by the Party. This episode led to a sustained campaign to give the NEC control of the manifesto (Minkin, 1980, pp. 363–6).

Arguments about relations between MPs and their constituency parties were fuelled by two causes: by the belief among many party activists that MPs, having been elected to Parliament wearing a Labour label, often subsequently neglected or opposed the Party policies; and by a number of particular cases in the 1970s when Labour MPs were in open conflict with their local parties. The remedy advocated was that MPs be required to present themselves for re-selection by their constituency parties before each General Election, a procedure finally adopted by Annual Conference in 1979.

A prolonged dispute about how to select the Party Leader provided the third and most contentious organisational question to divide the Party in recent years. It was especially contentious because it raised in a particularly dramatic way the problem of how to apportion power between the different institutions federated in the party. In the early years of Labour's history the person chosen by MPs was not automatically the leading figure in the Party. But when Labour became a governing party, and the leader of Labour MPs became Prime Minister, it was natural for the Parliamentary Leader to be identified as Leader of Labour as a whole. Thus it came about that the Party experienced the divisions of the 1970s with a Leader elected by Labour MPs alone. Arguments about reform turned on proposals to extend the electoral 'franchise' to other groups in the Party.

These proposals were not a constitutional novelty. Many socialist parties in other democracies select leaders by votes involving members outside Parliament. In Britain the Liberal Party has involved its rank-and-file members in leadership selection since 1976. But in the Labour Party, any proposal for change immediately raised the question of what should be the appropriate balance between the different parts of Labour's 'federation'. A 'universal suffrage' allowing the choice to be made by individual members of constituency parties would have excluded the unions. Yet any system of 'block' voting raised the problem of how to apportion block allocations between different groups, and how those groups would decide the direction in which votes should be cast. A long and often bitter argument culminated in a rule change at a Special Conference in January 1981. The new method retains block voting, allocating 40 per cent (minus a tiny amount for the socialist societies) to affiliated unions, 30 per cent to constituency parties and 30 per cent to MPs.

Different views are held about the significance of the organisational changes introduced by Labour in recent years. Many members of the Party see them as democratic, opening up leadership selection to members and thus producing a Party more responsive to the wishes of its rank-and-file. The change can also be seen as repairing the bridges between the PLP and the rest of the Party which were swept away in the storms of the 1970s. The overwhelming victory of Mr Kinnock in the 1983 leadership contest is seen as a particular illustration of the unifying power of the new arrangements.

Many critics of the Party, by contrast, see the changes as undemocratic. They argue that power is being transferred away from MPs accountable to the whole electorate towards small groups of activists who control the constituency parties and the trade unions.

3 Parties and Their Ideologies

No major political party in Britain is ideological in the most commonly understood sense of that word: no party of importance shapes its policies and actions by reference to a comprehensive, internally consistent and detailed social theory. Yet the fact that none of the parties is dominated by a single, comprehensive doctrine does not make ideology unimportant. All the parties are alliances of different groups, brought together by interest, accident and historical circumstances. These different groups contribute distinctive doctrinal elements to their parties. Though no party exhibits a single ideology all are deeply influenced by a variety of – sometimes conflicting – doctrines. Exploring party ideology involves exploring the different ideological strands within each party.

The Conservative Party: Ideology
The doctrinal content of British Conservatism is elusive. There are two reasons for this elusiveness. First, the Party has existed for longer than any of its main rivals, and in a long history has inevitably been influenced by a wide range of traditions. Second, the Party has been in government for longer than any of its rivals: since 1918, Conservative, or Conservative-dominated governments, have been in office for more than two-thirds of the period. Governments often have to act first and think of a doctrinal justification afterwards. The Conservatives, with their long history as a governing party, are therefore bound to have a chameleon-like quality.

The history of the Party is certainly a story of doctrinal flexibility. Modern Conservatism can trace its roots to the Party shaped by Sir Robert Peel in the 1830s. That Party was insular and traditional: it supported protection against foreign competition, was suspicious of industrialism and was closely associated with the Church of England. By the turn of the century, Conservatives officially stood for free trade and imperialism abroad, minimal government and industrial capitalism at home, but were already arguing about the appropriateness of such commitments to an economy facing serious foreign competition. By the middle of this century they had abandoned free trade (indeed did so in 1932), were reconciled to the Welfare State and the mixed economy, and were detaching themselves from identification with Empire in favour of support for the British Commonwealth (Harris, 1972, pp. 11–61). Three decades later, the Party has revived much of its early hostility to government intervention in social and economic affairs, supports free trade inside Europe and has abandoned both Empire and Commonwealth in favour of the European Economic Community.

Some observers have deduced from this variety that ideology is unimportant in Conservatism. According to this view the Party is opportunistic, allying itself with whichever groups in the electorate enable it to win office and whichever groups in society happen to be most powerful. Many Conservatives themselves provide corroboration for this view by dismissing the relevance of ideas to practical politics and by drawing a contrast between the Party and its supposedly more dogmatic opponents. Thus, according to a leading Conservative politician, Sir Ian Gilmour, 'so far . . . as philosophy or doctrine is concerned, the wise Conservative travels light. Conservative principles cannot be precisely tabulated' (Gilmour, 1977, p. 109).

It is undoubtedly the case that Conservative politicians are especially interested in power; after all, they have more experience of it than have their rivals. Yet the view that Conservatives are ruled by a unique drive for power is implausible: it is psychologically implausible because it pictures Conservatives as special individuals free from the normal human attachments to social and moral principles; and it is historically implausible because throughout its modern history the Party has actually been divided by debates over what it should stand for.

An alternative solution to the problem of identifying a Conservative ideology is popular with some modern apologists for the Party. It asserts that beneath the flux of policy change there are certain eternal values to which all Conservatives have been committed. This view faces the obvious difficulty of identifying those eternal values. One of the commonest candidates is the notion that Conservatism stands for the rights of private property (Norton and Aughey, 1981, pp. 15–52). The idea is unconvincing even at the level of rhetoric: 'property' to an eighteenth-century Conservative meant something very different from the 'property owning democracy' advocated by modern Conservatives in a mass consumer society. Nor have

Conservative Governments in practice always defended private property: they have taxed it, put legal restrictions on its use and even expropriated it through nationalisation.

It is therefore unconvincing to picture British Conservatives as either believing very little or as united by belief in some universal truths. The ideology of British Conservatism is elusive, not because it is non-existent nor because it is very general, but because it is composed of two very different traditions acquired during the Party's long history. The first, best labelled a 'Tory' tradition, values a strong state as a means of achieving a stable social order. Beer has shown that this tradition, which originated in the pre-industrial England, allowed the Conservatives to adapt easily to an age of big government, helping them after the Second World War to accept the Welfare State and the mixed economy (Beer, 1969, pp. 302–17). This 'Tory' tradition is in tension with a second tradition of 'liberal conservatism', a legacy of the alliance created before the First World War with free market capitalism. Liberal Conservatism suspects the state, favouring instead the operation of free market forces in the economy and the exercise of choice in social life.

Interpretations of Conservative ideology as representing these two traditions should be used with care. The Party, it needs to be emphasised, is not neatly divided into 'Tory' and 'liberal' factions. Although there is a growing tendency for policy division to be formally organised, different traditions are still widely dispersed. Most Conservative politicians have elements of the 'Tory' and of the 'liberal' in their makeup, and every individual Conservative and every Conservative Government has to strike some kind of balance between the two.

For three decades after the end of the Second World War the Party leadership neglected the tradition of liberal conservatism. Although party rhetoric praised the free market, in practice the Party accepted high taxation, a large publicly owned sector, high public spending on welfare services, and government management of the economy.

This ideological balance was destroyed in the mid-1970s. Mr Heath's Conservative Government, pursuing economic policies involving legal controls over pay and prices, emerged on the losing side in a bitter economic and constitutional struggle with the coal-miners. This defeat, and two successive General Election defeats in 1974, caused a crisis of ideology in the Party. That crisis was only resolved by replacing Mr Heath by Mrs Thatcher at the head of the Party, and by striking a new balance between 'Toryism' and 'liberalism'. Since 1975 – the date of Mrs Thatcher's succession – the Party has stressed the virtues of free market economics, has rejected the idea of active economic management, is committed to 'privatising' many publicly owned industries and is sceptical of many of the institutions of the Welfare State.

The great crisis of the mid-1970s produced a marked shift in official Conservative ideology. The full significance of this shift is nevertheless uncertain. Evidence can be produced to support three very different interpretations. An 'official' view, which Mrs Thatcher has expressed, is that the new ideas are actually a return to traditional Conservative beliefs in individual initiative and free market economics (Leach, 1983). An alternative view, however, points to the limited extent to which Mrs Thatcher's Administrations have actually dismantled big government (Burch, 1983). On this view 'Thatcherism', though undoubtedly a departure, is a pragmatic ideology, tempering its commitment to the free market with an eye to electoral popularity and the power of vested interests. A third interpretation puts a different gloss on the gap between free market rhetoric and the persistence of large-scale government intervention. This third view pictures 'Thatcherism' as a novel strain in Conservatism, caused by a unique cross-fertilisation between 'Tory' preferences for social order and 'liberal' preferences for a free market (Gamble, 1983a). Thatcherism, accordingly, is not engaged in building a freer society; it is creating a 'free market' with a 'strong state'. The strong state involves greater appeal to patriotic sentiments and more spending on the armed forces and on agencies of internal control, in part to restrain the victims of free market economics.

Whatever view is held of Thatcherism – whether it is a beacon of liberty, a set of pragmatic signals or a sign for authoritarianism – there is no doubt that it for a time settled the internal Party crisis caused by the failures of the Heath Government. The Labour Party was thrown into even deeper ideological crisis by the experience of government.

The Labour Party: Ideology
The Labour Party is more avowedly doctrinal than is the Conservative Party. The Party did not evolve in the manner of the Conserva-

tives; it was consciously founded to achieve particular aims. It has drawn its activists and its Parliamentary leadership from public sector intellectuals like teachers and lecturers who find systematic political philosophies attractive. While few at the top of the Party take its formal aims seriously, nevertheless the famous clause IV of the Party's constitution – adopted in 1918 – commits Labour to the radical socialist objective of securing 'for the workers by hand or by brain the full fruits of their industry ... upon the basis of the common ownership of the means of production, distribution and exchange'. The commitment suggests an obvious contrast with Conservatism, one often insisted on by Conservative apologists anxious to picture theirs as the party of pragmatic 'common sense'.

There is indeed something in the contrast. By comparison with the Conservative Party, debates about policy in the Labour Party are more likely to be linked to explicitly different conceptions of the Party's purpose. Labour is also in an institutional sense more obviously an ideological coalition, because there exists in the Party a tradition of factional organisation which encourages those with common beliefs to organise internal party pressure groups.

The Party has nevertheless never been guided by a single, coherent ideology. The variety of its doctrinal life has usually forced the Parliamentary leadership to create compromises reconciling different ideological traditions. Three of these traditions have been especially important. They can be called for convenience 'labourism', 'radical socialism' and 'social democracy'.

The first of these emphasises the Party's role as the political voice of the trade-union movement. The origins of this tradition go back to the birth of the Party at the turn of the century, when it was dominated by unions. The first sizeable group of Labour MPs elected in 1906 acted as the Parliamentary spokesmen of union interests. The domination of 'labourism' could not, however, survive the Party's emergence at the end of the First World War as the main radical movement in British politics. The formal commitment to achieving socialism, inserted in the 1918 Party constitution, was in part a sign that Labour had become more than a trade-union party and in part a sign of the rising influence of radical socialism (Beer, 1969, pp. 144–52). The radical socialism expressed in clause IV implied the necessity for revolutionary change. Yet the Party's radicalism has taken a distinctively British form. Marxism – the most important revolutionary socialist ideology of our time – has been only a marginal influence. Radical socialism in Britain has often been self-consciously nationalistic, looking back to a tradition derived from the Puritan Revolution in the seventeenth century. At the level of policy, radical socialism in the Labour Party is now strongly influenced by economic nationalism, involving support for import controls, opposition to membership of the EEC and suspicion of multinationals. Some of the most prominent modern representatives of the radical socialist tradition are Christians who link their socialism to an established native tradition of Christian Radicalism.

It should not be imagined that labourism and radical socialism form two distinct wings of the Labour Party, though it is probably the case that the former has been strongest in the unions while the latter has been strongest among activists in the constituency parties. The third ideological tradition, social democracy, for a long time dominated the Parliamentary Party. Social democrats in the Labour Party have been distinguished by a desire to use state power to reform the institutions of capitalism in order to promote both efficiency and equality of opportunity. The social democratic strand in Labour's ideology has obviously been in tension with radical socialism, because social democrats reject the wholesale dismantling of capitalism. But it is also in tension with the ideology of labourism, because to modernise capitalism has often entailed attacking the independent power of trade unions (Haseler, 1969).

The most effective leaders of the Labour Party succeeded by weaving elaborate compromises between the different ideological strands in the Party. This search for compromise was made easier by a widespread attachment in the Party to Parliamentarianism. In other words, people of all ideological persuasions were united by a belief that social change should come through winning control of Parliament in democratic elections. As Miliband puts it: 'of political parties claiming socialism to be their aim, the Labour Party has always been one of the most dogmatic – not about socialism, but about the parliamentary system' (Miliband, 1973, p. 13).

In the last decade, Labour has found successful ideological compromise elusive. Belief in Parliament as the authoritative source of social change has declined. 'Labourism' has been under attack because the Party's close association with the unions has been thought electorally damaging and because in social democratic eyes union power was a cause of Britain's economic problems. In the

1970s, radical socialism was given a renewed edge by the recruitment into the Party of a new generation of activists influenced more by Marxism than by the traditions of Christian socialism. In the same decade, one of the fundamental assumptions of social democracy – that the reform of capitalism could be paid for out of economic growth – collapsed with the onset of recession and mass unemployment.

4 Parties, Members and Activists

British political parties have many members but few activists. If the affiliated union membership of the Labour Party is counted, the total membership of all political parties exceeds eight million. By contrast, survey evidence suggests that no more than three voters in every thousand has ever held even the most minor party office (Butler and Stokes, 1974, p. 21). A study of the Labour Party at the end of the 1970s suggested that of about 250,000 members in the constituency parties only 55,000 could be considered activists (Whiteley, 1982, p. 115). The members with a long history of committed involvement must be even fewer.

The small group of activists is nevertheless important out of all proportion to its numbers in the population. Though the roles of activists vary in the different parties, in all they fulfil vital functions. To an increasing extent they are the group from which local and national political leaders are selected. The decline in recent years of non-partisan local government means that it is now almost impossible to become a councillor without being simultaneously committed to active support of a party. Selection as a councillor in turn gives access to positions of substantial influence. Leading councillors have a large say in deciding local government budgets running into hundreds of millions of pounds. In their own sphere elected local politicians can exercise far more control over policy than do their counterparts in Parliament or Whitehall. In competition for nomination as a Parliamentary candidate local activism is also an increasingly important recommendation, especially in the Labour Party: of Labour MPs elected in 1983, nearly a half had been local councillors (Burch and Moran, 1985).

Local activists are important not only because they inhabit the pool from which leaders are selected, but because they play a critical

part in the acts of selection. The choice of party candidates for
council elections is almost totally controlled at local level. The
choice of Parliamentary candidates, though more influenced from
the centre, is in most parties in the hands of selection committees
composed of local activists. In all parties local activists have some
say in making policy; in the Labour Party, that say, in the view of
some observers, can be great.

Activists also have important functions of a more subordinate
kind. Modern mass parties developed when electoral reform
expanded the electorate and introduced the secret ballot. Activists
became vital in identifying potential voters, making sure they were
registered, canvassing support during election campaigns and
prompting voters to turn out on election day. Though changes in
campaign styles have reduced the importance of 'doorstep' canvassing, superior organisation at local level can still account for several
hundred votes, thus determining the partisan outcome in many
marginal seats. Finally, members and activists are vital in raising
funds for parties.

The Conservative Party: Members and Activists
The Conservative Party has the largest direct membership of any
British political party; indeed its membership exceeds the direct
membership of all other parties combined. The Conservatives'
success in this respect is striking. Mass membership is usually
associated with radical groups of the Left. On the Continent
membership of leftist parties usually outstrips that of Conservative
groups. The achievements of British Conservatism are therefore
unusual. The Party's membership is not only greater than that of its
rivals, but also dwarfs that of supposedly 'mass' movements like the
Campaign for Nuclear Disarmament.

The generalisation that the Conservatives are the best-supported
and best-organised political movement in Britain can be offered with
certainty, but mystery surrounds the exact numbers of their members and activists. The Party – like most of its rivals – publishes no
accurate membership statistics; indeed, since members join through
local constituency associations it is unlikely that Party Headquarters
itself has an accurate record. The most reliable estimate of numbers
is now over ten years old, and is itself indirect: the Houghton
Committee on Financial Aid to Political Parties estimated an
average of 2400 members per constituency, giving a total of about

1.5 million (Houghton, 1976). The only previously published figure was issued by Conservatives themselves in 1953, claiming a membership of 2.8 million (Pinto-Duschinsky, 1981, p. 132).

These two figures show that the Party has in recent decades lost many members, though the two bald figures probably overstate the extent of decline. The 1953 figure is generally agreed to have overstated the Party's strength; conversely, Houghton's figures were calculated when the Party was demoralised by the failure of Mr Heath's government (1970–74) and by electoral setbacks. The accession to the leadership of Mrs Thatcher – a popular figure with committed Conservatives – and three successive general election victories may have restored some of the losses revealed by Houghton, though in 1984 the Party identified two hundred constituencies where membership had significantly declined in recent years.

Though the bald figures overstate the extent of decline, membership has nevertheless fallen significantly from the post-war peak reached in the early 1950s. The most important reason probably lies in the changing pattern of leisure and pleasure among the middle classes. The Party's attractions derived from its integration into local middle-class society; hence the unusually high proportion (about 50 per cent) of women in its ranks, engaged in the rounds of coffee mornings and jumble sales. The development of more sophisticated middle-class pleasures and the rise in the proportion of middle class women with paid employment has reduced the pool of available members.

The Party's decline as a social institution is clearly illustrated by the fate of the Young Conservatives. In recent decades the Young Conservatives, once famous for their social life, have become much more narrowly political in their interests. At the same time their numbers have fallen (from 157,000 in 1949 to 27,000 in 1978) as the young middle class have discovered less innocent pastimes than table tennis and ballroom dancing (Norton and Aughey, 1981, p. 213).

Uncertainty also surrounds the precise social characteristics of Party members. Only a few studies exist, and these are mainly of single constituencies, not necessarily representative of the whole party. The only wider evidence, provided by Pinto-Duschinsky, dates from the 1960s. The most certain generalisations are that manual workers and their families make a much smaller contribution to membership of the Party than to its vote; and a powerful social filter works so that each successive level in the hierarchy of constituency associations is more socially select than the one below it. Pinto-Duschinsky also found that constituency chairmen (the very elite of activists) included a majority of business proprietors over professionals like lawyers (Butler and Pinto-Duschinsky, 1980, p. 194).

Because our picture of the social make-up of the membership is sketchy we are also uncertain about one of the most interesting of all matters – its changing character. Throughout the post-war years the leadership has been sensitive to charges that the Party is socially unrepresentative. Periodic efforts have been made to broaden the social range of members, activists and MPs. The absence of good evidence spanning a long period of time makes it impossible to assess with sureness the success of these efforts. Some evidence from studies of particular areas (for instance, Lee's study on Cheshire) suggests a long-term move away from political leadership based on traditionally high social status, but local studies can only reflect the peculiarities of particular districts (Lee, 1963, pp. 93–105). Pinto-Duschinsky, the shrewdest modern observer of the Party, has offered the judgement that pre-war domination of constituency associations by aristocrats and great capitalists has given way to domination by professionals and proprietors of medium-sized businesses (Butler and Pinto-Duschinsky, 1980, p. 197). The change is modest and may reflect more the altered structure of the class system rather than an increase in the ability of the Party to recruit from a broader social range.

Uncertainty also surrounds the matter of what Conservative Party members and activists believe. Among academics and journalists there is a common view that activists are 'extreme' in their political outlook. If 'extremism' means opting for radical political solutions at variance with prevailing opinion among either electors at large or among Conservative voters, then there is little to support the view that activists do indeed hold extreme views. Over two decades ago Rose examined the political ideas of party activists through resolutions submitted for debate at Party Conferences but could find no significant evidence of extremism; Norton and Aughey concluded the same on more limited evidence for the early 1970s; Wilson found likewise in bringing Rose's work up to date (Rose, 1962; Norton and Aughey, 1981, p. 272; Wilson, 1977). It is true that impressionistic evidence suggests that in matters of crime and punishment Conservative activists support 'retributive' measures, especially the use of the death penalty. Such views are, however, hardly extremist unless the word is merely used pejoratively: survey evidence shows that they are like those widely held in the population (Reid, 1981, p. 294). Indeed, since survey evidence also shows that the working class hold more severe views on punishing criminals than do the middle class, it is likely that the Party's middle-class activist elite is actually less severe in its views about criminals than is the Party's working-class electorate.

The Conservative Party is the most successful mass political organisation in Britain, yet it has been neglected by scholars. By contrast, the Labour Party's membership has been the subject of long argument.

The Labour Party: Members and Activists

There are two classes of Labour Party membership – affiliated and direct. The bulk of affiliated membership is accounted for by the trade unions, a tiny remaining fraction representing affiliations by small socialist societies. Under existing legislation unions may, after commanding the agreement of their members in a ballot, establish a separate fund for political purposes. The fund is created by adding a small levy to union subscriptions. Members who object to the levy can 'contract out' of payment, but since the amount involved for individuals is tiny, and the method of contracting out cumbersome, only a minority do so.

Possessing a political fund is not identical with commitment to the Labour Party: some unions with political funds are not affiliated to Labour and most unions also use their funds for some purpose other than Party affiliation. The numbers affiliated by a particular union are also not identical with those who pay the political levy. In setting its level of affiliation a union makes a decision about how much financial support it wishes to give the Party and – since numbers affiliated decide the size of a unions' block vote – how much influence it wishes to exert. Crouch (1982) has remarked that union affiliation fees are not so much a reflection of membership levels as of the readiness of unions to buy 'shares' in the Party, in the manner of investors buying voting shares in firms. Despite particular variations, two trends have nevertheless been noticeable in the last thirty years: affiliated union membership (and thus union block votes and financial support) has become proportionately more important relative to the membership of constituency parties; and the union block vote itself is becoming increasingly concentrated in the hands of a few big unions (Kavanagh, 1982, pp. 210–13).

The growing relative significance of the union block vote is in part due to a fall in the individual membership in the constituencies. The precise scale of this decline is, however, uncertain, because there exists neither for the past nor the present an accurate measure of party membership. Those who know Labour best agree that membership of constituency parties peaked in late 1940s and early 1950s. Official estimates suggest that since then there has been a long decline: from just one million at the end of the 1940s to under 300,000.

These figures, though undoubtedly indicative of a trend, are not an accurate guide to the rate of decline. A minor reason for this is that they obscure important short-term variations. Seyd and Minkin (1979) have, for instance, argued that the Party's membership touched bottom in the late 1960s and recovered in the succeeding decade. More important, the figure is not a direct measure of membership. Until 1979, constituency parties affiliated on a minimum membership of 1000. It is known that only in a minority of constituencies did true membership equal or exceed this figure. All alternative measures of membership are imperfect. The Houghton Committee estimated membership to be 317,000 in the mid-1970s, but for technical reasons their method of calculation probably overstated the true figure. Whiteley adopted the indirect and imperfect method of asking a sample of delegates to the 1978 Party Conference for an estimate of the size of their constituency parties, and used their answers to produce a national figure of 255,000. The abolition of the '1,000 minimum rule' in 1980 virtually halved the official figure, and Whiteley has suggested that even this was an overestimate because it merely recorded the number of membership cards bought from headquarters. He is therefore probably right to believe that his 1978 figure of 255,000, though produced by imperfect methods, is the most reliable existing measure (Whiteley, 1982). At the moment Labour claims a membership of just under 300,000.

Whatever the precise figures, the Party has plainly suffered a great loss of individual members in the post-war years. Arguments about why this loss occurred are entwined with arguments about how the social composition of the party membership is changing. Two factors are most commonly cited to explain the loss of membership.

The first is disappointment with the Party's performance in government: thus the most catastrophic losses occurred in the difficult days of the Wilson Government in the late 1960s. The second factor is changing styles of political activity which have – as we shall see in the next chapter – drawn young radicals to pressure groups rather than to parties. The membership of the Young Socialists has suffered greatly from this last trend. An additional subsidiary cause may be the dispersal of traditional working-class communities by urban redevelopment, though the impact of this is uncertain because we are unsure how strong Labour Party membership ever was in such districts.

How far these developments have made Labour a less-working-class party is uncertain. Hindess (1971) argued that there had been a working-class withdrawal from the Party, but verification is hampered by the absence of good historical evidence. It would be surprising if the Party's working-class membership had not declined to some degree, because social change is cutting the absolute size of the working class. We just do not know, however, if independent of this change Labour's membership is becoming more middle class. The available evidence is contradictory, is drawn from studies of individual constituencies with their own peculiarities, and does not reach back beyond the recent past (Forrester, 1976).

There does, however, seem to be one undeniable result of economic change: as public sector employment has expanded, so Party membership has become dominated by those who work for public bodies. This feature is particularly noticeable among the most prominent local activists: for instance, a survey of Labour councillors conducted in six English local authorities in 1982 showed a remarkably high level of public sector employment (Gyford, 1983).

Our imperfect knowledge of the Labour Party's changing membership may be summed up as follows. Labour's total membership in the constituencies has declined over the post-war years but where this leaves present membership levels is uncertain. Labour is a more middle-class party than in the past, but how far this only reflects the changing class structure, and how far it reflects an independent withdrawal by working-class people from the Party, is also unclear. Even now, Labour remains the only Party able to recruit significant numbers of manual workers to party membership and to active politics.

There is also uncertainty about what Labour Party members

believe. The common caricature pictures local parties as dominated by radical socialists. The few studies of activists in particular localities give little support to this caricature, though any local study is plainly a prisoner of local peculiarities. The only systematic investigation is Whiteley's study of a sample of the local Labour elite, composed of figures like councillors and delegates to Party Conference. Though he found overwhelming support for some characteristic demands of radical socialism – such as nationalising profitable industries – and though radicalism seemed strongest among younger activists, the evidence nevertheless suggested that local parties were not dominated by 'extremists' (1983, pp. 30–9). The ferociously extreme local activist seems almost as mythical in the Labour Party as in the Conservative Party.

5 Minor Parties

Liberals and Social Democrats

The evidence of electoral studies suggests that the two main parties in Britain have a declining hold over the loyalty of voters. Yet one of the most remarkable features of modern British politics is the failure of any challenger successfully to capitalise on this dissatisfaction. For a brief period in the 1980s it seemed that an 'Alliance' of Liberals and Social Democrats would succeed in doing just that. The aftermath of the 1987 General Election destroyed such a possibility for the forseeable future. Immediately after the election Mr Steel, the Liberal leader, publicly pressed for a merger between the two wings of the Alliance. He was fiercely and publicly resisted from many sides: some Liberals were dismayed at the thought of losing their party's historic identity, while many Social Democrats objected to the disappearance of an institution of which they were founders. The most damaging opposition came from Dr David Owen, the formidable and commanding leader of the Social Democrats. Dr Owen not only resisted the merger proposal, but also made it clear that, whatever the outcome of talks, he would not join a merged party and would continue to offer leadership to disaffected and independent minded social democratic elements.

The ensuing events proved catastrophic for the political 'centre' in Britain. At both national and local level the Alliance broke up in acrimony. The public campaign to mobilise support for a merger, though it eventually resulted in the creation of a Social and Liberal Democratic Party (SLD), alienated activists and confused voters. Popular support for the centre groupings tumbled. Although the organisation of the centre is now too chaotic to allow an accurate estimate of membership figures it is likely that the new SLD commands a membership of less than half the combined total in the old Alliance. Meanwhile Dr Owen leads an indeterminate number of Social Democrats in their own party, prepared to fight the SLD at elections and capable, apparently, of draining off a crucial minority of votes.

To understand why the great hopes of the Alliance come to nothing we need to begin by realising that successful political movements are held together by common interests, common traditions and, occasionally, common principles. The Alliance was united neither on interests nor traditions, and had few shared principles. It consisted of two very different kinds of institution in the old Liberal Party and the Social Democratic Party.

Liberalism was federal in character (Finer, 1980, pp. 81–3): it was formally federal in the sense that there existed separate Liberal organisations for the different countries in the United Kingdom and for the English regions; and federal in substance because there was a deep and long-established tradition of local independent action, typified in recent years by the Liberal interest in community politics. From 1976 Liberal constituency associations also had the decisive say in the election of the Party leader. The structure of the Party was exceptionally complex with many different centres of power, reflecting the pluralistic character of Liberalism as a movement (Kavanagh, 1983).

This dispersed, sometimes chaotic, structure was often in severe tension with a Parliamentary leadership inevitably more attuned to the politics of Westminster. The tension was sharpened because, while modern Liberalism in the country was strongest in English suburbia, the Party's few MPs disproportionately represented rural and Celtic seats. There was a history of bitter quarrels over control of policy and of money. These quarrels were an important undercurrent in the scandal which caused the resignation of Mr Thorpe as Party leader in 1976.

The difficulties faced by the Parliamentary leadership in controlling the Party were illustrated by the character of the Liberal Assembly, the 'annual conference' and formally the supreme body of the Party. The Assembly was as argumentative as the Labour Party Conference, spanning a wide range of views from the most orthodox to the most eccentric. Unlike the Labour Conference, however, each participant had a single vote. The absence of a dominant union block vote made control from the platform very difficult. The Assembly was volatile in its behaviour, often inflicting embarrassing snubs on the leadership over sensitive issues like nuclear disarmament and rights for homosexuals.

The structure of the SDP was very different. It is true that it had some important marks of decentralisation. The Party was the only one of the 'Big Four' to select its leader by a secret ballot of all members, while its elected Council of over 400 activists met regularly to discuss and decide on party policy.

The marks of centralisation were nevertheless very strong. The SDP was the only major party whose members joined centrally rather than through a local association. It was also the only major party whose primary unit of organisation – the area – was larger than the territory of a single Parliamentary constituency (Bradley, 1981). Central control was the natural product of the way the Party was born. The SDP was the only existing party in Britain to result from a national initiative by politicians with an established reputation. The Party was the product of discontent among a section of Labour Party leadership with the direction taken by Labour in the 1970s, particularly with the challenge to the independence of the Parliamentary Party. The introduction in January 1981 of Labour's new system of leadership election (described above) provided the occasion for a break. Four former Labour Cabinet Ministers – Roy Jenkins, Dr David Owen, William Rodgers and Shirley Williams – founded a Council for Social Democracy. In March 1981 they formed the new party and were rapidly joined by over twenty MPs, all but one of whom were Labour defectors. In founding the new Party the leaders also appealed for members, an appeal rapidly answered by 65,000 people. In these circumstances the overwhelming ascendancy of the national leadership in the Party's early years is unsurprising. The founders were experienced politicians whose views and careers were given public prominence; by contrast, over 60 per cent of members, and even over half of the new Party's governing Council, had never before been members of a party (Döring, 1983).

Ideologically, the character of both wings of the Alliance was always puzzling and contradictory. Though some leading Social Democrats were members of past Labour Cabinets, the Party at large was an unknown quantity. Clues to ideology therefore relied heavily on the past careers and public statements of the most prominent national leaders. But past actions and present statements were often contradictory. The Party came out of the social democratic tradition in the Labour Party, a tradition which approved central management of the economy, using instruments like incomes policy, the creation of giant corporations in the public and private sector and the integration of the British economy into the European Economic Community. Many leading Social Democrats supported these policies when they were members of Labour Governments. After 1981 the most detailed statements of social democratic philosophy stressed different themes: using constitutional reform to devolve power away from the political centre; developing an economy where power was to be shifted from the top of the big corporations in the public and private sector; dismantling public monopolies in the interests of more competition (Owen, 1981). Yet at the same time, the Party's own structure was highly centralised, and it apparently remained committed to a centrally controlled incomes policy and to continued integration in a large European Economic Community.

Similar contradictions existed between different ideological strands in the Liberal Party. When it was displaced after the First World War as the main radical movement in Britain, the Party was the heir to two different sets of ideas: it stood for 'liberalism' in the sense of maximising individual choice, in the marketplace and social life, at the expense of big organisations like the state; and it stood for 'social reform liberalism', which involved using state power to provide welfare benefits and to regulate markets.

The influence of this social reform Liberalism endured. Some of it seeped into the Labour Party. Liberals themselves pioneered many of the ideas which in Britain after 1945 produced a centrally administered welfare state and a centrally managed economy (Gamble, 1983b). The modern Liberal Party supported a strong central government, a mixed economy with a large public sector and membership of the European Economic Community. In recent years the Party was also among the firmest supporters of a permanent prices and incomes policy.

Yet as Steed (1979) has shown, the libertarian tradition in

Liberalism also remained alive. The core of committed Liberals in the country tended to be suspicious of hierarchy and centralisation and to support the maximum amount of private choice. The picture is further clouded by the position of the most prominent Liberals, the small group of MPs in Parliament. The absence of a stable body of Liberal support in the electorate meant that Liberal MPs survived by cultivating their local ties, and their individual reputations, often at the expense of identification with the Party. Liberal Parliamentarians included an unusually high number of independent-minded political 'characters' whose attitude to organised Party politics was ambivalent. It was, in other words, always uncertain what ideological form Liberalism would have taken in government.

The differences in organisation and ideology between the Liberals and Social Democrats were reinforced by differences in membership base. The exact membership of the Liberal Party was never known, but a reliable guess would have put it at well over double the 50,000 in the Social Democrats. In other words, it always had much more 'muscle' at local level than had the SDP which, in addition, suffered from an excessive concentration of members among the middle class of south-east England (Döring, 1983).

In short, we can see that the once impressive Alliance was a fragile and unstable coalition. Renewed success for the centre depends, at a minimum, on the elimination of one of the rivals presently jostling for electoral support. The most likely victims are Dr Owen's Social Democrats. But whether renewed support will come, or whether the centre groupings will just become one of the range of minor parties, remains to be seen. It is to the other groupings that we now turn.

Nationalists, Communists and Fascists

Of the minor parties, the Nationalists are the most important. The Scottish National Party has enjoyed continuous representation in the House of Commons since 1967, and for a time in the mid-1970s was the most popular party in Scotland. Plaid Cymru, the Welsh Nationalist Party, has been attracting nearly a tenth of the votes in Wales since 1970. Nationalism is commonly spoken of as a single phenomenon but the two parties present striking contrasts.

Although the SNP made some of its earliest advances in rural, Gaelic Scotland, and although some of its founders aimed to recreate a traditional Gaelic culture, its main concern has been to exercise Scottish control over Scotland's industrial resources. It is essentially a modernising party devoted to the thesis that control from London has left Scotland with an out-of-date economy. After the Party's greatest modern setback – the failure to secure sufficient support in the 1979 referendum to implement the Labour Government's devolution proposals – an attempt was made by a group led by the former Labour MP, Mr Jim Sillars, to turn the Party in the direction of socialism. This attempt was defeated. An independent Scotland ruled by the present SNP would leave intact the structure of the market economy.

One of the most striking features of the SNP is negative in character: it lacks the interest, characteristic of most nationalist movements, in restoring a traditional culture or a national tongue. This proved a considerable strength during its great days in the 1970s. By addressing directly the central problems of Scotland's industrial economy it attracted considerable support in urban Scotland and drew support from across the whole class spectrum (Miller, 1981, pp. 153–216).

These features make the SNP very different both ideologically and socially from Plaid Cymru, the Welsh National Party. As the very name suggests, Plaid Cymru focuses its nationalism on preserving and extending the influence of the Welsh language. In doing this it reasons that defence of the language holds the key to preservation of national identity and national culture. The emphasis reflects both the social base of the Party and tactical considerations. Though the numbers able to speak the native tongue are a minority of the Welsh population, they are (at over one-fifth) a much larger segment than are Gaelic speakers in Scotland, who number under 2 per cent of the population (Rose, 1982, pp. 219–20). Plaid Cymru has been able to build electoral support best in those areas where the language, and the associated culture, are strongest. Its activist core is middle class, drawing heavily on public sector professionals like teachers and lecturers who stress 'cultural' more than 'material' issues.

Focusing on the language has also solved a tactical problem faced by all aspirant nationalist parties: how to engage in everyday campaigning in the interval before some measure of independence is achieved. In the last twenty years Plaid Cymru has been able, often with considerable success, to practise well-publicised campaigns for bi-lingual road signs, for the wider use of Welsh as a medium of instruction in schools, and for the establishment of a Welsh language television channel. It has also played a considerable part in reviving traditional culture, a revival signified by the reversal in the 1970s of the long decline in the number of Welsh speakers.

Plaid has in many ways been the less impressive of the two important nationalist groupings on the mainland: neither its Parliamentary strength nor its popular support ever reached the peaks achieved by the SNP, while the proportion of voters favouring the establishment of a Welsh Assembly in the 1979 referendum was tiny compared with the Scottish result – 20 per cent of Welsh voters were in favour, compared with 52 per cent favouring a devolved Assembly in Scotland. Yet in terms of its impact on important decisions, and in terms of its intermediate aim of defending Welsh language and culture, Plaid Cymru has probably been the more successful party.

Before the rise of nationalism in the last twenty years the most serious radical threat to the political order came from the Communist Party of Great Britain. The CPGB was founded in 1920 under the inspiration of the Russian Revolution. It has always had close links with international communism, and especially with the Soviet Union. Its greatest period of popularity occurred during and immediately after the wartime alliance with the Soviet Union when its membership briefly exceeded 40,000 (some claim it touched 50,000). In 1945, the Party for the first and last time had two MPs elected to Parliament.

Since then it has dwindled to electoral insignificance despite announcing its commitment to a 'parliamentary road to socialism'. The party's active support has come mainly from three groups: from a minority of well-placed activists and officials in unions; from a small number of working-class communities, principally in the Welsh and Scottish coalfields; and in the 1930s and 1940s from middle-class intellectuals. Though it remains a power in some unions, the Party is in an apparently irreversible decline. Membership is down to about 15,000 and few young recruits are being attracted. Though it now distances itself from the Soviet Union, it has suffered from the disenchantment of middle-class intellectuals with Russian communism. It is divided internally between the intellectuals, who want to modify traditional doctrines and tactics, and other members who want to maintain continuity with the past. Few young Marxist intellectuals now join the Communist Party. They gravitate instead to a wide variety of groups with tiny memberships, offering versions of Marxism which orthodox Communists find heretical. This fragmentation is in an obvious way a weakness, but it has also proved to be a kind of strength. Marxists and Marxist ideas are now widely disseminated among a range of radical groups, in the women's and peace movements, in environmental groups and even in the Labour Party.

Marxism has long been a respectable creed in Britain, especially among the intelligentsia. The same is not true of Fascism, whose supporters have been pariahs since the war against Hitler. The best-publicised post-war Fascist group was the National Front, formed by merging three separate bodies in 1967, but recently fragmented again by internal divisions. The Front's membership perhaps reached 25,000. The peak of its electoral success came in 1974 when ninety General Election candidates received an average of just under 3 per cent of the vote.

These unimpressive figures understate the importance of British Fascism. Its ideology combines vigorous economic nationalism (attacks on the EEC and on multinationals, calls for central direction of the economy) with violent abuse of non-whites, especially of immigrants. These views are not at all unusual in Britain. Survey evidence has shown that a much larger proportion of voters (principally in the working class) are sympathetic to Fascist views, especially on race, than actually vote for Fascist groups. One analysis of opinion poll evidence suggested that about 5 per cent of the electorate are potential Fascist voters and another 10 per cent are sympathetic (Harrop *et al.*, 1980). More startling still, Husbands found in a survey of opinion in selected urban areas that 17 per cent of those interviewed expressed views which were strongly in favour of National Front policies, while another 13 per cent could be classed as mild NF sympathisers (Husbands, 1984, p. 135).

Support for Fascist politicians in Britain is drawn disproportionately from the young, male working class, but contrary to popular caricature it is not drawn from mentally disturbed or violent dregs of that class. Though Fascist leaders often have peculiar personalities (as do leaders of many bigger parties), Fascist voters are not at all mentally odd. There is widespread popular support for Fascist attitudes, especially hostility to blacks. This is converted into Fascist voting not by some individual psychological peculiarity but most commonly by environmental influences: the Fascist vote rises where blacks are especially visible or, as in some parts of London, because there already exists a historically established tradition of racialism (Whiteley, 1979).

Fascism's most serious difficulty in attracting a significant body of support lies less in the character of popular attitudes than in the character of the leaders that it has produced. The leaders of Fascist groups have been so intensely anxious to establish their own personal superiority that most energy has gone into factional rivalry. The National Front, the most significant Fascist Party in the 1970s, has now been split by internal feuding. Even so, one study of 16-year-olds in the West Midlands in 1983 found that 30 per cent put one of the two main Fascist groups as their first choice party (*Times Educational Supplement*, 25 May 1984). There is evidently a significant, and probably growing, body of support awaiting mobilisation by a unified Fascist movement. There is some evidence that Fascists are now trying to infiltrate the Conservative Party, a tactic apparently modelled on left-wing penetration of the Labour Party. In 1983, a Young Conservative report alleged that the scale of infiltration was serious (*The Times*, 10 October 1983). The decline in Conservative Party membership (especially in membership of the Young Conservatives) certainly helps any small groups of activists determined to take over local organisations. Considerable dispute still exists, however, about the scale and seriousness of Fascist infiltration of Conservatism. We need more evidence before a considered judgement is possible.

6 Parties in Decline

British political parties are in decline. The fall in electoral support for the two major parties charted in Chapter 3 has coincided with their decline as organisations. Though exact figures are impossible to find, Labour and Conservative have together certainly lost in aggregate around two million individual members since the peaks reached in the late 1940s and early 1950s. Labour's proportional loss has been greatest but the largest absolute loss has been suffered by the Conservatives. Of course the expansion of smaller parties has provided some compensation: the revival of Liberalism, the birth of the Social Democrats and the appeals of nationalism all attracted people into party membership. This compensation is nevertheless slight and has been largely cancelled out by the collapse of the centre Alliance. A cautious estimate would be that today there are about one and a half million fewer direct subscribers to a party than thirty years ago.

This decline is due to both social and political forces. Altered tastes have made party institutions less central to the leisure of the middle and working classes; disappointment with party performance in office has caused disillusionment; new styles of political participation have become popular, especially among the young.

Declining membership has also damaged the professional efficiency of the parties. Between 1963 and 1981, for example, the number of paid agents in constituency Labour Parties fell from 200 to 74 (Pinto-Duschinsky, 1982). Even the rich Conservatives have been forced into economies.

These cuts are connected to the financial consequences of institutional decline. Most party income in Britain comes from two sources: from individual members, either as subscriptions or as funds raised by events like jumble sales; or from donations by institutions, notably companies and unions. Opponents of the two main parties have commonly charged that their incomes are largely from the latter sources.

The notion that Labour depends on the unions for money is, literally, a half-truth: successive estimates of total Labour Party income (local, regional and central) made at different times since the war suggest that just over half of the Party's income is from unions (Pinto-Duschinsky, 1981, pp. 225–6). The contribution of companies to total Conservative funds is even smaller: the latest available authoritative figures – from Pinto-Duschinsky's monumental study of political finance – suggests that in the decade after 1967–68 only 30 per cent of total income came from companies.

It is true that the picture changes if attention is concentrated on national party finances and on particular years. Pinto-Duschinsky has estimated that 90 per cent of the Labour Party's general election funds, and 60 per cent of Conservative central income, comes from unions and companies respectively (1981, pp. 137, 162). Institutional income also tends to be highest at a critical time in party policy-making, around election campaigns.

Organisational decline has nevertheless created serious financial problems for the parties. More efficient fund-raising in the constituencies has helped Labour compensate for the loss of membership subscriptions, but continued decline in numbers will obviously harm these very fund-raising activities. At national level the Party has been cushioned financially by a long-term rise in the amounts received from unions. This rise was largely due to the steady increase (dating from the late 1930s) in union membership, which in turn swelled the numbers contributing to the political levy. Since the end of the 1970s this expansion has been reversed, TUC membership falling by 1,500,000 between 1979 and 1983. In addition, the levy is itself threatened by the recent TUC–Government agreement to hold periodic ballots on the continuation of political funds.

The position is made even more serious because in recent years over 60 per cent of those contributing to a political fund have come from five big unions (Transport Workers, Engineers, General and Municipal, Public Employees, Shopworkers). The five combined lost over 700,000 members between 1979 and 1983.

Though the Conservative Party remains the richest party in Britain, it too faces great problems. The loss of around half the total membership in the last three decades, though serious in itself, is not the most worrying sign of decline. Even more ominous is the fivefold fall in the three decades to the end of the 1970s in membership of the Party's youth wing. The Young Conservatives in their great days were important both as a training ground for activists and – because of their famous social life – as a useful source of income. The Party's reliance for 70 per cent of total income on local fund-raising events and individual subscriptions makes the overall decline in member-ship especially worrying. The problem is intensified by the long-term failure of company contributions to keep pace with inflation. Both parties – alongside most others represented in Parliament – now receive state aid, but this meets only a small proportion of their obligations.

7 Conclusion

The financial and membership problems faced by major parties, though important in themselves, have an added significance as a sign of wider political change. Parties in their modern form began to develop with the appearance of a mass electorate in 1867. For a century they were a major – perhaps the major – means of representation for the great interests in the community. But no law of nature dictates that the Conservative Party be the voice of business or Labour the voice of unions. Rich and sophisticated groups are perfectly capable, should they feel so impelled, of organising representation independently of parties. This has indeed been happening, with the result that pressure groups now seriously rival parties in the system of representation. We next examine the developing forms of pressure group politics.

5

Pressure Group Politics

Men rejoice when they divide the spoil.

Isaiah, 9.3

1 Outline

This chapter begins by examining the nature of a pressure group and by distinguishing between types of group. It then examines in detail the most important groups, those created by the structure of the modern economy. This is succeeded by an account of a second major kind of group, created by associations uniting individuals with shared preferences. This section also examines the recent rise of movements devoted to the pursuit of radical aims by mass mobilisation. The final section of the chapter analyses the general character of pressure group politics, examining in particular the highly influential theory that a corporatist system of pressure group organisation is developing in Britain.

2 The Nature of Groups

A pressure group is conventionally defined as any group which tries to influence public policy without seeking the responsibility of government. This definition makes pressure groups one of the commonest means by which individual citizens participate in politics, for almost all of us are, often without realising the fact, members of such groups. The scale of government intervention in social and economic life means that almost no activity is untouched by public control. Even the most innocently non-political associations are drawn into politics, if only intermittently: the gardening association resisting a proposal to build a road over its land becomes a pressure group; water-skiers who band together to fight public restrictions on their activities become another (for an example of the latter see Dowse and Hughes, 1977).

Pressure groups are central to economic life: trade unions, firms, associations of businessmen, professional bodies, all spend much of their time dealing with government. But pressure groups also penetrate even the most apparently solitary activities: the individual who retreats from the world by entering a monastic order has joined a pressure group; the angler who joins a fishing club to pursue his solitary sport has joined another. Pressure groups follow us from birth to death: the midwife who delivers us is a member of a pressure group; the minister who buries us is a representative of another.

It will be plain that there exists an extraordinary variety of groups. This variety is a great obstacle to understanding, and even complicates the elementary task of definition. The conventional definition with which we began, in picturing groups as institutions trying to influence policy without accepting responsibility for government, seeks to distinguish groups from political parties. This distinction, though useful, cannot be pressed too far. Many small political parties – such as nationalists in Wales and Scotland – are advocating a particular cause rather than offering to govern the United Kingdom. Conversely, many of the most powerful pressure groups are not separate from government; they are absorbed into the state, playing a large part in making and executing public policy.

The variety of group life even complicates the simple act of labelling. 'Pressure group' is now so widely accepted as the generic label that its attempted replacement by some other title would only cause confusion. The implications of the phrase are nevertheless unfortunate. 'Pressure' suggests that all groups stand outside government, trying to extract concessions by campaigning to arouse popular opinion or support in Parliament. The most powerful groups actually only try to exert pressure in this way as a last resort. For the most part they are not the adversaries of civil servants and ministers, but are natural collaborators and agents of government in policy-making and policy implementation.

Care must also be taken over the use of the word 'lobby'. That term derives from the practice of entering the lobby of the legislature to accost Parliamentarians. Nowadays Parliament is of only minor importance to many powerful groups. 'Lobbying' has become a useful shorthand to describe the general attempts made by groups to influence government. This shorthand will be used here.

The great variety of groups not only makes definition difficult; it also complicates the task of arranging groups into some ordered classification. The problems are reflected in the many different methods of classification on offer. The commonest distinction is by aim. This is the basis of the division usually made between protectional groups, who are concerned to defend the sectional interests of their members, and promotional groups, who are concerned to promote the cause of others (as the human members of the Royal Society for the Prevention of Cruelty to Animals, for instance, promote animal welfare). A similar distinction lies beneath the division commonly made between interest groups and attitude groups.

An alternative means of classification divides groups by the tactics they typically use. This distinguishes three kinds: those who put most effort into lobbying civil servants and ministers in Whitehall; those who cultivate Parliamentary contacts; and those who devote most energy to arousing public opinion. A related classification distinguishes groups by their relations with government, dividing 'insider' groups with ready access to policy-makers from 'outsiders' enjoying no such favoured position (Grant, 1984).

Few groups fall neatly into any of these categories, but rough-and-ready distinctions are nevertheless invaluable in bringing some order into what would otherwise be unmanageable variety. But the best systems of classification do a bit more than this: they allow us to distinguish between sets of groups who are different in a variety of important ways. In the succeeding pages we will see that one of the most important dividing lines in the world of pressure groups lies between *functional* groups and *preference* groups, to adapt language suggested by Cawson (1982, pp. 37–43).

Functional pressure groups are created by the economic structure. Britain's is a complex industrial economy organised on the principles of market capitalism. The most powerful pressure groups represent those who carry out key functions and whose co-operation is needed if government is to work at all effectively. The rules of the market economy create the two most important kinds of functional group, those representing business and those representing labour. Business forms an important functional group because the rules governing control of property in a capitalist economy give to firms and to individual businessmen a large say in carrying out the functions of investment and production (Lindblom, 1977, pp. 170–

2). Workers are important because their co-operation or obedience is needed if production and services are to be carried out.

High technical and social complexity also creates a third important kind of functional group. Some workers claim that their jobs demand such a high level of technical or administrative skill that they deserve the status of a profession. Associations representing professions make special demands on government and, we shall see, exercise special powers.

Functional groups representing business, unions and the professions are the most important part of the pressure group universe. They are the involuntary creation of the economic structure, which is why the broad outlines of functional groups are the same in all advanced capitalist economies. By contrast, preference groups result from free associations between individuals united by common tastes, attitudes or pastimes. Since human tastes are almost infinite, the range of such groups is very wide. Three important kinds should be distinguished.

The first and most numerous are *social institutions*: those many organisations (churches, leisure organisations) uniting people with a common belief or a common attachment to some pastime. Social institutions plainly only behave as pressure groups on occasions. They can thus be distinguished from *pure pressure groups*, whose whole purpose is to exert influence on public policy. Some of the most successful and widely publicised lobbying organisations of recent years – for instance, the Abortion Law Reform Association (ALRA) and the numerous organisations promoting the interests of homosexuals – fall into this category. The best-known pure pressure groups have been London-based lobbies with a small membership, devoting most of their energies to cultivating policy-makers in Whitehall and in Westminster. In this they can be distinguished from *political movements* (for instance, the Campaign for Nuclear Disarmament and associated peace groups). Though the dividing line between pure pressure groups and political movements is not sharp, the latter tend to have more diffuse aims, are usually more anxious to recruit a large membership, rely heavily on arousing public opinion, and devolve most authority and activity away from London to local groups (Byrne and Lovenduski, 1983).

Among the most striking features of pressure group politics in recent decades have been the multiplication of preference groups, the expansion of pure pressure groups and the rise of political movements pressing radical causes. We examine these developments in section 4, but look first at functional groups.

3 Functional Groups: Capital, Labour, Professions

Business and Power
Of all the great interests now represented in the system of pressure group politics the business community has the longest history of effective political activity. In the eighteenth century the merchant and financial interests in the City of London were closely connected to government. In the nineteenth century merchant and banking interests were critical influences on British imperial policy, while a succession of particular groups – like railway companies at the height of the boom in rail construction – manipulated considerable numbers of Members of Parliament (Butt, 1967, p. 81; Wooton, 1975, pp. 13–54). The voice of business was given added influence later in the century by the evolution of the Conservative Party into a broad alliance representing industry, finance and landowners.

These forms of business representation developed before the extension of democratic politics, the rise of big government and the concentration of firms into large combines. Traditional representation was therefore personal and informal. It was typically carried out by individual capitalists who moved naturally in the same society as political leaders. Indeed, until well into the twentieth century it was common for leading businessmen to combine careers as successful capitalists with active political life in the House of Commons (Haxey, 1942, pp. 32–59). In such circumstances lobbying was as likely to be for the narrow interests of the particular individual concerned as for the collective interests of the business community.

This informal, personal system of representation still exists, but it is of declining importance. The representation of business interests in national politics is now mainly directed at civil servants and ministers in government, rather than at politicians in Parliament, and is conducted by formal organisations rather than by individual capitalists. These organisations are of four types: giant firms, employers' associations, trade associations and peak associations.

We saw in Chapter 1 how changes in economic structure have concentrated production in a small number of giant firms. Many industries are now dominated by a handful of enterprises. A few are dominated by a single firm. These giants have great advantages in dealing with government. They are run by managerial bureaucracies who speak the same language as public bureaucracies. (There is indeed a growing tendency for personnel to be swapped between firms and government.) They are rich, and can hire the best experts to make representations about future decisions and to trawl through the detail of existing policies. Some firms even have special departments given over completely to relations with government (Grant, 1982, pp. 513–6). The biggest enterprises have to be listened to by ministers and civil servants because the decisions they make about investment, production and marketing deeply affect how public policy can be made and executed.

The biggest firms often make little use of employers' associations. Many employers' associations were originally formed in particular industries to meet the rising challenge of trade unions in the late nineteenth and early twentieth centuries. They turned to politics because the power of the state was an important weapon in the conflict between workers and employers (Devlin, 1972, pp. 23–5). For over eighty years bodies like the Engineering Employers' Federation have been important voices inside and outside government in arguments about trade-union law, about the regulation of work and about central problems of economic policy like the control of incomes.

Trade associations are even more important and more numerous. Every British industry of importance has at least one, and often several, associations. Trade associations began to develop in significant numbers late in the nineteenth century as part of organised attempts to limit competition between firms, often in the face of rivalry from more efficient foreign enterprises. The associations soon turned to lobbying government, in order to obtain protection for members from foreign competition. As state control of the economy grew, governments welcomed approaches from the associations, seeing them as sources of advice, as institutions which could confer approval on government decisions and as a means for executing the details of policy.

Employers' associations and trade associations practise interest representation as only one function among many. By contrast, peak associations concentrate on interest representation rather than on the regulation of an industry or negotiation with employees. Peak bodies are generally loose federations of trade associations, employers' associations and individual firms. Most attempt to represent particular sections of business: for instance, the Retail Consortium is a federation dominated by the big chain stores, while the British Roads Federation unites a wide range of construction, haulage and motoring interests, principally to press the case for public spending on roads and motorways (Grant and Marsh, 1974; Dudley, 1983).

A small number of peak associations have the larger ambition of speaking for the whole business community. The best known of these is the Confederation of British Industry (CBI). The CBI was founded by merging three separate associations in 1965, largely at the prompting of government, which wanted to deal with a single, authoritative representative of business. The Confederation has only partly succeeded in this role. Its greatest achievement has been to establish itself as the most prominent of all business interest associations. Less publicly, it is a considerable presence in government. It maintains continuous contact with a wide range of government departments. A staff of four hundred and a large budget give it considerable resources in dealing with those departments. It nominates members to a wide range of state bodies, including the National Economic Development Council, the governing boards of many public agencies and a wide range of government advisory committees. The Confederation's roots in the business community and its dealings with government put it at the centre of a potentially very influential network of influence (Grant and Marsh, 1977).

Despite all these advantages the Confederation has never succeeded in making itself the authoritative voice of business. It has been bedevilled by internal divisions, because of the impossibility of reconciling all the varied interests of different industries (Grant, 1983). Many firms find their own industrial trade associations a better means of representation, while some of the biggest firms bypass all associations in favour of direct negotiations with government. (The biggest UK manufacturing firm, GEC, is not even a member of the Confederation.) But the CBI's greatest weakness is that, while it draws members from every sector of the economy, it is dominated by big manufacturing enterprises. Small firms are poorly represented in its ranks; indeed small business is generally poorly organised as a national pressure group. An even more serious deficiency is that the Confederation is of little importance in representing the interests of firms in the service sector, the most successful part of British business. The Retail Consortium speaks for the wide range of firms connected with the retail trade, while the highly successful financial institutions in the City of London have their own channels of influence. The 'City' is so distinctive and important that it deserves a separate description.

The most distinctive feature of interest representation as practised by the City of London is that it has relied little on formal lobbying or pressure group organisation. The City's power has depended instead on a freedom to run its own affairs greater than that enjoyed by any other important economic interest.

The City has been able to stand aside in this way from orthodox pressure group politics because its social and economic structure makes it much more united than its manufacturing industry (Moran, 1981). This unity is partly a product of geography. The headquarters of most of the great financial institutions are within a few minutes' walk of each other in the City of London itself, and thus form a small, cohesive community.

Geography is reinforced by the social characteristics of the City. Its different parts – the banks, the Stock Exchange, the insurance market in Lloyd's – have all been dominated by a social elite far more exclusive than is the case in manufacturing industry. A small number of families, often connected to each other by kinship and by economic interests, and drawn from upper-class society, have exercised disproportionate influence in City life (Wilson and Lupton, 1959; Whitley, 1974). This social unity has enabled the City to act in an informal but united way, keeping it apart from orthodox forms of pressure group politics.

The City's distinctiveness also owes much to the Bank of England. The Bank is Britain's 'central bank': that is, it is a public institution carrying out important government functions in economic management and in regulating economic institutions. But the Bank has also traditionally organised City interests and put their views in government. Until 1946 the Bank was a privately owned body, and even now it remains very close to the financial community. It is the only important public agency concerned with economic management actually located in the City of London. Its personnel are more like those who work elsewhere in the City than like civil servants in Whitehall. Its daily operations bring it into close and continuous contacts with financial markets.

The Bank is the key to understanding why the City has developed a system of interest representation separate from the formally organised lobbying practised by groups like the CBI. Its role in economic management and regulation give it access to the most important policy-makers in government; its City connections make it the natural voice of City interests inside government. With such a powerful sponsor, the City for a long time had little incentive to either ally with other parts of business or to go directly to government on its own account.

In recent years this pattern has begun to change. The Bank of England has grown more distant from City interests. The City itself has found difficulty in running its affairs free from government intervention. Trade associations and other lobbying organisations have become increasingly important. Direct contacts between Ministers and civil servants, on the one hand, and City interests on the other, have become increasingly common. The City is, in short, beginning to resemble the formally organised interests usual elsewhere in the business community. Nevertheless, at the moment it still retains much of its distinctive, informal approach to interest representation.

Business interests have a long history of intervention in British politics. There are, however, considerable differences of opinion about the amount of power exercised through these interventions. Those who favour the view that business is exceptionally powerful stress two features: its capacity positively to influence the decisions of government by lobbying; and its ability to pre-empt decisions by activities in the marketplace. These two elements of business power merit separate consideration.

The view that business is a particularly effective lobby rests partly on the belief that in a market economy like Britain's the most successful businessmen are almost automatically part of an elite of wealth, and are thus well placed to lobby other elites in government. In addition, since policy making and execution are activities involving high levels of technical and administrative complexity, influencing policy demands a detailed grasp of its details and its implications. Businessmen often have that grasp because of their own expertise and because they have the resources to hire other experts. The best example is provided by tax policy where, even when business loses the argument about the substance of policy, it can still use its lawyers and accountants to squeeze maximum advantage from loopholes in legislation. The business community also undoubtedly has the resources to influence opinion throughout society. It has the money to launch mass publicity campaigns, while key institutions like the national newspapers, which are almost wholly owned by big corporations, are overwhelmingly sympathetic to its interests.

The argument that business is not just a highly effective lobby but that it also possesses an especially potent pre-emptive power has been commonly argued by Marxists. The most influential recent statement of the case is, however, contained in Lindblom's analysis of business power in market economies (1977). Lindblom argues that the root of business power lies in the rules of property which govern such economies. These rules confer privileges on firms and private individuals, by putting into their hands the right to make key economic decisions about production, investment and employment. Government therefore has to defer to business, because without the co-operation of capital no policies of economic management could be effective.

Most businessmen would deny that they are a particularly effective lobby or that they exercise special power through the market-place. This denial is supported by many observers of British politics. Particular doubt has been expressed about whether business is indeed an especially influential lobby. Deep differences of interest divide the business community, separating, for instance, the City from manufacturing industry. These divisions both impede united lobbying and pit businessmen against each other in politics. It is also true that the impressive resources and access enjoyed by business have often failed to produce desired policies: there exists a long list of government decisions made and executed in the face of business opposition in post-war Britain. There are also good grounds for scepticism about the effectiveness of business pressure groups. The Confederation of British Industry, the best-known peak association, has a history of internal divisions and resignations. More generally, Devlin's study of trade associations found that while some were rich and well organised, others were poor and politically incompetent (Devlin, 1972, pp. 63–4).

The argument that property rights in a market economy confer power on business undoubtedly has force. But it should be noted that the exercise of these rights can be restricted in varying degrees by the opposition of trade unions, by the reactions of consumers and, above all, by the range of taxes and regulations which government can impose on business. Businessmen can in turn influence unions, consumers and governments; but this complex to-ing and fro-ing is a long way from Lindblom's picture of business as a great power securely defended by its property rights.

Arguments about the power of business are often fierce because, since Britain's is a market economy, conclusions about business power can affect judgements about the attractiveness or otherwise of market capitalism. Similar ferocity often surrounds discussion of the power of trade unions.

Trade Unions and Power

Academic observers of British politics often argue about the power of business; but the most contentious public arguments in recent years have concerned the influence of trade unions. Surveys of public opinion have shown that a large section of the population believes unions to have great and undesirable power. This reputation derives from the fact that organised labour is able to exercise influence in three different ways: through the connections existing between many large unions and the Labour Party; through the influence exercised over civil servants and ministers by the unions' peak association, the Trades Union Congress; and through the capacity of organised labour to extract concessions by using, or threatening, industrial action

Links between unions and the Labour Party are, as we saw in the last chapter, more visible and formal than are those between the Conservative Party and the business community. The unions originally created the party; the block voting system gives them over 90 per cent of votes at annual Labour Party Conferences; and unions sponsor nearly a half of all Labour members of Parliament. In the last fifteen years formal links between the unions and the Party have been strengthened. During the 1970s a TUC–Labour Party liaison committee exercised significant influence over the policies of the Labour Party and Labour Governments (May, 1975, pp. 37–52). In 1981 constitutional changes agreed at a Party Conference gave the unions – through the block vote system – 40 per cent of the votes to be cast in contests for the leadership and deputy leadership.

The trade-union movement's central place in the system of interest representation rests even more, however, on the key part played by the Trades Union Congress in dealing directly with government. Congress enjoys some special advantages in speaking as the voice of organised labour in Britain. British unions have never suffered the serious divisions over religion or political ideology experienced by many trade-union movements abroad. Since its foundation in 1868 Congress has therefore enjoyed a special position as the authoritative voice of labour. Its claim to speak with authority has been reinforced in the last two decades because an increasing number of unions representing white-collar workers have joined. Despite a decline in membership in the 1980s, the overwhelming majority of trade unionists are now members of the TUC.

The importance of Congress in interest representation is the result of a series of national crises, notably those created by the two world wars and by the growing crisis of the British economy in the last two decades. Before the First World War the TUC was a Parliamentary lobby; indeed its executive was called the 'Parliamentary Committee'. The full-scale mobilisation of the economy in the First World War, especially after 1916, drew the unions into close co-operation with Whitehall and, in some cases, into direct representation on public bodies. Co-operation and representation did not survive long after 1918, but during the 1930s, under the leadership of Walter Citrine and Ernest Bevin, Congress began to renew its connections with government. This renewal proved a prelude to the dramatic and enduring changes produced by the Second World War. The appointment of Bevin as Minister of Labour in 1940 created close working relations between government and the unions, the most distinctive features of which were: regular consultations about economic policy between the TUC leadership and the highest levels of government; the representation of the trade unions on a wide range of public bodies in both advisory and executive capacities; and negotiations between government departments and the TUC over the details of many policies.

Since the early 1960s, when governments began to respond to a growing economic crisis by greater intervention, the institutional connections between unions and government have expanded: the TUC has an almost unbroken line of representation on the National Economic Development Council (founded 1962) where its members discuss broad issues of economic policy with senior businessmen and senior ministers; it nominates members to the governing bodies of important public agencies like the Health and Safety Executive and the government's Advisory, Conciliation and Arbitration Service; it was deeply involved in the 1960s and 1970s in negotiations over, and sometimes in implementing, pay and prices policies; and it continues to be represented on a broad range of advisory bodies and tribunals both nationally and regionally (May, 1975, pp. 61–91). The public presence of trade unions in policy arguments is great: the General Secretary of Congress is a widely known national figure and the leaders of the largest unions are usually considerable public personalities, better known than most leading businessmen.

The common view that unions are extremely powerful rests in part on the belief that the Labour Party connection, coupled with the more orthodox activities of the TUC as a pressure group, gives unions access to two great levers of power. But the development of industrial relations over the last twenty years has convinced some observers that the greatest source of union power lies outside conventional politics, in the use, or threat, of strikes and other industrial action. The most dramatic illustrations of this power were provided by the miners, when in 1972 and 1974 they triumphed in trials over incomes policy with the Conservative Government. Both Finer and Brittan have argued that industrial action, by disrupting the economy and social life, gives organised labour a uniquely powerful weapon (Finer, 1973; Brittan, 1975). Middlemas has argued, though in a different tone, that 'trade union hegemony has broadened out further [in Britain] than in any comparable Western nation' (1979, p. 452).

Arguments about union power have a great political significance because it is widely believed that the unions use their power in malign ways. It is commonly argued that they enjoy special legal privileges, have defeated the laws of democratically elected governments and have perpetuated restrictive labour practices damaging to the economy. Those who dissent from these estimations argue, conversely, that the trinity of union power – in the Labour Party, in the activities of the TUC as a pressure group, and in industrial action – is less impressive in reality than in appearance. In the eyes of Marxist observers like Miliband the connection with the Labour Party has actually been a weakness rather than a strength, because it has tied the unions to Parliamentary politics and sapped their will to use industrial strength (Miliband, 1973, pp. 318–49). In analysis of the Labour Governments, 1974–79, Coates has also argued that in government the pressure of events and the power of business soon combine to destroy union influence. Coates claims that in the 1974–

79 period union 'victories' in policy-making were very limited, while the pressure of economic crisis wrenched important decisions out of their grasp (Coates, 1980, pp. 258–84).

The view that the unions actually exercise only a limited influence through their Party connections is not widely believed outside the labour movement itself. By contrast, there is widespread scepticism about the effectiveness of the TUC as a pressure group. Though Congress undoubtedly benefits from the absence of any serious rival to its position as the peak organisation for the labour movement, its ability to act in a decisive and authoritative way is seriously limited by the structure of trade unionism. There exists in the union movement a strong resistance to central control which restricts both the authority and the resources of Congress. This institutional weakness affects the quality of trade-union representations, because unions often lack adequate bureaucratic and technical expertise when they go into Whitehall. The inadequacy is particularly important because modern policy-making is exceptionally intricate. Those with detailed, expert knowledge can exercise great influence both when a policy is being made and when it is being executed; those who lack expertise are greatly disadvantaged.

These institutional weaknesses also exist in individual unions. Many of the biggest unions are loose federations of different industrial and regional groupings. Paid officials are comparatively few in number, much power is at local level and bureaucracies are poorly funded. This is in striking contrast to the biggest firms, who have clear managerial hierarchies and armies of accountants and lawyers poring over the details of government policy.

These, then, are the most important grounds for scepticism about the ability of unions to lobby in Whitehall. Those who quarrel with the view that the strike weapon gives unions a unique, third, power can hardly deny that in recent years it has been used to spectacular effect. Both Mr Heath's government (1970–74) and Mr Callaghan's Labour Administration (1976–79) could blame their loss of office in part on damage suffered at the hands of strikes among key groups of workers. It is commonly argued, however, that even the economic sanctions available to unions do not match the control over prices, production and investment wielded by firms in a market economy (Marsh and Locksley, 1983). It is also plain that readiness to strike, and the effectiveness of strikes, varies greatly according to economic circumstances. Strikes were most common and most effective during the heyday of full employment in the thirty years after the Second World War. Since then, workers, faced with the prospect of unemployment, have often been reluctant to strike, while employers and governments have become increasingly sophisticated in combating the effects of industrial action. But the effect of strikes in big industries still can be spectacular. The argument about how far industrial action gives unions a special kind of power therefore continues.

Like many of the arguments discussed in this book, different views about the power of unions arise only in part from different evaluations of evidence. Estimates of union power also carry a heavy weight of moral judgement because they are bound up with estimations of the worth or otherwise of our social institutions. But though the arguments are highly charged they have at least been thoroughly debated by observers of British politics, and important evidence has been accumulated. By contrast, we are only just beginning to study and understand the place of professions in interest representation.

Professions and Power
Debates about the nature of a 'profession' have long engrossed social scientists. One of the most convincing accounts has been offered by Johnson, who pictures professionalism as a strategy used by a wide range of occupations. This strategy, when successful, gives those in the occupation control over important aspects of work: over who enters the occupation, over the skills and technology it uses, and over its relations with clients (Johnson, 1972, pp. 41–7; Dunleavy and O'Leary, 1987, pp. 300 ff).

The rise of professions is in part the product of continuing economic development, which creates new technologies, new skills associated with those technologies and new demands for specialised services. The occupations in Britain using the strategy of professionalism include the 'established' professions (like medicine and the law); newer 'caring' professions created by the rise of services fulfilled through the welfare state, such as the various branches of social work; and occupations created by the discovery or systematisation of technical knowledge (engineers, architects, accountants).

Professional identity and professional organisation are powerful weapons. Three sources of influence are especially important: control over the occupation itself; the use of professional organisations to lobby; and the development and diffusion of a professional ideology. The first of these is the most potent. If an occupation has its claims to professional status accepted, it gains the right to regulate its affairs substantially free of public control. The best-developed example is the legal profession, which controls a whole range of matters deeply affecting the wider community. These include the price of legal services, the amount of competition between members of the profession, its internal organisation, the numbers who practise law and the content of much legal training. Self-regulation of this type is a particularly effective way for a group to defend its interests because it dispenses with much of the need for lobbying: the interests of a group are simply perceived as a matter for private decision, neither the state nor other groups in society having any presumptive right to intervene. But even when an activity is publicly funded and publicly controlled the acceptance of profes-sional judgements can confer great influence on particular groups. In the National Health Service, for instance, the belief that certain decisions can only be properly made by qualified medical profes-sionals gives such groups a large say over how public money is spent.

Occupations claiming the status of professions vary in the extent to which they are allowed to exercise influence through independent regulation of work: lawyers and doctors, for instance, enjoy more independence, and thus more influence, than do schoolteachers. All professions can, however, organise to take part in pressure group politics. Professional associations have considerable advantages in lobbying government and Parliament. They often perform collective bargaining functions, and thus have the additional resources of a trade union. These include a mass membership, the ability to withdraw the co-operation of the labour force, and a considerable income from subscriptions. To this they add the reputation for expertise and impartiality which is widely suggested by the image of a profession. Governments usually welcome professional organisa-tions into policy-making. They look to them for expert advice in making new policies. They are glad of professional approval for policies already made. They find professionals invaluable in execut-ing policies when they are put into effect. In most parts of govern-ment – from the most public, like the provision of education, to the most esoteric, like the formulation of company law – professions are central to the making and execution of public policy.

Just how potent a professional association can be is illustrated by the case of the British Medical Association. The BMA is probably the best-organised pressure group in Britain. In 1981 it had a budget of over four million pounds, and employed over two hundred staff (Jones, 1983). It is recognised in government as the voice of doctors on a wide range of medical issues requiring 'expert' judgement. In addition, it is listened to with respect on important social questions (such as when and how workers can be judged medically unfit for work) and on some of the most difficult moral problems of our day (such as the age at which contraception should be freely available, or the circumstances when new-born babies can be left to die). To all this it adds a key position in collective bargaining over doctors' pay and conditions, possessing the ability, in an extremity, to withdraw the labour of its members from the National Health Service.

'Self regulation' and lobbying by professional associations are two important ways in which professions exercise power. The third source of influence, through the impact of professional ideologies, is more elusive. Professions typically develop a dominant set of beliefs encompassing both the perceived duties of the profession and views on a wide range of substantive questions. The ideology of the teaching profession, for instance, lays down codes of conduct for teachers and makes assumptions about how subjects should be taught. The prestige of individual professions, and the activities of particular groups of professionals, can transmit these ideologies widely. Many policy-making communities are heavily influenced in this way by professional groups. In social work, for instance, professionals play a key part in debates about policy (Wilding, 1982). In other subtle ways professional ideologies influence everyday life and the everyday actions of government: medical ideologies influence beliefs about which drugs are socially acceptable; educational ideologies influence the organisation of schools and the content of the curriculum; architectural and planning ideologies influence public decision about building, and thus influence the physical surroundings of our home and work.

Political scientists have so far paid little attention to professional ideologies and how they connect to the demands of other powerful interests in the community. Some debate has taken place about how far the ideology of judges is shaped by the interests of property owners (Griffith, 1977; Robertson, 1982). Dunleavy has examined the role of planning and architectural ideologies in the building of high-rise council flats in the 1960s, and has shown how these ideologies grew up in professions linked by ties of patronage to powerful interests in the building industry (Dunleavy, 1981, pp. 104–43). But work on professions by political scientists is only beginning. We know little about the limits of professional power or about why the power of different occupations varies. Beyond the well-documented case of medicine we even know little about the formal organisation of professions as pressure groups.

4 Preference Groups and Power

The heart of the pressure group system consists of those groups created by a developed market economy. But the vast majority of groups have a more voluntary character, resulting as they do from the association of like-minded people with a shared preference. We earlier distinguished three kinds: social institutions, pure pressure groups, and political movements.

The first of these are the most numerous. They include associations with no overt political character uniting people with common beliefs (for instance, in churches), or in common pursuits (for instance, in clubs for sports and hobbies) or in service to a common cause (for instance, in some of the 140,000 registered British charities). These institutions rarely see themselves as pressure groups, and often resent any suggestion that they are involved in politics. They consequently often avoid such public activities as lobbying politicians or campaigning to influence opinion in the community at large. The pervasiveness of government intervention nevertheless inevitably sucks them into politics. Churches have obvious interests in political issues, such as the debate about the legal control of abortion. Political control of international sport has also in recent years forced the governing bodies of many major sports to deal with governments.

These obvious political interventions are, however, only the tip of the pressure group iceberg. The everyday operations of a wide range of social institutions are deeply affected by public intervention: churches and other charities take a close interest in taxation policy, because detailed changes in tax law can affect their income; churches and sporting organisations are affected by physical planning policy, because they are often substantial property owners; churches and secular charities take a close interest in the making and execution of social policy because they provide a wide range of services, such as education, help for the homeless, care of orphans and aid for victims of drug abuse.

Social institutions provide, in particular, some of the most important pressure groups in local politics because many of the public activities that affect them deeply – education provision, planning controls, housing services, child care – are administered by local government. Newton's study of Birmingham illustrates the central role played by many voluntary organisations in implementing social policy and in spending public money at the local level: even at the end of the 1960s, the City Council was making grants of over one million pounds annually to voluntary organisations carrying out public services (Newton, 1976, pp. 63–75). In 1983, the Greater London Council alone was making donations to over 2000 voluntary bodies.

Precisely because they provide important voluntary services, institutions like churches, charities and leisure organisations are welcomed by government into policy-making. This is one reason why the best-established institutions so often reject 'politics' in the sense of lobbying and public campaigning. As Dearlove has demonstrated in a study of local politics, established and 'respectable' charities have such good contacts with local authorities that they often do not feel the need to exercise overt pressure (1973, p. 157). In some cases the divide between the public and the private has virtually been obliterated. Charities like the Family Fund (which gives financial help to the families of the handicapped) and institutions like the National Association for the Care and Resettlement of Offenders, are sponsored and funded by the state (Barker, 1982). In some instances quasi-government bodies have been set up to organise whole categories of social institutions and to distribute public money: these are the functions of, for instance, both the Arts Council and the Sports Council.

Social institutions are intermittent and often reluctant participants in pressure group politics. By contrast, 'pure' pressure groups organise individuals with a particular set of shared policy preferences and attempt to bring these preferences to bear on government. They include the groups most readily associated in the public mind with pressure group activities, such as bodies like the Society for the Protection of the Unborn Child (which unites those wishing to reverse the permissive legislation on abortion passed in 1967) and the League Against Cruel Sports.

Specialised groups are nothing new. Their origins can be traced back to the eighteenth-century campaigning groups who originally agitated on questions like electoral reform and Catholic emancipation. Indeed, the half century or so before the emergence of modern disciplined parties was a golden age for the specialised pressure groups. They deeply influenced a wide range of social changes, including the abolition of slavery, Catholic emancipation and the reform of poor relief (Hollis, 1974, pp. 1–26). A few contemporary groups, like the Lord's Day Observance Society (founded 1831), actually date from this golden age. Others, like the pro-abortion lobbies, are directly descended from Victorians with 'advanced' ideas who wanted to control the breeding habits of the population.

Though specialised pressure groups are not novel, their recent rate of birth seems to be unprecedented. Almost all the existing groups are post-war creations; indeed in the *Guardian Directory of Pressure Groups* – a listing dominated by specialised groups – one-half of the groups recorded were actually founded after 1960 (Marsh, 1983, p. 4). Their voices have been loud and persistent in recent public arguments. In the mid and late 1960s, in particular, they achieved a set of substantial victories: pressure groups were highly influential in changing the laws on capital punishment, abortion and homosexuality, and in stimulating public debates about poverty and about homelessness.

Pure pressure groups nevertheless enjoy much less influence than their public prominence might suggest. They suffer from two disadvantages. First, unlike functional groups they control no great resource – like property or labour – and are therefore weak in bargaining with government. Second, unlike functional groups and such social institutions as churches they have little to offer recruits in the way of selective benefits available only to members. Their membership therefore tends to consist of a small number of enthusiasts for a common cause.

The most successful groups compensate for these deficiencies in various ways. They cultivate contacts with professionals, so that their lobbying is informed and sophisticated. This tactic has been employed by both sides in the abortion debate (Marsh and Chambers, 1981). They also try to build alliances with functional groups. The pro-contraceptive lobby, for instance, has contacts with the medical profession, with the large firms who market contraceptive devices and with important public agencies. Thus in 1984 the main contraceptive manufacturers combined with the Health Education Council (a public body) and the Family Planning Association (a pressure group which encourages contraception) to fund a study of so-called 'unplanned' pregnancies in Britain.

Although these tactics can link 'pure' pressure groups to more-powerful institutions they can also create difficulties. Pure pressure groups are usually devoted to pursuing politically radical (or at least 'progressive') causes. Those who sympathise with such causes are often suspicious of what they see as elitist lobbying based on contacts between experts in London. In numerous areas – covering animal welfare, defence of the physical environment, opposition to nuclear power, abortion, contraception and connected women's rights issues – pure pressure groups have consequently been rivalled in recent years by broader political movements.

These movements have a number of distinctive features. They aim for large memberships, and in some cases succeed: at the time of writing, membership of the Campaign for Nuclear Disarmament (at about 80,000) exceeds that of the old Social Democratic Party, while the broader peace movement claims 250,000 supporters. These movements reject London-based lobbying in favour of mass action using marches and demonstrations. Their organisation is usually decentralised, emphasising local initiative: the Campaign for Nuclear Disarmament has around 1200 local groups. They are often – as in the case of the Women's Movement – loose federations of sympathisers rather than formal associations with members committed to a single cause. Their aims often go beyond changing the law to altering wider sets of social attitudes and social institutions. They tend to be dominated by young recruits from the middle class who are suspicious of established institutions and established ways of exercising political influence (Byrne and Lovenduski, 1983).

The movements that have grown so rapidly in recent years see themselves as something novel in British politics. It would be truer to say that they revive old traditions of campaigning. Mass agitation was pioneered before 1850 by the movements for electoral reform, Catholic emancipation, and Chartism (Hollis, 1974). Even particular campaign techniques associated with the new movements are often nineteenth-century inventions. Wearing badges as a sign of support for a cause was pioneered by the original campaign against the slave trade. Popular campaign songs were used by the nineteenth-century campaigners against alcohol, as in splendid old parlour favourites like 'Father's a drunkard and mother is dead' (Turner, 1972). Nor is there anything novel about groups trying to alter social attitudes instead of merely changing the law: the temperance movement and the early campaigns against cruelty to animals had precisely these wider objectives.

The decline of the great nineteenth-century campaigning movements coincided with the rise of nationwide political parties. The emergence after the 1860s of the Liberal Party as the natural home of radical causes channelled into Liberalism the energies that had previously gone into popular agitation for particular causes. The recent revival of political movements coincides with the decline of parties, especially of the Labour Party, the successor to Liberalism as the natural home of radicals. The new movements therefore have an importance beyond their effect on policy, because they are becoming the most important means by which the young middle class enter politics. A generation ago politically inclined young people almost automatically engaged in political activity through a party; now they increasingly do so by supporting a campaigning movement.

The spread of pure pressure groups, and the rise of more broadly based political movements, are two of the most striking developments in modern British politics. So sudden have been the changes that we are only just beginning to understand why they happened. Some of the forces at work are peculiar to Britain. The electoral system, for instance, by discriminating against small political parties with geographically dispersed support, encourages the formation of pressure groups as an alternative form of political action. In West Germany, by contrast, the 'environmentalist' movement has been able, under a different voting system, to mount a considerable electoral challenge to the established parties. In some degree the new groups also seem to be the product of the way policy debates happen in modern political systems. It has often been observed that there is an 'issue attention cycle' by which, partly through the mass media, particular issues become the focus of intense campaigns until, with the arguments exhausted, they are pushed aside by other issues attracting equally intense attention. This cycle helps explain why so many of the new groups have short, highly publicised lives. Take as an example the Anti-Nazi League, a group devoted to public confrontation with Fascists: in a few short years in the late 1970s the League went from insignificance to a membership numbering over forty thousand, then back into insignificance.

This cyclical theory cannot, however, explain the sheer multiplication of groups, nor the durability of so many. Three rather different general explanations can be offered. The first – recalling some of the themes of our second chapter – suggests that the new groups display the marks of a 'post-affluent' political culture: they often explicitly reject the kind of politics practised by the old class-based parties; they commonly concentrate on issues involving questions of personal morality (abortion, homosexuality) or openly campaign against what they believe are materialist values (as do the environmental groups); and they draw members disproportionately from the young, well-educated middle classes, exactly as Inglehart's theory of post-affluence would lead us to expect. Cotgrove has refined this explanation in a study of the environmental movement. Noting that the new environmentalist organisations draw members from occupations in the tertiary 'service' sector of the economy (welfare work, the creative arts and academic life) he suggests that such occupations insulate those employed in them from the values of the market, and attract those who already reject such values. The new movements can therefore be seen as part of a wider rejection of business culture (Cotgrove, 1982).

An alternative explanation sees the proliferation of pressure groups as a rejection, not of the culture of business, but of class-based politics. The 'post-materialist' account undoubtedly makes sense of some of the newer middle-class-dominated groups, especially those concerned with issues like peace and the protection of the environment. But many of the new groups organise people who are anything but affluent: single parents living in poverty; council tenants living on ramshackle estates; blacks living in the squalor of inner cities. These groups are in effect an alternative to the Labour Party's claim to represent working-class interests as a whole. As the hold of class declines, so individuals form groups according to the almost infinite range of tastes and conditions which define human beings. Thus we get pressure groups catering for divorced fathers, homosexual ramblers, and connoisseurs of real ale, to name only three formed in recent years.

A third and very different explanation for the spread of the pressure group habit is suggested by those theories of 'sectoral' politics which we encountered in previous chapters. If new production sectors and consumption classes are replacing the old occupational class groupings, then we might expect change in the pressure group world to reflect the rise of the new groupings. In a stimulating study of the anti-nuclear lobby, Ward has argued that theories of sectoral politics help explain the rise of groups concerned to subject the physical environment to greater public regulation. He suggests that the environmental movement draws its members heavily from public employees (Ward, 1983). These people benefit materially from stricter environmental regulation, because public control curbs market forces and enhances the prestige and resources of the public institutions who do the regulating. It is certainly striking how often environmental groups are allied to particular functional pressure groups. The National Union of Mineworkers, seeing a threat to jobs in the development of nuclear power, has supported those who campaign on environmental grounds against the construction of nuclear power stations. The pressure group 'Transport 2000' is an alliance between, on the one hand, those who support public transport because they believe it safeguards the physical environment and, on the other, rail unions who stand to lose jobs and members if public transport contracts.

This third interpretation contradicts the 'post-materialist' view of the new pressure groups. One of its striking advantages is that it gives a better understanding of the numerous local groups which have mushroomed in recent years. Some of the most startling changes in the pressure group system are taking place in local communities. The new local groups are far from 'post-materialist'. They are typically concerned with such issues as tenants' rights, defence of local transport and education services, and the attempt to prevent the decline of the local economy (Dunleavy, 1980a, pp. 156–9). They mobilise supporters who live very far from the world of a post-materialist bourgeoisie. In short, the local groups seem to be movements growing out of the common location of individuals as consumers of public services like housing, education and transport.

5 Understanding Pressure Group Politics

Complicated and contradictory changes are happening among British pressure groups. 'Preference' groups are multiplying at a great rate. Movements with highly democratic structures where most initiative lies at local level are becoming especially prominent. But this picture of growing openness and diversity is not matched elsewhere in the pressure group world. Business is being increasingly dominated by a small number of giant firms and by a few representative associations with strong, highly professional bureaucracies. Organised labour is witnessing a similar process of concentration. A small number of professions have forged privileged links with the state.

These contradictory developments have created a crisis of understanding in the study of pressure groups. Until a decade or so ago the theoretical analysis of groups was dominated by a model usually called 'pluralism'. As the name implies, pluralism depicted the world of pressure group politics as a highly competitive place where there existed a plurality of groups possessing a plurality of powers and enjoying a plurality of relations with government (Burch and Wood, 1983, pp. 39–41).

The pluralist model did not suggest that all groups had equal influence, or that all interests would be adequately represented. It was a natural and expected outcome of competition that some groups would be more successful than others in political bargaining, just as in economic bargaining some firms prospered while others failed.

This image of groups now seems unreal, especially when applied to functional groups. At the heart of the pressure group system competition and diversity are being displaced, in favour of domination by a small number of institutions – a few giant firms, trade and peak associations and a small number of unions. These organisations are often not in competition with each other for influence, but are engaged in a close and stable collaboration with the state. The decline of diversity and competition is the reverse of what the pluralist model would lead us to expect. Furthermore, these tendencies are not a particular result of short-term circumstance, but are the product of enduring features in the economic structure and in the structure of the modern state. The point has been well made by Cawson, who points out that the same institutions – big firms and big unions – exercise great power both in the economy and in government (1982, pp. 36–7). Economic concentration and the growth of giant organisations are destroying that dispersed system of power pictured by pluralist theory.

In the last decade 'corporatism' has emerged as the most influential rival to the pluralist model. An extended debate has been conducted about how far the pressure group system in Britain is – or promises to become – corporatist. The debate has involved two distinct arguments: whether corporatism exists, or is ever likely to exist, in Britain; and whether it is a desirable system of social organisation. The first argument involves an assessment of evidence; the second turns largely on prescriptive judgements about what is desirable. Only the first debate is examined here.

Fierce argument has occurred over the meaning of 'corporatism'. A wide variety of competing definitions are on offer, the most commonly used of which is Schmitter's. 'Corporatism', he says, is:

> a system of interest representation in which the constituent units are organised into a limited number of singular, compulsory, non-competitive, hierarchically ordered and functionally differentiated categories, recognised or licensed (if not created) by the state and granted a deliberate representational monopoly within their respective categories in exchange for observing certain controls on their selection of leaders and articulation of demands and supports. (1979, p. 13)

The development of corporatism, according to this definition, involves a number of features: groups are able to compel individuals to join instead of having to compete for members with rival groups; groups organise individuals who perform particular (economic) functions in the community; group leaders control their members, rather than vice-versa; groups are given power by the state to regulate the economic sectors in which they operate; and groups control and discipline their members under the guidance of the state, and speak to the state on their members' behalf.

It is not difficult to see why this model of pressure group organisation seemed in the 1970s to make sense of what was happening to British politics. Changes in both the economic structure and in the national organisation of pressure groups strengthened the dominant position of a small number of organisations. The state offered trade unions special privileges – like closed shops – and in return asked unions to control their members. Successive Conservative and Labour Governments tried to practise economic management in a partnership between the state, business and unions, with the partners sharing the tasks of making and enforcing policy.

The usefulness of corporatism in understanding pressure group politics has nevertheless been challenged, both by subsequent debates and by subsequent events. Close scrutiny of the model itself revealed that it was unsatisfactory in several respects. It turned out that among those who used the term, the many definitions involved two quite different notions of what corporatism involved: some saw it as a system of state control, through which the state licensed groups in order to put public policy into effect; others saw it as a system of social organisation in which powerful groups independently controlled key areas of social life, where the state was only the pawn of these groups (Martin, 1983). The two sets of arrangements were very different: some thought corporatism involved the creation of a strong, authoritarian state; others thought it produced a weak state colonised by powerful interests.

There also existed very different explanations for the development of corporatism. For some, like the sociologists Pahl and Winkler (1974), it was the result of the logic of economic organisation in advanced industrial societies. Since Britain had plainly become such a society, fully developed corporatism could be expected shortly; indeed Winkler (1976) announced its imminent arrival. By contrast, the historian Middlemas identified only a corporatist tendency, the origins of which he traced to the great historical crises created by the two world wars (Middlemas, 1979). Others saw corporatism as a strategy developed under market capitalism by business and its political allies to control the workforce through the official trade-union movement (Panitch, 1980). On this last interpretation, the prospects for the development of corporatism depended on the behaviour of workers and their unions; most observers concluded that the small size of trade-union bureaucracies and the tradition of local independence in unions were great obstacles to any system of corporatist control.

The development of pressure group politics in recent years has reinforced doubts about the usefulness of the corporatist model. While many attempts were made in the 1970s to practise corporatism, most came to grief. Attempts by governments to manage the economy in partnership with the CBI and the TUC as the representatives of business and labour were failures, and were abandoned when Mrs Thatcher was elected Prime Minister in 1979. Though the CBI and the TUC had a considerable public presence, and enjoyed some moral authority over their members, they never wielded the kind of control demanded for corporatism. Any corporatist system involving a strong state would cut against values deeply engrained in Britain. These values – spanning the trade unions, the City of

London, other parts of business and the professions – emphasise independent regulation and control free of central government activity.

Such values are an obstacle to corporatism but they do not stifle it completely. Perhaps the most convincing formulation has been offered by Middlemas. He does not claim that we have seen fully developed corporatism but argues instead that from the First World War Britain experienced *corporate bias*, an inbuilt tendency to drift in the direction of corporatism like – to use Middlemas's image – the bias in the wood used in the game of bowls which drags it in a particular direction (1979, pp. 371–85). The implication is plain: just as the bias in a wood can be corrected, so the bias to corporatism can be redressed by particular historical events, by the actions of individuals and by the values prevailing at any particular moment.

The debate about the usefulness of the corporatist model in understanding pressure group politics was largely generated by developments among the key functional groups in business, unions and the professions. By contrast, developments among 'preference' groups seem to fit the pluralist model. There exists strong competition, and new groups have appeared in profusion. These contrasts have been neatly explained by Cawson. He divides the pressure group universe into corporate and competitive worlds. The corporate world is inhabited by groups who are the involuntary creation of an advanced market economy. Control over productive power is concentrated in a small number of institutions, and in sectors where economic regulation relies on a partnership between those institutions and the state. The competitive world is, by contrast, inhabited by groups created through the free association of individuals with shared preferences (Cawson, 1982, pp. 43–4).

Cawson's model illuminates the complicated development of pressure groups in Britain because it explains why in some areas groups are multiplying and competing while in others there is pressure towards amalgamation and co-operation. But in developing a model, Cawson – quite legitimately – simplifies and distorts. No simple divide exists between a corporate and a competitive sector. Among functional groups the trend to corporatism is far from complete. Conversely, many preference groups exhibit strong corporatist tendencies. Some of the most obvious examples of the latter are in the important area of leisure: the Arts Council and the Sports Council are both embryonic corporatist bodies, trying to organise groups into disciplined associations ready to bargain with the state. While functional and preference groups do inhabit different worlds, they are frequently connected by important links. These links often take the form of particular tactical alliances: recall how both pro- and anti-abortion groups have cultivated the medical profession, and how public sector unions have allied themselves with environmental pressure groups. Some social institutions also qualify as functional groups. The Church Commissioners, who administer the property of the Church of England, have the rights and powers of any large-scale controller of property in a market economy. Many other social institutions are coming increasingly under the control of giant firms: consider, for instance, the impact of commercial sponsorship of sport on the operations of associations like the Test and County Cricket Board and the Football League.

An adaptation of Middlemas's formula perhaps best describes the different developments among pressure groups. Functional and preference groups are not neatly divided into corporate and competitive sectors. In the world of functional groups there exists a bias to corporatism which is often checked by influences favouring competition; conversely, among preference groups there exists a bias to competition which is often checked by corporatist influences.

6 Conclusion

Political scientists have often taken an excessively narrow interest in pressure groups, concentrating on the most overtly 'political' organisations and on specialised problems of tactics and influence. The great importance of pressure groups is more general. They are now the most obvious and important way in which communal interests and preferences influence what happens in the political arena. The importance of groups therefore lies only partly in their capacity directly to intervene in politics; it lies also in their ability to control economic resources and to shape social values. Understanding pressure groups therefore demands far more than an understanding of their immediate political activities.

In Chapters 4 and 5 we have looked at a range of important institutions in Britain. These institutions are themselves social hierarchies with their own leaders. Chapter 6 turns to a more general examination of the social identity of leadership groups.

6

Rulers and Representatives

> The rich ruleth over the poor, and the borrower is servant to the lender.

> Proverbs, 22.7

1 Outline

'Elites', says Parry, are 'small minorities who appear to play an exceptionally influential part in political and social affairs' (1969, p.13). The bulk of this chapter examines the social origins, economic connections and education of elites in Britain. The examination of social composition in this manner is an established tradition in elite studies but in recent years doubts have been cast on its value. Section 2 describes these doubts and explains why the study of elite origins and connections is nevertheless important. Section 3 summarises the evidence about the most important parts of the political elite, simply defined to include Members of Parliament and Ministers. Section 4 examines administrative elites, notably the higher civil service and key public officials like judges and those at the head of the armed forces. Section 5 summarises evidence about economic elites because – as we saw in Chapter 4 – heads of large firms and big trade unions are also important political actors. Section 6 stands back from the detailed evidence to sketch the most important features of elite recruitment in Britain. But it is a legitimate criticism of studies of elite recruitment that they tell us little about the political culture of elites or about the actual distribution of power. Section 7 examines these subjects.

2 The Study of Elites

Social scientists have long studied the social origins and connections of those occupying top positions in politics, administration and the economy. In recent years the point of these studies has been widely questioned (Crewe, 1974). The three particularly pertinent objections have been raised: that studying the social structure of elites tells us nothing about whether or not those formally in elite positions actually exercise power; that the significance of social origins for elite behaviour and attitudes has never been satisfactorily established; and that the particular social characteristics identified in most studies are arbitrarily chosen, depending more on what information happens to be easily available in directories like *Who's Who* than on any well-thought-out criteria of relevance.

These are forceful criticisms, but of course they are reasons for caution rather than arguments for abandoning the study of elite origins. The first criticism reminds us that in studying social origins we learn nothing directly about the exercise of power. We do, however, learn a great deal about individuals who, because of their elite position, have an especially great capacity to exercise power. The second criticism reminds us that knowing the social origins of an elite group does not allow us to make simple inferences about the group's views: it is not true, for instance, that elite members of working-class origin are especially likely to be sympathetic to left-wing policies. A variety of studies have nevertheless shown that social background is far from irrelevant: it affects both beliefs and actions in complicated and presently only half understood ways (Whiteley, 1978). The final criticism – that elite studies rely too heavily on a small range of evidence derived from standard directories – undoubtedly points to a major shortcoming. Students of elites face a special problem: while interviews with representative samples have proved a powerful way of discovering the attitudes and social characteristics of the population at large, the rich and powerful have been much less willing to submit to such interviews. We are therefore forced to use often imperfect published information as alternative evidence. These imperfections should be recognised and, where possible, rectified; but even imperfect evidence is better than none at all.

The caution necessary in using evidence provided by directories like *Who's Who* is well illustrated by the example of evidence about education. Directories usually tell us where prominent people were educated. In Britain, about 5 per cent of the population are educated at 'public' schools, most of whose pupils pay sizeable fees. The proportion of public school products in an elite group is therefore usually taken as a measure of how exclusive are the social origins of the group. The measure is defective in two ways. First, the definition of a public school is imprecise. Bodies belonging to the 'Headmasters' Conference' – a pressure group for independent education – are conventionally called public schools. But members of the Conference range from the most socially select like Eton and Harrow to those catering solely for day pupils from the local community. Second, a minority of those educated in public schools – especially as day pupils rather than boarders – are non-fee-paying scholars, whose social origins cannot therefore be inferred from their attendance at a public school.

These difficulties can be eased in a number of ways. We can distinguish between different categories of schools to get a more refined sense of the social origins of a group. This is the main point of examining the proportions of an elite provided by old Etonians (Eton is recognised as the leading public school), or by products of the 'Clarendon Schools', nine of the leading institutions. We can also compare different elite groups, and compare over long periods of time; for while a public school education may be an imperfect measure of social origins at any single moment, changes over time, and marked differences between groups, are good indications of variations in social composition.

Arguments about the usefulness of educational evidence as a sign of social origins are especially important, because the study of British elites has been dominated by the attempt to discover how far elite members are representative of different occupational classes in the community. These concerns are sometimes the object of satirical comment: why, it is asked, be interested in the proportion of an elite which is of working-class origin, rather than in how far that proportion mirrors the social distribution of other human characteristics, like religion, nationally, or even colour of hair?

The answer is threefold. First, class origins are of special interest because class remains the most important line of political division in Britain. In a different society different social characteristics would require study. The religious upbringing of English elites is of little account because religion is of little account to the English – but in Northern Ireland the religious affiliations of elites are of crucial interest. As values change, so attention to the social characteristics of elite groups also changes: for instance, the rising expectations of women in the last generation have alerted us to the tiny number of women near the top of the most important institutions. If a political party appealing to red-haired people attracted substantial support, then the proportion of Cabinet Ministers and senior civil servants with red hair would be a legitimate subject of enquiry.

Interest in the class origins of elites thus reflects the central place of class in British politics. A second reason for being interested is that class origins illuminate the importance of inheritance in elite selection. Knowing how many millionaires are the offspring of the rich indisputably tells us a great deal about how wealth is transmitted between generations. But Cabinet Ministers, generals and senior civil servants also control valued social resources just as surely as do millionaires: these resources include esteem, income and the opportunity to exercise power. Knowing how many were born to families already exercising disproportionate control over these social goods is as illuminating as knowing the economic origins of the very rich, because it gives us a sign of the role of inheritance in allocating social rewards.

Finally, knowing the class origins of elite members tells us much about the role of merit in elite selection, and about the social consequences of what is usually called 'meritocracy'. Almost every major institution in Britain now claims to be meritocratic: that is, recruitment and promotion are supposed to depend on some measure of achievement, rather than on 'ascribed' characteristics like social origins or race. Evidence about class origins helps tell us how far the formality of meritocracy is practised in reality. The evidence also tells us something about the results of meritocratic selection. It was once believed that elites selected by merit would be especially representative in their class origins, because able people of humble station would rise to the top. In the succeeding pages we can test the accuracy of this expectation.

3 Political Elites

Most studies of political elites in Britain concentrate on the House of Commons and on government (especially Cabinet) Ministers. It is worth noting in passing that sub-national elites, especially in local government, have been neglected. The concentration on Members of Parliament and on Ministers is in part due to the fact that information about many of their social characteristics can be gathered from standard directories, but it also rests on more substantial grounds. Ministers, especially Cabinet Ministers, occupy the most desirable and sought-after positions in British politics. They can take decisions affecting millions of lives and allocating billions of pounds. Membership of the House of Commons, though less important, nevertheless brings social esteem and a measure of fame. Above all, a seat in the Commons is a necessary qualification for most Ministerial careers. The connections of MPs in different parties are also a valuable guide to the relations between parties and particular interests in the community.

Table 6.1 summarises some of the most important available information about the social composition of the major parties in the House of Commons in this century. The most important columns in the table are those which amalgamate the evidence about MPs in the Parliaments elected between 1918–35 and 1945–74. (The 1935 Parliament lasted a decade because of the intervention of the Second World War.) These composite portraits are of special value because they iron out the variations produced by short-term factors, notably the changing fortunes of parties at particular elections. But amalgamating the figures plainly runs the risk of obscuring changes which, though marginal, may be signs of the future. The table therefore supplements the evidence by comparing the last Parliament returned before the upheaval of the First World War (December 1910) with the most modern figures available.

The figures provide evidence on two matters. Those for schooling can be taken as a guide (though not a perfect guide) to social origins. Those concerning occupation refer to the known occupations of members before election. The two sets of figures thus give us some idea of both the class origins of MPs and of their class location in adult life.

It is sensible to begin with the Conservatives since they have been the dominant party for much of the century. The overwhelming picture conveyed by the figures for Conservative MPs is one of stability. The twentieth century has seen extraordinary political and social change in Britain: the extension of the suffrage to almost all adults, revolutions in styles of life and in the relations between the sexes, the rise of the Welfare State. Within the Conservative Party strenuous efforts have been made to widen the social range of its Parliamentary candidates, partly in response to these changes. The

TABLE 6.1 *Education and occupations of MPs, 1910–87 (per cent of total in each of the two major parties)*

	1. December 1910		2. 1918–35		3. 1945–74		4. 1979		5. 1983		6. 1987	
	Conservatives	Liberals	Conservatives	Labour	Conservatives	Labour	Conservatives	Labour	Conservatives	Labour	Conservatives	Labour
Education												
Elementary only	0.3	6.6	2.5	75.5	0.7	20.1	0 ⎱	4.8 ⎱	8.2 ⎱	21.5 ⎱	6.3 ⎱	16.2 ⎱
Secondary only	8.4	31.9	no data	no data	5.2	10.1	8.2 ⎰	14.8 ⎰	⎰	⎰	⎰	⎰
Public school	72.0	38.2	78.5	9.0	75.7	17.9	73.0	17.0	64.1	13.4	68.0	14.0
Eton	33.0	8.4	27.5	1.5	20.2	0.9	15.0	0.4	12.4	1.0	10.8	1.0
Oxford/Cambridge Univs	46.6	29.7	39.5	7.4	49.6	15.9	49.2	20.4	45.7	14.4	41.6	14.9
All universities	57.3	51.4	50.1	18.2	61.7	44.0	68.0	57.0	71.7	54.1		
Occupation												
Employers/managers	no data	no data	52.0	4.0	41.6	9.6	34.0	5.0	no data	no data	no data	no data
Manual workers	0	1.8	4.0	72.0	0.1	21.1	1.0	19.8	no data	15.3	no data	no data
'Professions'	56.2	53.6	52.0	24.0	40.4	40.7	45.0	43.0	no data	no data	no data	no data

Sources: Column 1, calculated from figures in Thomas (1958); Column 2, calculated from figures in Guttsman (1963); Column 3, calculated from figures in Mellors (1978); Column 4 from figures in Butler and Kavanagh (1980), but figures for manual workers in Labour Party from Burch and Moran (1985); Column 5 from Burch and Moran (1985); Column 6 from Butler and Kavanagh (1988).

Notes: (a) Not all columns sum to 100%, due to missing or omitted data. (b) 'Public school' indicated by membership of Headmasters' Conference. (c) 'Occupation' means job before entering Parliament; 'worker' figure for 1918–35 includes those in routine non-manual jobs.

end result was that at the end of the 1970s the proportion of public-school-educated MPs was slightly higher (at 73 per cent) than in 1910. The statistical over-representation of the public schools is extraordinary: recall that under 5 per cent of the population receive a public school education. Examination of the composite figures for 1918–35 and 1945–74 confirms the stability suggested by the figures for the beginning and end of the period.

There is indeed some evidence in Table 6.1 to suggest that those from the very poorest backgrounds are being filtered out even more effectively than happened in the past: the proportion who began their adult lives as manual workers has dwindled since the inter-war years from the tiny to the infinitesimal. It is easier for a camel to go through the eye of a needle than for a poor man to enter Parliament as a Conservative MP.

This impression of social stability at the top of the Conservative Party is confirmed by other evidence. There has been no significant long-term change in the proportion of women Conservative MPs: only eight women were returned to the Party's benches in 1979, only thirteen in 1983 and only 17 in 1987. Nor, as is clear from Table 6.1, is any obvious alteration taking place in the balance drawn from the professions or from business ('employers and managers'). This is unsurprising, as the dividing line between the two categories is uncertain. Many 'professional' Conservative MPs are in occupations like law and accountancy which have close connections with the business community. Some MPs nominally classified as lawyers are actually businessmen.

Striking social stability is the most impressive feature of the Conservative Party in Parliament during this century. Nevertheless, even that social monolith has not been immune to change. Some of the changes are even hinted at in Table 6.1. Thus in 1983 the numbers educated at public schools fell for the first time below 70 per cent. There is also evidence that both the very rich and those most closely connected to great centres of power in the business community are in a proportional decline. One sign of this is the slow but persistent fall in the percentage of MPs educated at Eton, the most prestigious of public schools. Rubinstein also found, by examining the wills of dead MPs, that the real wealth left by Conservative members has declined (1974, p. 168). There are evidently fewer outstandingly rich individuals among the Party in Parliament. Most striking of all, great capitalists close to the centres of economic power are less numerous. As late as the 1930s Conservative MPs contained a sprinkling of men like Sir Alfred Mond, a founder of Imperial Chemical Industries (ICI). Such individuals are far less apparent now: Stanworth and Giddens found in their study of chairmen of the biggest firms in the economy that whereas nearly a fifth of those active before the Second World War were (mostly Conservative) MPs, the figure was only 4 per cent by the early 1970s (1974, pp. 81–101).

The declining number of outstandingly rich MPs has accompanied another development – the rise of the career politician. Hardly any Conservative MPs now win a seat at a first attempt in their 20s, a common occurrence when family connections gave the offspring of the rich a safe seat for the asking. The typical new Conservative Member is now in early middle age; has served an apprenticeship by fighting a hopeless constituency at least once; and, increasingly, has a record of local government service. He also lives off politics to a growing extent: off a Parliamentary salary whose real value has grown in recent decades, and off politically created work like journalism, business consultancy and lobbying.

During the post-war years the Conservative Party has tried to make its MPs more socially varied. In practice, however, the Party in Parliament has become less so. The extremes – very young, very old, very rich, and (by origin) very poor – have become less common. The Party is dominated by middle aged, middle class males.

Some have concluded that the rise of the middle-class professional politician in the Conservative Party is part of a convergence in the social composition of the two parties who have dominated all modern Parliaments (Johnson, 1973). Table 6.1 certainly gives some support to this view. The number of Labour MPs with only an elementary education fell sharply between the inter-war years and the end of the 1970s. More striking still, while nearly three-quarters of all Labour members in the inter-war years had once been manual workers the same was true for less than a sixth of those returned in 1983. Conversely, the proportions with a university education and a professional job in adult life are now at levels very close to those in the Conservative Party. The pattern of political apprenticeship – fighting a hopeless seat, serving in local government, entering Parliament in early middle age – also resembles that among Conservatives.

The extent of social convergence between the two parties is

nevertheless limited. Labour still retains a substantial core of ex-manual worker MPs, and in recent years the decline in the numbers in this group has been slowed down, if not quite arrested. But much more significant is the fact that the middle-class group of Labour MPs is very different from its Conservative counterpart. The typical graduate Conservative MP was educated at one of the two most prestigious universities, Oxford and Cambridge; the typical graduate Labour MP went to a less select provincial university. The professions supplying Conservative MPs are the established high-status occupations like the law, enjoying close connections with private enterprise; Labour MPs with professional jobs are typically drawn from less-prestigious public sector professions, notably teaching. Though the proportion of Labour MPs educated at public schools shows a modest increase by comparison with the years before the Second World War, a large amount of this is accounted for by scholarship boys of modest origins educated as day pupils. This fact hints at one of the most remarkable features of the modern Parliamentary Labour Party: a strikingly large number (over half in a survey of the 1979 intake) are the children of manual workers (calculated from Roth, 1979). No other elite group, and few high-status occupations, contains such a high proportion of members upwardly mobile from the working class. An unusually large number of Labour MPs also have fathers who worked in heavy industry, like steel and coal mining: the 1979 Parliament contained nineteen MPs who had worked as miners but thirty-five more who were the children of miners (Roth, 1979, p.2).

The Parliamentary Labour Party has thus not simply shifted from working-class to middle-class domination. A more complex mutation has occurred: before the Second World War the typical Labour MP achieved mobility out of the working class in his own adult life by entering Parliament; in the post-war years the typical Labour MP rose out of the working class through education and then capped this social success by election to the House of Commons.

Analysis of the changing social and educational composition of Cabinets confirms many trends evident in the case of MPs and emphasises the continuing differences between the Conservative and Labour leaderships. Because Cabinets usually only have around twenty members we must combine several to obtain figures sufficiently large to allow analysis. Table 6.2 compares selected features of all Cabinet Ministers provided by the two main parties for the period 1916–55, and for the years since, to mid-1984. (The figures on class origins for 1955–84 follow the convention used by Guttsman, from whom the figures for 1916-55 are obtained: 'working' or 'middle' class is indicated by fathers' occupation, 'aristocrat' by descent from a hereditary title in the grandparents' generation.)

TABLE 6.2 *Education and class origins of Cabinet Ministers, 1916–84 (per cent of all Cabinet Ministers in each major party with selected characteristics)*

	1916–55		1955–84	
	Conservative % (N = 98)	Labour % (N = 65)	Conservative % (N = 77)	Labour % (N = 56)
Education				
Elementary/sec. only	4.0	50.7	2.5	37.5
Public	76.5	26.1	87.1	32.1
Eton/Harrow	45.9	7.6	36.3	3.5
No univ.	30.6	55.3	19.4	37.5
Oxbridge	63.2	27.6	72.8	42.8
All univs	71.4	44.6	81.6	62.5
Class background				
Aristocrat	31.6	6.1	18.1	1.8
Middle class	65.3	38.4	74.0	44.6
Working class	3.0	55.3	2.6	41.0
No data	—	—	4.0	12.6

Sources: Figures for 1916–55, calculated from Guttsman (1963), pp. 106–7; 1955–84 figures Burch and Moran (1985).

The evidence for the Conservatives is especially revealing, since it contradicts a common assumption that the Conservative Party is now led by meritocrats of humble origins. This belief originates from the fact that the Party's two most recent leaders (Mr Heath and Mrs Thatcher) are precisely in this mould, the former the son of a carpenter, the latter a shopkeeper's daughter. One reason for the elevation was undoubtedly the desire to present Conservatism as a Party open to all with talent. The evidence indicates, however, that no great long-term broadening has occurred in the social origins of Conservative Cabinet Ministers. In some ways, if anything, the composition of Cabinets after 1955 became more select: proportions educated at public schools increased, as did the numbers from

Oxbridge, while Ministers of working-class origins became even scarcer. There are, however, some signs that those with the greatest wealth and most distinguished connections are in decline: Ministers from aristocratic families have fallen markedly in numbers, as have those from Eton and Harrow, the two most socially select public schools. There is also evidence that this decline is accelerating: of new entrants to Conservative Cabinets since 1970, only 15 per cent were educated at Eton or Harrow (Burch and Moran, 1985). In summary, the evidence for Conservative Cabinets suggest a narrowing of social range: as among MPs as a whole the very rich are declining in number, but there has been little compensating recruitment among those of humble social origins. Conservative Cabinets have become more uniformly middle class.

The social evolution of Labour Cabinets is more complicated. The development of Labour's leadership in Parliament is often pictured as involving the increasing exclusion of those of humble origins. The pattern is more subtle than is suggested by such a picture. Early Labour Cabinets had a significant aristocratic contingent, in part because Labour did not have in its own ranks individuals with the appropriate specialist qualifications to occupy particular offices, like the Lord Chancellorship. The aristocratic group declined to insignificance after 1955 and disappeared completely in the 1970s: of new entrants to Labour Cabinets after 1970 not one was an aristocrat or a product of Eton and Harrow (Burch and Moran, 1985). At the same time, the proportions of Cabinet Ministers with a university education rose sharply, the proportions born in families of non-manual workers rose a little, and the proportions who were children of manual workers fell. The working-class contingent nevertheless remained substantial. The typical modern Labour Cabinet Minister was not a public schoolboy on the make: he was someone who achieved social mobility through education and who promoted further mobility by a successful political career. Mrs Thatcher (the state-educated daughter of a shopkeeper) is socially atypical of both the Conservative leadership and of Conservative MPs. By contrast, the present leader and deputy leader of the Labour Party (Mr Kinnock and Mr Hattersley) nicely typify the social range of the Parliamentary Labour Party: both educated at state schools and at provincial universities; the first the son of a labourer, the second of a clerk.

We examine the wider implications of changes in the social

composition of political leadership in section 7 of this chapter. Here, however, we turn to administrative elites.

4 Administrative Elites

In Britain, as in all modern states, public servants organised in administrative hierarchies play key parts in making and implementing public policy. Those at or near the top of those administrative hierarchies are universally recognised as occupying crucial positions: they control vital information, are a key source of advice for elected leaders, often make policy independently and even more frequently shape the way it is executed. In short, they are a powerful group who merit examination. In Britain, most argument has focused on the social and educational makeup of the higher reaches of the home civil service. But policy advice and execution also come from elsewhere: from the diplomatic service, the armed forces, the judiciary. These groups are therefore also examined here.

Recruitment and promotion in the home civil service are formally rigorously meritocratic. For over a century, entrance has been by competitive tests, supplemented latterly by interviews. A complex series of tests and reviews is also designed to ensure that promotion is according to ability. Arguments about the social composition of the service have turned on how far this formal commitment to meritocracy is realised in practice. Most debate has focused on entrants to what is now called the Administrative Trainee Grade, mostly selected from applicants who are imminent or recent graduates. The justification for this concentration is that the small number of Administrative Trainees (in 1983 only forty-seven took up appointment) provide a pool from which the most senior civil servants are eventually selected.

Two sets of questions about recruitment to the higher civil service have proved especially contentious: how socially representative are recruits? And how far is the statistical over-representation of groups from particular classes and institutions the result of unconscious social bias among those who do the selecting? (No serious observer now argues that there is any conscious social bias.) Table 6.3 summarises evidence on the first of these two questions. The figures show (and unsurprisingly) that certain familiar minorities – those from the public schools and Oxbridge – are represented in numbers out of all proportion to their presence in the population, and even out of proportion to their presence in that select group of people possessing a degree. There are nevertheless signs of a modest increase in social diversity, signified by the rising proportions coming from non-fee-paying schools. The belief that diversity is growing is reinforced by evidence not summarised in Table 6.3: there has occurred a long-term decline – dating from the 1920s – in the proportions of the most senior civil servants (of Assistant Secretary rank and above) from the elite 'Clarendon' schools, and a rise in the proportions coming from the homes of manual and routine non-manual workers. The extent of change is nevertheless modest. Opening up the higher civil service to meritocrats of humble origins has chiefly benefited the offspring of the lower middle classes; the proportion of recruits to the administrative class with fathers in semi-skilled or unskilled manual work actually fell between the late 1940s and the late 1960s (Kelsall, 1974, p. 179). The dominance of Oxford and Cambridge also remains overwhelming. Their graduates are not only most numerous among new entrants; they enjoy an even greater preponderance in the most powerful and prestigious departments and, within departments, at the most senior levels.

None of this shows that the civil service practises social discrimination. Indeed, powerful arguments can be marshalled to support the view that the social and educational characteristics of senior civil servants are not merely compatible with, but are the inevitable outcome of, meritocratic selection. Educational achievement in our society is closely connected to class origins; where criteria of 'merit' are in turn closely tied to academic ability – as they undoubtedly are in the civil service – those of working-class origin will be greatly under-represented. Likewise, since Oxford and Cambridge attract some of the most able students it is to be expected that meritocratic selection will disproportionately favour their candidates.

It has nevertheless been argued that the inequalities resulting from selection by merit are reinforced by social biases built into the system of recruitment, a criticism apparently partly accepted by the civil service (Atkinson, 1983). The most striking evidence in support of this view was presented in figures of the varying success rates of different groups of applicants for the Administrative Trainee grade, provided to the House of Commons Expenditure Committee when it investigated recruitment in the 1970s. The Committee found, for instance, that while 21 per cent of all applicants were from Oxbridge,

TABLE 6.3 *Social and educational background of 'open competition' entrants to the administrative class/administrative trainee grade of the home civil service*

	1921–32	1933–9	1949–50	1961–5	1971–5	1981	1982–3
a. Children of manual/routine non-manual worker	no data	no data	27%	18%	no data	no data	no data
b. Educated at non-fee-paying schools	20%	19%	26%	29%	65%	56%	no data
c. Oxbridge educated	84%	89%	74%	80%	50%	56%	66%

Sources: Kelsall (1974) for first four columns; House of Commons Expenditure Committee (1977) for 1971–5; Civil Service Commission (1983) for 1980s figures.

the two ancient universities accounted for 50 per cent of those accepted (1976–7, p. xviii). Given the known uncertainties of selection by examination results at 18 – when universities choose their students – it seemed implausible to ascribe the differences wholly to the higher quality of Oxbridge applicants. Even more striking was the disproportionate success of public school products: in the mid-1970s they provided, for instance, just over 8 per cent of applicants from provincial universities but over a fifth of successful applicants from this source. That difference too seemed inexplicable in meritocratic terms, because there is no evidence that public-school-educated undergraduates at provincial universities are more able than their contemporaries from non-fee-paying schools.

It is tempting to conclude from these figures that the inequalities produced by meritocratic selection are being reinforced by residual social biases among those doing the selecting. The evidence is nevertheless inconclusive. The most striking social feature of the higher civil service – its domination by Oxbridge graduates – seems to be the result of pure meritocracy. Thus, an inspection of the figures on success rates for Administrative Trainee applicants (published annually by the Civil Service Commission) shows that Oxbridge's greater success rate is most pronounced in the initial qualifying tests. These are written examinations, marked with no knowledge of the candidates' background, and therefore allowing no exercise of social bias by the marker. By contrast, at the Final Selection Board, where selectors see the candidates and know their backgrounds, non-Oxbridge candidates have a slightly higher success rate than their Oxbridge rivals (Civil Service Commission, 1981, 1982, 1983). If unconscious social biases are at work we ought to find selectors favouring Oxbridge applicants when they see them in the flesh.

These are contentious areas where the evidence is often contradictory and incomplete. Nevertheless, one conclusion seems plain: the statistical biases in recruitment to the higher civil service – favouring Oxbridge and the public schools – are at most only trivially influenced by social bias. The social inequalities reflected in civil service recruiting patterns result from the rigorous application of meritocratic rules and not, as is sometimes claimed, from failure to observe those rules.

Whatever the particular influences shaping the social characteristics of senior civil servants, it has generally been thought that the home civil service is among the most socially open of all administrative elites in Britain. Table 6.4 provides some evidence on this matter. Using the evidence collected by Boyd (1973) and gathered for the 1980s by me, it examines the educational background of five elite groups. In the table, type of school is taken as a sign of social origin. As we saw earlier there are serious defects in this procedure. It is justifiable only on two grounds: that, while imperfect, evidence about education is the only available long-term indicator of social origins; and that, while isolated figures of the proportions educated at non-fee-paying schools may mean little, comparison of figures between groups and over time does provide an indication of variations in the social range of elite recruitment.

It will be apparent that substantial differences exist between different administrative elites. The diplomatic service, the judiciary and the army are closed socially and show little sign of change since before the Second World War. By contrast, the Royal Air Force and the upper ranks of the home civil service ('under-secretary' is the third highest rank) are more open socially, and have seen their social composition change substantially. The differences extend to more discriminating measures of openness not revealed by the table. In the upper reaches of the civil service, which is often caricatured as the domain of languid old Etonians, under 2 per cent (five in number) were from that school in 1983, and only one-eighth were from the elite Clarendon Schools. By contrast, 8 per cent of judges were old Etonians and almost a quarter in all were from Clarendon Schools. Even in the cases of the RAF and the civil service, however, the opening up of elite positions to those not educated in the public schools has been slow and far from continuous.

Table 6.4 also cannot tell us how far down the social hierarchy the increased opportunities extend: no studies exist which directly investigate the class origins of these elites in the 1980s. The experience of the home civil service, examined earlier, would suggest that few gains have been made by children of manual workers. The chief beneficiaries of meritocratic selection are the academically able offspring of the lower middle class who manage to reach Oxford or Cambridge: in 1983, 70 per cent of ambassadors, 80 per cent of high court judges, and 63 per cent of civil servants of under-secretary rank and above, were Oxbridge products.

It is plain from Table 6.4 that the rate of social change in different elites has varied. Before the Second World War all the institutions –

TABLE 6.4 *Per cent of selected administrative elites educated at fee-paying schools, 1939–83*

	(1) 1939 %	(2) 1950 %	(3) 1960 %	(4) 1970 %	(5) 1983 %
Ambassadors	73.5	72.6	82.6	82.5	76.3
High court judges	80.0	84.9	82.5	80.2	79.0
Major Generals and above	63.6	71.3	83.2	86.1	78.9
RAF Vice-Marshals and above	66.7	59.1	58.4	62.5	41.1
Civil servants, under-secretary and above	84.5	58.7	65.0	61.7	58.8

Sources: Columns 1–4 calculated from Boyd (1973) pp. 93–5; calculated from *Whitaker's* and *Who's Who.*

judging from the evidence of education – had a similar social composition; by 1983 the backgrounds of ambassadors, judges and generals were different from those of senior civil servants and senior air force officers. The contrasts are even more marked when we turn to economic elites.

5 Economic Elites

Britain's economy works on market principles. This means that a considerable slice of the nation's productive resources are privately owned, both by individuals and by institutions like firms. Business elites consist of individuals who own substantial amounts of productive property and those who occupy top positions in the most important firms. But the structure of a private-enterprise economy has also created a second economic elite additional to that based on ownership and control of private property Trade-union leaders, deriving their power and authority from their position as representatives of those who sell their labour, also form an elite.

Knowing the social composition of elites formed by labour and by owners of capital illuminates the general character of political elites in Britain in several ways: it provides a further point of comparison by which we can judge how socially open are elites in Parliament, Cabinet and administrative institutions; it identifies individuals and institutions who – as we saw in Chapter 5 – are themselves important political as well as economic actors; and it highlights the characteristics of those who control valued economic resources in the community.

Little systematic work has been carried out on the social origins and educational experience of national trade-union leaders. The impressionistic evidence nevertheless points overwhelmingly to one conclusion: the trade-union elite is remarkably different from other top groups in the economy or in the more formal political arena. British trade unions, by contrast with unions in most other industrial countries, have small and weak bureaucracies. Paid officials are comparatively scarce and most full-time officers are recruited from the rank-and-file membership. While ability counts in officer selection, 'meritocratic' criteria are considerably qualified by other considerations. Unions organising manual workers place a particularly strong emphasis on class origins. It is very difficult to rise in such unions without some adult experience as a manual worker – indeed, without experience in one of the jobs organised by the union. The consequence is that by education, class origins, and occupation in early adult life, the trade-union leadership more accurately mirrors the characteristics of the population than does any other elite group. Most were reared as the children of manual workers – as were most people in Britain. Most left school at the earliest legal leaving age – as do most adults. Most have worked at manual or routine white-collar jobs – like most of the employed population. Hardly any have entered higher education – a denial shared by the vast majority of Britons. The public-school-educated are as scarce among leading trade unionists as they are among the population at large.

There are some signs of change in this state of affairs. Unions are acquiring larger professional staffs, and are recruiting them increasingly from the products of higher education. Unions organising white-collar workers –the fastest-growing part of the movement – are much readier than are those organising manual workers to recruit officers by conventional meritocratic criteria, ignoring class origins and stressing the kinds of skills usually acquired by extended education. These changes nevertheless remain marginal. The trade-union leadership is more representative in its class origins and early adult experiences than any other elite in Britain.

In this it contrasts markedly with the business elite. Stanworth and Giddens's historical examination of the changing characteristics of the chairmen of the largest firms in the economy suggests that no significant widening has occurred in the social range from which business leaders are selected. They found no discernible long-term decline in the proportions of company chairmen educated at fee-paying schools, and some evidence of a rise in the proportion educated at the most select schools like Eton, Harrow and other 'Clarendon' institutions (Stanworth and Giddens, 1974, pp. 81–101). Whitley's wider study of the educational background of all directors of leading financial and industrial enterprises in the early 1970s confirms that the leaders of business are recruited from a social elite, but suggests that significant differences exist between industrial companies and financial institutions: for instance, while 'only' 13 per cent of directors of large industrial firms were old Etonians, the same was true of a third of directors of big banks and insurance companies (Whitley, 1974). The socially elitist character

TABLE 6.5   The financial elite, 1983 (% educated at different institutions)

Eton	31.9
All fees	80.8
Grammar	8.5
Oxbridge	68.0

Sources: Calculated from standard directories.
Note: 'Financial elite' is: chairmen of 'big four' clearing banks and leading merchant banks in Accepting Houses Committee; chairmen of twelve largest insurance companies; directors of Bank of England.

of the financial community persists into the 1980s as Table 6.5 shows. The domination of a single school, Eton, is extraordinary: no other elite – not even the top of the Conservative Party – contains such a high proportion of old Etonians; even among ambassadors and high court judges – two other socially exclusive elites – products of Eton accounted in 1983 for only 3 and 8 per cent respectively.

The especially closed character of the financial elite is due to two factors. Almost all elites, as we have seen, are disproportionately drawn from individuals already born to privilege. Early material advantage, family connections and the close links between class and educational success give such people a flying start in the race to the top. Those born to wealth have these advantages in their business careers, but they also have a second resource. The rules governing the ownership of property give the rich legally enforceable claims in business life. Elite position can be inherited in business in a way that is impossible in other institutions. A Hambro or a Rothchild inherits ownership of productive property which can be used to influence business decisions and to stake a claim to a business career. In no other institution can a claim to elite status be transmitted from one generation to the next by force of law; nor, outside business, can wealth be used to buy elite position.

Thus far we have looked in detail at statistical evidence bearing on the social composition of different elite groups. It is now time to stand back from the detail in order to acquire a more general sense of patterns and developments.

6 Elites in Britain: Variety, Change and Stability

Two questions are prompted by the evidence examined in the preceding pages: to what extent do different elite groups in Britain have similar social origins? And to what extent have changes in the social composition of elites occurred over time? The answers to these questions emphasise the surprising diversity existing between different elites, the ambiguous consequences of meritocracy, and the growing tendency towards elite specialisation. Each are examined in turn.

Variety in Elite Background

Two contrasting theories of how elites are recruited in modern Britain have recently enjoyed popularity. The first, which is part of the official ideology of most powerful institutions, insists that recruitment depends on merit, that opportunities are equal for all, and that elites contain a high proportion of able people born to a humble social position. The constrasting theory, popular with many left-wing radicals and some students of elites, argues that what social scientists call 'closure' is the most important influence on elite recruitment (Heath, 1981, P. 61). Those who believe in the existence of 'closure' suggest that, however much social mobility occurs lower down the hierarchy, powerful mechanisms close off elite positions to the vast majority of those not born to a family already occupying elite status.

Neither of these views is completely borne out by the evidence. There does indeed exist some evidence of closure. In almost every elite group members are drawn disproportionately from privileged social minorities. The pattern exists whether privilege is indicated by attendance at a public school or by more direct evidence of family origin. The Conservative Party, the business community, the diplomatic service and the judiciary are not dominated by an aristocracy of merit, let alone by meritocrats representative of all social classes. Even in the Labour Movement family dynasties have begun to develop (Johnson, 1973).

It is, however, plain that 'closure' varies greatly in different elite groups. There is no single path to the top in Britain. Eton and the other great public schools enjoy a marked ascendancy in the financial elite, but there is not a single old Etonian or product of the other Clarendon schools at the top of the Royal Air Force, and very few near the top of the home civil service. Oxbridge provides over 80 per cent of High Court judges but only a minority of Labour MPs and less than 10 per cent of top army officers.

Although there is no single route to the top, there do exist definable paths of advancement for different clusters of elite groups. The following are most obviously identifiable.

Cluster 1 consists of institutions whose elites contain a substantial proportion of self-made men, individuals from modest social backgrounds who do not possess a university education. It used to be thought that industry was the natural home of the self-made man. In fact he is commoner at the top of the trade unions, the Labour Party and the Royal Air Force. Probably – though no systematic evidence exists on the point – he is also common at the top of important provincial and local elites in Britain: these include groups like chief constables, chief officers in large local authorities, top administrators in regional health and water authorities, and leading executives of the big provincial building societies.

Cluster 2 covers institutions whose elites contain a substantial proportion of university-educated meritocrats from working- and lower-middle-class origins. They include the Parliamentary Labour Party, Labour's front bench in Parliament and the less prestigious and less powerful departments of the home civil service.

Cluster 3 covers a range of institutions whose elites contain a large proportion of middle-class functionaries, individuals educated at good, but not the very best, public schools and at Oxford or Cambridge. They are commonest on the back benches of the Conservative Party, in the diplomatic service and among the judiciary. Impressionistic evidence suggests that among Conservative MPs in this group a high proportion are 'first generation' public school, the offspring of families newly mobile into the group able to afford a good public school education for their children.

Elites in *Cluster 4* contain a markedly high proportion of upper-class patricians, who were educated at the most exclusive public schools and who are the children of fathers who also enjoyed elite status. Such figures are commonest in the business community and – to a less marked degree – in the top reaches of the Conservative Party. The conventional marks of merit, though not irrelevant, count for less in this fourth cluster. This is not because the individuals concerned are without ability. They are often, because of inherited advantages, outstandingly capable; but their initial crucial opportunity to achieve elite position comes from inherited privilege, not from demonstrated capacity.

One simple way of illustrating the differences between these four clusters of institutions is to imagine what advice we would give to ambitious young people who wanted to rise to the top in Britain. The advice would vary by gender, class origins and education. Girls would have to be advised that their chances of entering any elite were slim. Young men of working-class origin with limited education would do best to consider careers as trade-union officials; those from lower-middle-class homes without a university education would be best advised to try the Royal Air Force, and perhaps local government and the police force. Ambitious university graduates from working-class or lower-middle-class homes should look for seats as Labour MPs or should consider the home civil service, especially if they have reached Oxbridge. Anybody from a middle-ranking public school who also reached university would do best to consider the diplomatic service or law; those who cannot or choose not to go to university would find the army a possible route to the top. Those with parents already in elite positions who have attended an exclusive public school are unlikely to need our advice: family connections already point to a business career as the way to ensure elite status.

The four clusters of institutions are illustrated in Figure 6.1.

The Impact of Meritocracy

It is tempting to explain variations in the social origins of different elite groups as a consequence of the uneven application of 'meritocratic' principles in elite selection. Some features of elites can indeed be accounted for in this way: we have already seen that much of the 'closed' character of the business elite is due to the importance of property inheritance. But selection by merit does not universally widen the range of social groups from which elites are selected. Indeed, meritocratic elites can actually be more exclusive in their social composition than are elites recruited by other means. The only elite in Britain which is a mirror of the occupational class composition of the population – the trade-union leadership – is selected by rules where class origins are at least as important as conventional marks of merit. One of the oddities of elite recruitment is that the most open and the most closed elites in Britain – the union

	Cluster 1	Cluster 2	Cluster 3	Cluster 4
	Self-made men	Lower-class meritocrats	Middle-class functionaries	Patricians
Examples of personnel	Trade-union leaders, RAF senior officers, chief constables, building society chiefs	Labour MPs, higher civil servants (home civil service), Labour ministers	Ambassadors, judges, Conservative back bench MPs, generals	Bankers, Conservative cabinet ministers, chairmen of big industrial corporations
Class origin	Working/lower-middle	Working/lower-middle	Upper-middle/middle	Upper-middle/aristocracy
Education	Secondary, non-fee-paying	Non-fee-paying secondary, university	Middle-rank public school, Oxbridge	Elite public school, Oxbridge
Criteria of initial selection	Merit, but ascription in unions favours men of working-class origin	Merit; some ascription in Labour Party favours those from working class; residual ascription favouring upper middle class in civil service	Mixed merit/ascription	Largely ascription

FIGURE 6.1   *The variety of elites in Britain*

Note: 'Ascription' – selection by 'ascribed' features like birth rather than by demonstrated merit.

leadership and the leadership of the financial community – are both recruited by non-meritocratic criteria.

The failure of meritocratic selection significantly to broaden the base of elite recruitment is not difficult to explain. In most institutions the conventional shorthand signs of ability – social confidence, fluent speech, ease with the written word – are those most likely to be exhibited by individuals from privileged backgrounds. These advantages have been reinforced by the way important institutions now increasingly recruit their future leaders from the university-educated. Graduates – especially those from Oxford and Cambridge – are commonly marked out from the beginning of their careers for rapid promotion, often by being placed in special fast 'streams'. Since the proportion of children of manual workers in universities is small, educationally determined meritocratic selection does little to advance those from the humblest social origins. Those likely to achieve mobility into elite positions are an intellectually gifted minority from the most earnestly ambitious parts of the lower middle class, educated as day scholars at minor public schools and at Oxbridge. Thus, two recent heads of the home civil service have been the Oxford-educated children of, respectively, a Salvation Army Officer and a school teacher; while at the start of the 1980s Nottingham High School – one of the best of the old direct grant grammar schools – provided both the Permanent Secretary to the Treasury and the Governor of the Bank of England.

Under meritocratic selection, elites are still disproportionately staffed by those already born to privilege and educated at the great public schools. The most outstanding schools have great advantages in meritocratic competition. Their pupils already come to them from privileged backgrounds. The schools strengthen these advantages with, literally, the best teachers that money can buy, an unrivalled acquaintance with the great universities, and a social atmosphere designed to promote qualities of confidence and leadership. In the last twenty years there has occurred in the best public schools a conscious adaptation to a more meritocratic world, with increasing attention to academic standards. A place at the greatest schools is now something to be competed for rather than inherited; even at Eton the proportion of pupils who themselves were the children of old Etonians fell from 60 per cent to 43 per cent in the decade after 1970 (Sampson, 1983, p. 143).

In summary, meritocratic selection has done little to open elites to those of working-class origin. The children of the working class have the best chance of advancement in the Labour Movement, where non-meritocratic criteria like class origins remain important. A minority of the lower middle class have benefited from meritocracy, but those from the most-privileged backgrounds have found little difficulty in adapting to competition in a more meritocratic world.

The Growth of Specialisation

The persistence of particular patterns of elite recruitment does not mean that elites in Britain are unchanging. The twentieth century has witnessed a revolution in the scale of social organisation. Huge organisations have become the norm in government and in the economy. The demands made on those at the top of big organisations – demands of time, skill and commitment – have increased. The most obvious effect has been a growth in the extent to which elites are specialised. Before the First World War, for instance, it was perfectly possible to combine a successful career at the top of business and at the top of politics. Neither sphere demanded the exclusive commitment of time and ambition now required. Organisations were smaller and simpler, and could be run in a much more informal way than is now the case. The traditional organisation of elites was well summed up by the phrase 'the Establishment', a label suggesting a small group which dominated most significant institutions, was educated at a narrow range of institutions, was part of a close community bound by ties of friendship and kinship, and which mixed socially in such characteristic institutions as the great London clubs. The phase 'the Establishment' was actually coined at a moment in the mid-1950s when this well-integrated community, and its social institutions in London's clubland, was in decline. In the 1980s elites specialise increasingly in their own institutions and deal with each other in increasingly formal ways. The most striking sign of the change is the decline in the social integration between the top of the Conservative Party and the business elite.

The implications of this growing specialisation for the outlook of elites and for the distribution of power are uncertain. Does the decline of a traditional 'establishment' also mean the fragmentation of control into many different hands, or does it only involve a refined division of labour between sections of a unified ruling elite? We look next at the debate about power.

7 Power, Ceremony and Secrecy

The question of whether a single, unified elite rules Britain has provoked fierce argument. Lack of agreement stems in part from factors which we have already encountered several times: though it seems at first glance as if the question can be settled by straightforward appeal to evidence, in practice the 'facts' are incomplete and often contradictory; there is dispute about what constitutes appropriate evidence and the examination of evidence is often bound up with highly sensitive moral evaluations.

Arguments about the distribution of power in Britain are generally conducted in terms of a range of competing models. We encountered some earlier, in a different setting. Thus *pluralism,* which we discussed in Chapter 5 as a model of pressure group politics, has also been a highly influential model of the distribution of power. Pluralists have asserted that no single elite rules, that power is widely dispersed between different groups, that the resources (money, numbers, organisational skill) are likewise widely dispersed, and that it is possible for any significant interest group to share in decision-making.

It has proved increasingly difficult to maintain this optimistic account. Consequently, pluralism itself has evolved a variety of more pessimistic versions. Models of *pluralist stagnation* stress how the variety of powerful groups checkmate each other and prevent government reaching any effective decisions (Beer, 1969). In this view, nobody controls Britain; the country is trapped in a paralysed balance between powerful pressure groups. *Pluralist elitist* models have abandoned the notion that pluralism allows wide public participation in decision-making, substituting the claim that a range of groups, controlled by their own separate oligarchies, are engaged in competitive bargaining about policy. According to this view few people take part in decision-making, but the elites who dominate separate groups have divided interests and, because of division and bargaining, are often forced to appeal to their own rank-and-file members. Thus, while the pluralist elitist model allows little place for continuous popular participation in politics, the mass of citizens can periodically exercise a decisive influence when elites are divided. This model is only a short step from the *corporatist* models which we encountered in Chapter 5, where politics and the economy are pictured as under the control of a small group of closed interests.

Pluralist models have traditionally been contrasted with elitism, which in turn is normally divided into *ruling class* and *ruling elite* versions. Ruling class models argue that the base of power lies in control of economic resources, and that in Britain these are in the hands of a small class of capitalists (Leys, 1983). The cut-and-thrust of everyday politics, which so impresses pluralists, is dismissed by supporters of the ruling class model as irrelevant to the underlying distribution of power. This account obviously derives from Marxism. Ruling elite models, by contrast, derive from a variety of sociological theorists – notably Mosca and Pareto – who were contemptuous of democracy and who believed that government was inevitably controlled by a small minority. A ruling elite model would picture power in Britain as the monopoly not of a class of capitalists but of a small, self-selecting political class.

The apparently endless dispute between advocates of different models of the distribution of power in Britain arises in part from lack of agreement about what constitutes appropriate evidence. Three issues are involved in answering questions about the significance of elites in British politics. First: are those who control Britain sufficiently small in number and sufficiently free of popular restraint to be called an elite? Second: are those who exercise control united by common beliefs distinguishing them from the rest of the population? In other words, is there a distinct elite ideology? Third: are controllers a unified social group? In other words, do they have common social origins and economic connections? Pluralist models concentrate on the first of these questions, especially as revealed by participation in decisions, but neglect questions of elite ideology or social coherence. Ruling elite models stress ideological coherence and the social cohesion of the political class, but neglect the details of decision-making (Hewitt, 1974). Ruling class models examine the social origins and economic connections of those who occupy top positions in government and the economy, but likewise neglect the details of decision-making.

The debate about power in Britain has been considerably complicated by important recent changes in the social atmosphere of government. As recently as the end of the Second World War it was possible to speak of a distinctive elite political culture in Britain. Those involved in government were comparatively few, and were part of a community largely congregated in central London which overlapped to a considerable extent with upper-class 'society'. Despite the decline of rule by the aristocracy, and the rise of the Labour Party, government had not shaken off its aristocratic roots. A political class, both right and left wing, shared common assumptions. Confidentiality (or, as critics called it, secrecy) was believed to be essential to good government. This belief was expressed in doctrines like 'collective ministerial responsibility' which obliged all ministers to defend government policy and concealed from the public the debates and divisions about policy inside government. Likewise, the doctrine of 'individual ministerial responsibility', which asserted that ministers were responsible for everything done in their name, shielded civil servants from public scrutiny. The institution of the 'lobby' gave a selected group of journalists privileged access to information about government, and in return controlled what they could reveal.

Public debate among the political class was also constrained by powerful conventions. Inside government, policy was made by bargaining between powerful interests, but this took place behind a facade of Parliamentary rule (Middlemas, 1979). Public doctrines said that Parliament ruled Britain, that dissent should be expressed through Parliament and that laws enacted by Parliament should always be obeyed. Parliament itself was tightly controlled by the Executive, while the conventions of Parliamentary life reinforced the sense of community between all Members. The House of Commons had a strongly ritualistic character, which separated the Parliamentarian from the wider society and defused inflammatory political debate. Many things encouraged this formalistic quality: the faintly church-like Gothic architecture of the place; the unreal hours of work in the afternoon and evening; the carefully cultivated atmosphere of a good late-Victorian club; the highly elaborate quality of Parliamentary language and procedure; even the emphasis on 'correct' Parliamentary dress, which insisted that Parliamentarians of all classes dress in a conventionally 'respectable' middle-class way. Debate in Parliament spanned a wide range of issues about policy, but even the most violently contrasting views had to be sieved through Parliamentary language. In the words of the standard handbook of Parliamentary procedure: 'Good temper and moderation are the characteristics of parliamentary language. Parliamentary language is never more desirable than when a Member is canvassing the opinions and conduct of his opponents in debate' (Cocks, 1971, pp. 418–9). Among words and phases judged unparliamentary in the past have been such everyday terms of abuse as 'coward', 'hooligan', 'hypocrite', and 'swine'.

The political culture of the elite, therefore, allowed wide debate about the substance of policy but imposed great procedural restraints: goverment had to be carried on confidentially; the supremacy of Parliament could not be challenged; political debate had to be conducted in a ceremonial and ritualistic way governed by a 'gentlemanly' code. The pervasiveness of these ideas is shown by the fact that one of their finest post-war statements is in an introduction to British government written by Herbert Morrison, a leading figure in the Labour Party from the 1920s to the 1950s (Morrison, 1954).

In the 1980s this distinctive elite political culture, though not dead, is in serious decline. Important changes have taken place in values. In the most extensive up-to-date comparative study of elite beliefs in Western democracies, British politicians and civil servants emerged as among those most favourable to the idea that government should involve open party controversy and popular debate (Aberach, Putnam and Rockman, 1981, pp. 170–208). Contrary to popular caricature, the values of the British political elite are, by international standards, now highly favourable to popular controversy and the open expression of social and political differences.

These values are reflected in important recent changes in political practices. Both ceremony and secrecy have declined. Some of the signs are trivial but revealing. They include the growing readiness of politicians to be cross-examined by interviewers in public, and the increasingly common use of informal modes of address, like first names, in public exchanges between the elite. In Parliament, ceremony and ritual have increasingly given way to a more 'business-like' atmosphere, while traditional standards of Parliamentary language and Parliamentary dress have been widely challenged. The fact that MPs now abuse each other in everyday language across the floor of the House of Commons, and often wear casual clothes, may appear trivial changes; but they reflect the declining restraint of ceremony and ritual and the declining distinctiveness of the political class.

With the decline of ceremony and ritual, confidentiality (or secrecy) has suffered. British government could be carried on in secrecy when the political class was small, when business was done by word of mouth, and when the cohesion of the political class was cemented by distinctive institutions and distinctive rituals. It has not survived the explosion of bureaucracy, the growth of committees in government, and the rise of investigative journalism to challenge the traditionally controlled 'Lobby' system. Both collective and individual ministerial responsibility are in decline: leaks of disagreements inside Cabinets and inside Departments are commonplace, while the practice of shielding anonymous civil servants behind Department ministers has likewise become less usual.

British government is often said to be obsessed with secrecy; but this obsession, in so far as it exists, is a product of the growing difficulty experienced by elites in maintaining traditional standards of confidentiality. The most important reason for the decline of confidentiality is the growing scale of government and the formality and specialisation which scale had imposed. As elites have been compelled to deal with each other in an increasingly formal way, so more information has been committed to paper. In bureaucracies – and British government is a series of large bureaucracies – documents are routinely copied to large numbers of affected individuals, a practice encouraged by the development of the photocopier. So-called 'secret' documents are therefore almost always seen – and can be copied and leaked – by large numbers of people. Take a single example. In 1984 a junior Foreign Office clerk was jailed for sending to the *Guardian* newspaper a copy of a 'secret' memorandum from the Secretary of State for Defence to the Prime Minister. This 'secret' document was, it has been calculated, seen – and could therefore be leaked by – at least fifty-five people, in addition to those to whom it was addressed. This was because the routines of copying and filing inside government put the document into the hands of numerous officials, some of them quite junior (*The Economist*, 31 March 1984).

Rulers and representatives in Britain therefore operate in an increasingly informal and open political atmosphere. Whether this also means that power is being more widely shared than in the past is a matter for dispute. Pluralists will see in these changes a confirmation of their view that the political system is open and responsive. By contrast, those who think that the levers of power lie in the structure of the economy rather than in the machinery of government, will argue that whatever cultural changes are taking place economic concentration is placing strategic power in the hands of an ever-smaller number of economic controllers. The different views will remain unreconciled, in part because they rest on different assumptions about the very nature of power. Does the increasingly open atmosphere of government in Britain mean that citizens at large are able to voice their interests and influence policy accordingly, or are the 'interests' voiced in such debates only the desires stimulated and manipulated by powerful economic forces? Any answer involves a judgement about how individuals' interests are to be identified. The identification of interests, as Lukes (1974) has shown, in turn involves judgements about human purpose; in other words, involves us in moral evaluations. At this point in the argument empirical evidence ceases to have any decisive part to play.

8 Conclusion

The study of power and elites is one of the most contentious areas of the social sciences. It is possible to describe the social arithmetic of elites with a tolerable degree of accuracy, but the implications of that social arithmetic for the distribution of power are a subject of serious dispute. Perhaps the most remarkable long-term feature of the social structure of elites in Britain is the limited scale of change in patterns of recruitment, and the slow pace at which that change has been accomplished. Change there has nevertheless been, the end result of which is a perceptible widening in the social origins of many, though not all, elite groups. How far this change is in turn a cause of the alterations in the political culture of the elite is uncertain. At least part of the decline in elite consensus about the 'rules of the political game' can be traced to the stresses produced by policy failure and national decline. We examine these matters in our next chapter.

7

The Decline of the British State?

She that was great among the nations, Princess among the provinces, how is she become tributary.

Lamentations, 1.1

1 Outline

The British state has been in decline for over a century: this is the single most important feature of British politics. Our final chapter begins by describing the nature of decline. This is followed by a description of the system of Welfare Democracy which was developed during and after the Second World War as a response to that decline. The failure of Welfare Democracy to reverse decline, and the great crisis of the mid-1970s which helped destroy the Welfare Democratic consensus, are next outlined. This is followed by an account of the New Economic Order which since then has been supplanting Welfare Democracy. In section 4 the implications of this New Order for the future of the British state are examined, together with a brief review of some alternative responses to the experience of decline.

2 The Decline of the British State

The Shape of Decline
The British state reached its zenith in the middle of the nineteenth century. For a few brief decades Britain was the greatest power on earth; indeed, she probably enjoyed a more complete world dominance than has been achieved by any state, before or since.

This supremacy rested on three pillars: economic superiority, military might, and imperial possessions. As the first industrial nation Britain had immense advantages. She dominated world production in the goods of the early industrial revolution, like cotton textiles, iron, steel, coal and heavy engineering products such as ships. Her bankers were the organisers of world trade, the sponsors of economic development in other countries and the regulators of the international financial system. Military might – notably sea power – reinforced her domination. It helped her to impose international free trade, thus opening the markets of other nations to the goods and services produced by her more advanced economy. The Empire in turn gave her privileged access to markets, to raw materials and to territories of strategic military value. The domestic political and social significance of Empire was immense. Ideologies of Imperialism penetrated almost every part of British society. The pacification and administration of the Empire absorbed much of the country's surplus labour force.

By the 1980s the economic, military and imperial pillars supporting British power had all collapsed. By almost any measure her economy had been in decline, relative to her international competitors, since the 1870s. Sterling, once the chief medium of world trade, had become a second-rank currency. The country's share of world trade had likewise dwindled. As recently as 1950, for instance, her share of world markets in manufactured goods was over a quarter; by the 1980s it was less than a tenth (Pollard, 1983, p. 352). The great industries through which Britain had dominated the world economy – textiles, steel, shipbuilding – were decayed. In the most technologically advanced sectors of the contemporary world economy – like automobiles and electronics – she was chiefly an assembler and consumer of goods originating elsewhere.

The collapse of military power was, if anything, even more complete. Britain's 'finest hour' – Churchill's description of her defiance of Nazi Germany in 1940 – was also her final hour, the last occasion when world history turned on her military efforts. During the Second World War decisive military strength shifted to the United States and the Soviet Union. By the 1980s Britain was a junior ally of the United States and a minor country within the American sphere of influence.

The disappearance of imperial power was the most extraordinary change of all. Within two decades of the end of the Second World

War the most extensive empire in history melted away, to be replaced by nearly fifty independent states. The attempt to preserve some of the old imperial influence by joining former colonies into a British Commonwealth was a failure. The loss of Empire was also accompanied by a decline in less-formal kinds of power. In the decades after the Second World War the United States displaced Britain from those parts of the world – like the Middle East – where she had once been the dominant influence.

The decline of the British state was necessarily also an English decline. Britain is a multinational kingdom dominated by England. The British state was an English creation, formed by the integration or conquest of lesser nations in the British Isles. In almost every sphere English domination is, and has long been, overwhelming. She is the most populous and wealthy country in the kingdom. The key institutions of the state, the greatest financial enterprises and the biggest industrial firms are controlled from London. The most prestigious institutions in education and entertainment are located in England. Although economic decline has in some ways strengthened English dominance – because the economies of the Celtic nations have suffered disproportionately – the decline of the British state is a decline of an English-dominated political arrangement.

'The collapse of British power' – to use Barnett's (1972) phrase – is one of the unsolved mysteries of modern history. Nobody knows why it occurred; or, to be more exact, many accounts have been offered, none of which commands common acceptance. For some, both the era of British power and the era of British decline are episodes in the continuing development of a world capitalist economy (Gamble, 1981). To understand Britain's moment of greatness and her subsequent fall we must therefore look to the changing characteristics of the world economy and the world political system. Others have also linked decline to international events, though of a more historically particular kind. The two world wars are often seen as important culprits, dissipating Britain's wealth and destroying the international economic and political arrangements on which her power rested (Strange, 1971). The extraordinary post-war economic successes of Germany and Japan, the two main defeated nations in 1945, convinced some that Britain's misfortune was not military involvement alone, but victorious involvement which preserved old industries and old values ill-adapted to survival in the post-war world.

This last argument connects to the most popular explanations for

British decline, those which stress the role of domestic institutions and values. Most of these try to account for relative economic decline, but an exception is Barnett's (1972) massive history of the loss of military and imperial might, which pictures collapse as the product of a loss of spirit and will by the rulers of Britain. Accounts of economic decline, though they differ in their particular explanations, often share a common assumption that Britain's pioneering role as the first industrial nation was the source of her modern difficulties. For some, the fatal legacy of early economic development was an industrial structure incapable of responding to modern demands. According to this view Britain was saddled with out-of-date equipment, and with industries too small and too fragmented into different firms to engage in the scale of investment and production necessary to compete in giant world markets. Other observers have stressed the role of particular institutions. For many, the main culprit was an excessively powerful trade-union movement which obstructed the efficient use of manpower and machines. By contrast, some observers sympathetic to labour have argued that decline was due to fatal misjudgements by those responsible for economic policy, especially in the Treasury (Pollard, 1982). Some accounts have linked the Treasury to the great financial institutions in the City of London, arguing that Britain's decline was due to the way that interests of financiers shaped policy at the expense of manufacturing industry (Blank, 1979).

The view that manufacturing industry in Britain works in a uniquely hostile culture is also a central theme of the most currently fashionable accounts of the causes of decline. According to these accounts, one of the distinguishing traits of British culture is disdain for the life of business, especially the business of making and selling manufactured goods. This disdain has drained talent away from industry into 'unproductive' activities, especially into the public sector. The most influential and subtle account is Wiener's *English Culture and the Decline of the Industrial Spirit* (1981). According to Wiener, Britain failed to develop a culture appropriate to an industrial society. There persisted – especially among the middle and upper classes – an ambivalence about business activities, a nostalgia for the past and a cult of rural life. Business, especially manufacturing industry, suffered low esteem. It neither attracted the most talented people nor secured the most favourable government policies.

A different cultural account has stressed the significance of political values. This view seems to be heavily influenced by the post-Second World War successes of state-sponsored capitalism in Japan and France. It argues that there is absent in Britain any 'strong state' tradition. As a result, there exists widespread hostility to central control and direction of institutions like unions and firms. It has consequently been impossible for the state to intervene, in the manner of the Japanese or the French, to shape industrial structures and to direct investment in the interests of modernisation (Shonfield, 1965).

It is often said that decline – especially economic decline – broke the prevailing post-war consensus in British politics during the 1970s. This is true, but it is less commonly said that this consensus was itself the product of earlier experiences of decline. The economic and social changes introduced during and after the Second World War were designed to remedy the failures of pre-war governments and to reorganise declining traditional industries. These changes introduced what can be called Welfare Democracy.

Welfare Democracy and Decline

The most important assumption in Welfare Democracy was that the state would be responsible for the economic and social well-being of its population. Public provision of social services was expanded into a comprehensive Welfare State. There occurred a significant expansion of public ownership. Free market forces, though they remained important, were regulated or displaced in a 'mixed economy' of private and public sectors. Government was committed to economic intervention in order to promote full employment, economic growth and the reversal of British industrial decline. Policy was made through what Crouch (1977) has called 'bargained corporatism', involving the striking of agreements between the state and the most powerful organised interests in the community. The extent of consensus should not be exaggerated. Significant policy differences still existed between the two major parties.

Many in the Conservative Party only reluctantly accepted the consensus as the price of working-class co-operation and electoral success. But whatever the particular arguments, and whatever the motivations of particular groups, Welfare Democracy was still supreme.

Many critics of the Welfare Democratic consensus have pictured it as a cause of Britain's decline. The argument is usually put with particular force by those who object to the Welfare State, to the pursuit of full time employment by government and to the creation of a sizeable public sector (Jay, 1976). But whatever their effect, the policies and institutions which formed the subject of consensus during and after the Second World War were a result of, and an attempt to cope with consequences of, a decline which was already well established.

For a couple of decades after the end of the Second World War it seemed that the policies and institutions created by the wartime crisis had indeed reversed decline, at least in the economy. Except in a few areas dominated by the old industries of the Industrial Revolution, full employment was created and maintained. Britain's rate of economic growth equalled, and for a time exceeded, that recorded when she led the world economy in the nineteenth century. The benefits of prosperity were widely, if unevenly, distributed throughout almost the whole population. To most people growing up in the two decades after the Second World War the notion that the country was in decline would have seemed improbable; Britain had rarely known such peace and never known such prosperity.

The story of how this sense of achievement was destroyed has been told many times (for instance, Beer, 1982, pp. 48–76). Two episodes were crucial. The failures of Mr Heath's Conservative Government between 1970 and 1974, especially its humiliating exit from power in the middle of a crisis over incomes policy, intensified Conservative disenchantment with the terms of the post-war consensus and brought to prominence in the Party a generation of leaders determined to break with that consensus. The second episode was the economic crisis of 1975 6, which forced the Labour Government into attempts to cut public spending, put the control of price inflation above the promotion of economic growth and led to the final abandonment of the commitment to full employment.

The fundamental causes of the end of the post-war consensus have been greatly argued over, but the immediate reason was the continued decline of the British state. Britain's post-war prosperity was due to her participation in 'the long boom', the great period of sustained economic growth among advanced capitalist economies lasting from the Second World War to the early 1970s. Her absolute prosperity increased greatly during this period; her relative power continued its decline, relegating her to the position of a minor state distinguished chiefly by economic weakness. When 'the long boom' was succeeded by world recession in the 1970s she lacked the economic resources, the military strength or the imperial presence necessary to shape world events or to protect herself from their consequences.

The destruction of the post-war consensus produced a wide range of policy responses, concerned largely with the problem of economic decline. The most intellectually and politically influential of these has involved the creation of a New Economic Order. The New Economic Order is not the only existing solution of the problem of decline, but it has a distinction shared by no other remedy: it has been tried, at first hesitantly and incompletely by the Labour Government after 1976, and then with increasing vigour under the Conservative Government in office after 1979.

In Section 3 we examine its intellectual origins and practical implementation.

3 The New Economic Order

Intellectual Origins
The most important intellectual origins of the New Economic Order lie in the tradition of classical economies and in the revival of that tradition by economists like Hayek and Friedman. These modern writers are sometimes collectively called 'monetarists'. The label is unfortunate because it obscures the very considerable technical and philosophical disputes dividing those herded into the category. Monetarists are divided about precisely how the supply of money to a community should be regulated and these divisions reflect deeper philosophical differences about the proper scope of state power.

Two propositions are nevertheless widely accepted by those conventionally labelled monetarists: that the preservation of liberty depends on the existence of a free market economy, where government confines itself to providing rules and conditions allowing economic agents freely to strike bargains; and that the powers of government should be exercised according to legally prescribed rules which minimise discretionary choice by public officials. From these more general propositions come the particular arguments which have attracted the label 'monetarist': that in economic management the most important job of the state is to safeguard the quality of a nation's currency; and that it best does this by observing a fixed rule governing the rate at which money is supplied to the economy, thus eliminating discretionary decisions from the main form of state economic intervention.

Advocates of these views of course objected to the consensus which governed British politics from the Second World War to the middle of the 1970s. Nationalised industries, the institutions of the Welfare State, the practice of manipulating demand in the economy to achieve full employment: all these seriously breached the principles of market economics. The political bargaining associated with Welfare Democracy also violated the principle that government intervention should be determined by non-discretionary rules.

Attacks on the Welfare Democratic consensus by economists were reinforced during the 1970s by criticisms from academic political science. These criticisms were unexpected. Political science had long been sympathetic to extensive government intervention and to bargaining between the state and sectional interests. In both Britain and the United States one of the main roots of politics as an academic subject lay in the study of 'public administration', a discipline which sympathetically examined the workings of big public institutions. By the 1960s the dominant intellectual tradition in political science was 'pluralism', a set of doctrines picturing government as a process of bargaining between the state and sectional interests in society. But in the 1970s these sympathies gave way to arguments critical of big government and of bargaining between government and private interests. The most powerful case was put forward by advocates of the 'overload' thesis. According to this view, government in Britain was suffering from 'overload' because its responsibilities had come to exceed its capacities; or in King's words, 'the reach of British government exceeds its grasp' (King, 1976, p. 15). Two forces were commonly held to be at work: the expectations of citizens were continually rising, with a consequent increase in the demands on government; and the resources available to the state to meet expectations were fixed or even declining.

The growth of 'excessive expectations' was commonly ascribed to party competition. Political parties were forced to outbid each other in the contest for votes by offering extravagant promises to the electorate (Brittan, 1975). In Britain, some critics argued, party competition was also peculiarly adversarial because the electoral system encouraged two-party competition and discouraged compromise between the parties. The ability to supply the goods and services demanded by the population was thought to be limited by a number of factors. Some writers, such as Rose and Peters (1978), argued that the usual sources of public revenue, like taxation, just could not yield the money necessary to pay for the growing demands on the state. Others, like King (1976), argued that the increasing complexity of social institutions now made it exceptionally difficult for government to secure the obedience and co-operation necessary to carry out ambitious policies; hence there had occurred an increase in the number of government policies which simply and spectacularly failed. According to these arguments, therefore, to economic, military and imperial decline we ought to add an absolute decline in the 'governability' of Britain. Some of the suggested remedies were similar to those advocated by economic critics of the Welfare Democratic consensus: means would have to be found to diminish popular expectations; government would have to reduce the range of its responsibilities and confine itself to tasks requiring less ambitious and complex organisation.

It should not be assumed that these ideas have simply been translated into action by government. In analysing the New Economic Order, as in analysing any other set of public policies, we must distinguish between the intellectual origins of the policy, the policy which those in government said they were implementing, the policy which was actually implemented and the impact of the policy. To these matters we now turn.

The New Economic Order: Implementation and Impact
The beginnings of the New Economic Order in British Government can be traced to the crisis which occurred in 1975–6. The origins of that crisis lay in weaknesses of the home economy and in the fragility of sterling as an international currency – in other words, they were a legacy of Britain's past eminence and her decline from those heights. The particular form taken by the crisis was a sharp fall in the exchange value of sterling relative to other currencies, the acceleration of price inflation, and the collapse in 1975 of the attempt to limit wage rises by a voluntary 'Social Contract'.

The crisis did not produce a complete break with the politics of Welfare Democracy. The government was, for instance, able in 1975 to renogotiate its wage restraint bargain with the unions, thus securing wage restraint for three more years. To solve the sterling crisis, however, the Labour Government felt obliged to seek help from the International Monetary Fund. The formal price of that help was a commitment by the government to set and observe targets for levels of public borrowing and the growth of the money supply. The real costs could be seen in the abandonment of many of the elements of the Welfare Democratic consensus. There occurred a determined, and partly successful, attack on public spending, including spending on some welfare services. Full employment – the coping-stone of Welfare Democracy – was removed from the aims of economic policy. The fight against price inflation was put above all other aims. There also occurred a less tangible alteration in the intellectual climate, with Ministers of a Labour Government joining in criticisms of many of the aims and institutions of Welfare Democracy.

Labour had been the chief political agent in the original creation of Welfare Democracy. During the Second World War, Labour Ministers in the coalition took the lead in preparing and implementing reforms; the post-war Labour governments (1945–51) carried out many of the wartime plans and commitments. It is not surprising, therefore, that between 1976 and 1979 the Government found the business of dismantling Welfare Democracy and putting down the foundations of the New Economic Order an agonising experience. It did the job reluctantly, imcompletely, and to a chorus of criticism from its own supporters. Mrs Thatcher's Conservative Government, elected in 1979, continued the task in a much more enthusiastic way.

The Conservative programme was shaped by a conscious desire to break with the Welfare Democratic consensus and was expressed in the language of the Party's 'liberal' tradition (on which, see Chapter 4). It stressed the importance of individual liberty, the superiority of free market forces in social choice and the necessity of dismantling much of the public sector. The particular detail was plainly influenced by what is conventionally called 'monetarism'. The centrepiece of economic management was a 'Medium Term Financial Strategy', under which targets were to be announced for the levels of public borrowing and monetary growth. Within the limits set by these targets market forces would operate in wage bargaining and in firms' decisions about costs, investment and production. A start would be made on dismantling some of the institutions of Welfare Democracy by 'privatising' parts of the public sector: local authorities would be compelled to sell council houses to tenants; profitable public concerns would be sold to private buyers; some unprofitable public bodies would be reorganised with an eye to a future sale; cuts would be made in the level of taxes on incomes and in the overall level of public spending (Hood and Wright, 1981).

The practical implementation of this programme after 1979 differed from the blueprint offered to the electorate. It came closest to realisation in respect of 'privatisation' proposals: 750,000 local authority dwellings had been sold to tenants, and important utilities, like gas supply and telephones, have been sold to private investors. The extent to which 'monetarism' had been implemented was more doubtful. A Medium Term Financial Strategy had indeed been published, but its implementation failed two key tests of monetarism: the targets set out in the Strategy were persistently breached; and in the conduct of economic policy the Government was if anything less bound by fixed rules, and more given to discretionary intervention, than had been its predecessors.

Explanations for these gaps between stated intentions and achievements will differ according to political viewpoint. They may be a simple failure on the Government's part to deal with the causes and symptoms of British decline. A more sympathetic account views what has happened as a series of setbacks which can be redressed with the passage of time. Some left-wing observers ignore the technical failings of monetary policy and argue that the measure of monetarism's impact is the creation of mass unemployment and the resulting reduction in working-class power and confidence (Hall and Jacques, 1983). Some observers argue that it is wrong to picture the modern Conservative Party as engaged in restoring a traditional liberal market order. On this view – which we encountered in Chapter 4 – the decline of Britain and the crisis of Welfare Democracy produced 'Thatcherism', a novel fusion of elements in Conservative ideology involving the establishment of a free market society controlled and policed by a strong, possibly authoritarian, state.

All these interpretations plainly involve difficult and uncertain judgements about the intentions of those who control government, and about the connections between intentions and policies. Establishing the most important features of the New Economic Order is a different business. It involves looking at the content and consequences of policy and comparing that state of affairs with conditions under Welfare Democracy. When we do this, we recognise six established features of the New Economic Order. They are discussed in turn below.

(1) *The development of mass unemployment.* The single most important particular feature of Welfare Democracy was full employment. This has now been abandoned. The process began before the Conservatives entered office in 1979: under the previous Labour Administration unemployment nearly tripled to one and a half million. Under the Conservatives registered unemployment rose to over 3 million, though it has since fallen. Considerable argument surrounds the official measures. Some observers believe that there is much less unemployment than government statistics suggest. According to this view, there exists a large hidden labour market where individuals registered as unemployed do a variety of paid jobs–driving minicabs, cleaning windows or acting as bookies' runners. Against this view, other observers argue that a hidden economy populated by hundreds of thousands of window cleaners, minicab drivers and bookies is hardly likely to go unnoticed, and is equally unlikely to be supported by the poverty stricken council estates of Liverpool or Glasgow. They also argue that the 'fall' in unemployment has much to do with successive official redefinitions of what constitutes unemployment and successive restrictions of entitlement to unemployment benefit. Few observers on either side of the argument expect 'full employment' as once understood to return.

(2) *The state as manager of decline.* The appearance of mass unemployment has coincided with the accelerated decline of manufacturing industry, once the base of Britain's power. Between 1979 and 1981 – when unemployment first truly reached mass proportions – the numbers working in British manufacturing industry fell by 13.6 per cent. The comparable reduction in West Germany was 1.3 per cent, the same as in the United States. In Japan, numbers employed actually rose by 3.5 per cent (Dyson and Wilks, 1983, p. 13). Under Welfare Democracy the state tried to reorganise and to revive declining industries and declining regions. Under the New Economic Order, industries and regions incapable of competing have been forced to face the consequences in the marketplace. In this way, whole areas of manufacturing industry have withered. Although the

rhetoric of the New Economic Order pictures it as a way of reversing decline, it involves in practice something very different, the final stage of Britain's fall from the position of industrial eminence which she once enjoyed. The state, which under Welfare Democracy tried to reverse decline, is now in the business of managing it in as socially peaceful a way as possible.

(3) *Reduction in trade-union power*. The orderly management of decline has been helped by one of the chief consequences of mass unemployment, a reduction in trade-union power and confidence. Unions were a key influence in Welfare Democracy. If the system could be said to have had a date of birth, it would be 13 May 1940 when Ernest Bevin, the greatest trade-union leader of his day, joined Churchill's coalition government. For the next three-and-a-half decades organised labour suffered few reversals in government or in the workplace, and achieved a remarkable range of victories. As recently as the mid-1970s the power of unions seemed to some the most distinctive feature of British politics.

Since that time the balance of power has tilted against organised labour. The battles have been bloody – often literally so, as in the sometimes violent struggles on picket lines – and not all have resulted in reverses for the unions. The overall outcome has nevertheless been to their disadvantage. In the workplace, managers and employers have reasserted power lost often as long as a generation ago. In government, the drift of economic policy since the great crisis of 1975–6 has likewise been against the unions. Mass unemployment has hit with particular severity some of the most traditionally powerful and militant unions, such as those in the engineering and construction industries.

(4) *International integration of the economy*. This fourth feature of the New Economic Order marks not so much a break with the past as an acceleration of trends long observable. Britain's economic and political powers have long been deeply influenced by the changing structure of the world economy. Since the Second World War the most noticeable tendency has been the growing organisation of economic activity on an international scale. The key institution in this change has been the multinational corporation, whose character is signalled by the way it organises its investment, production and marketing across a range of countries.

Britain's decline, as Gamble (1981) has persuasively argued, should be seen against the changing international economic and political system. Her fall from power turned her from a central influence in world politics and economics into a minor member of the group of highly developed economies located principally in Western Europe and North America. She played an important role – through the financial institutions of the City of London – in providing financial services for the increasingly unified international economy. But in manufacturing she ceased to be a world leader in either technology or production, and was increasingly relegated to assembling goods produced elsewhere. The biggest British firms themselves became multinational in character; in the case of many, by the 1970s British operations had become a minor part of their activities.

The New Economic Order has hastened this absorption into a wider international system. In recent years the biggest financial markets and financial institutions have become almost totally multinational. The City of London is now one part of an international system of markets trading round the world and round the clock. The declining manufacturing sector is dominated by multinationals, to whom Britain is a minor market and a minor part of their operations. The decisive contribution of the New Economic Order in this process has been twofold: it has allowed the domestic economy to face the consequences of foreign competition, and offered important parts of that domestic economy the opportunity to loosen links with the declining home base. The most significant move in the latter respect was the abolition in 1979 of official controls over investment abroad. This change helped the integration of the City of London into the world financial system and accelerated the pace at which British investors were able to put their resources into foreign markets. In the two years after the abolition of exchange controls, for instance, the level of direct and portfolio investment abroad was more than double the level in the two years before abolition.

(5) *More inequality*. We saw in Chapter 1 that there is considerable argument about how far class inequalities altered during the first seven decades of this century, and in particular how far the institutions of the Welfare State diminished those inequalities. It is undeniable, however, that the rise of the New Economic Order has significantly increased both class and regional inequalities in Britain.

The greatest alterations in the relative fortunes of occupational classes have occurred at the top and bottom of the social scales. The very rich have benefited from one of the most persistent policy features of the New Order – the desire of successive governments to cut levels of taxation on all incomes. There have been significant reductions since 1979 in taxes on the incomes of the highest paid. The rich have also benefited in a number of subsidiary ways: the rise in levels of indirect taxes is known to bear on them more lightly than on the less well off; they have suffered least in the recession; and the growing integration of Britain into a wider international economy has allowed the richest individuals, and the biggest firms, to participate in more buoyant foreign markets.

By contrast with those at the top of the economic ladder, those at or near the bottom have become relatively worse off under the New Economic Order. The very poor have long been disproportionately drawn from those who rely on state benefits, particularly in the form of benefits for unemployment. The gap between the value of these benefits and the value of wages has widened since the early 1970s. The poor have also suffered from the shift to indirect taxes and from sharp rises in the cost of goods and services like gas and electricity. Since the mid-1970s there has also, of course, been a great increase in the numbers experiencing the lot of the very poor because the force of the recession has pushed so many more on to the dole.

The changes in economic structure contributing to greater class inequality have also led to greater inequality between regions. No part of Britain has escaped some of the effects of decline. In even the most prosperous areas there exist districts (for instance, some inner London boroughs) where physical decay is advanced and jobs scarce. But the recession of recent years has widened the gap between the poorest and richest regions, especially as measured by the crucial indicator, unemployment.

The impact on regional inequality has been determined by the nature of industrial decline and by the changing shape of the world economy. Those (few) parts of Britain well integrated into the most-advanced parts of the world economy have continued to advance. This largely means London and the South East, together with a few pockets of buoyancy elsewhere, such as those parts of Scotland participating in the international oil industry. For some of the poorest areas, by contrast – in districts of Northern Ireland, North West England and North East England, for instance – the dream of full employment has been replaced by the reality of full unemployment.

(6) *Increased central control.* The political rhetoric accompanying the New Economic Order has attacked central control by the state and advocated a society marked by more decentralisation of power and authority. In practice, there is occurring a long-term growth in the power of central government, at the expense of public agencies outside Whitehall and of sub-national political authorities, especially local government. Growing centralisation is due to two connected features of the New Economic Order: the attempts to cut public spending, and to direct what remains to purposes approved by central government. Welfare Democracy not only involved high levels of public expenditure; it also developed a very wide range of institutions with the power to raise revenue and to spend money. Public spending was accounted for by local authorities; by nationalised corporations like the Coal Board; by public agencies which provided such goods and services as health care, water and transport; and by agencies like the Arts Council and the University Grants Committee which disbursed funds at their own discretion to a wide variety of institutions. Some public bodies could also raise money, either by imposing taxes (such as local authority rates, a property tax) or, like nationalised industries, by charging for services.

Even under Welfare Democracy it was recognised that these arrangements were a source of friction, particularly when central government wanted to limit the growth of spending. The friction has been intensified because cutting the real level of public spending is a central aim of the New Economic Order. Doing this involves controlling the numerous spouts outside central government through which public money flows.

The best-known case concerns local government. Already under pressure after the economic crisis of 1975–6, when Labour was in office, local authorities have experienced determined attempts by the Conservative Government since 1979 to limit both their spending and revenue-raising powers. Central government has also increased its power elsewhere. The administration of the health service has been (and continues to be) re-designed to allow Ministers and senior civil servants a greater say over health costs. The discretion exercised by the University Grants Committee was reduced during the squeeze on university spending between 1981 and 1984. The polytechnics – previously administered by local authorities – have been brought under the partial control of a national body itself closely influenced by central government. The government has intervened increasingly in the operations of nationalised industries, particularly to cut those unable to survive the more competitive atmosphere of the New Economic Order.

It should not be assumed that the changes summarised here are happening in a smoothly inevitable way. The institutions and policies of Welfare Democracy were in the interests of large and often powerful groups. The changes brought about by the New Economic Order have been bitterly resisted. Indeed, two central aims of the New Order – cutting the overall level of public spending and reducing the total level of taxation – had not been achieved by the mid-1980s.

Within less than a decade great changes have nevertheless occurred. The key features of the New Economic Order may be summarised as involving changes in the character of the economy and consequential changes in the role of the state. The economy is being most closely integrated into a wider multinational economy, in which it has a minor role. Some groups in Britain—those keyed to the most-advanced parts of the multinational economy—are benefiting. Other regions and groups are bearing the brunt of decline, with consequent increases in regional and class inequalities. In the political sphere the central machinery of the state—national government—is managing this decline: opening the economy to the effect of international economic forces; struggling with the problem of preserving social order where decline causes discontent; exercising a tighter grip over public spending institutions outside the centre.

The New Economic Order developed by successive Administrations since the mid-1970s is not the same as the Order which politicians promised or intended to introduce. What happened in government and the economy was only loosely related to intentions. Some outcomes – such as greater class inequality – were consciously engineered in the belief that a thriving market economy demanded more inequality to provide incentives. Greater regional inequality was an unintended outcome of economic change. The creation of mass unemployment and the accelerated decline of manufacturing industry were the inevitable but unacknowledgeable result of exposing the economy to competitive forces. It is not certain how far growing central control was an unintended consequence of efforts to cut public spending and how far the natural outcome of a philosophical commitment to 'strong state' regulation of a market economy.

The most important reason for the fall of Welfare Democracy was its failure to stem British decline. But the future of the New Economic Order and of the British state also involves difficulties. To these we now turn.

4 The End of Britain?

The political system of a country is not simply a skin enclosing its economy and society, changing in shape as economic and social structures alter. Political institutions are indeed deeply affected by their environment; but they persist, decline, or merely change according to forces other than economic circumstances. Their fate is shaped by the pattern of political organisation, by the influence of political ideas and by the intervention of decisive personalities. So it is with the British state, which survived the loss of military might and the descent from imperial grandeur, Indeed, one of the striking features of preceding chapters is the way they document compara-tive stability – in political values, electoral behaviour and elite recruitment – in an age of social and economic change. It must not be assumed, therefore, that because Britain is in economic, military and political decline the state too is doomed.

Decline, especially in the accelerated form experienced recently, nevertheless creates serious problems for the state. Britain has been relegated to a minor role in an international economy populated by developed nations. This change has involved the partial disappear-ance of a separate British economy, and the creation of economic structures crossing state boundaries. The South East is part of a 'metropolitan' economy encompassing parts of North America, some regions of Western Europe and the great newer economies of the East like Japan. Northern Ireland and the depressed parts of mainland Britain are part of a peripheral economy of depressed areas like Southern Italy and the Republic of Ireland. One of the decisive contributions of the New Economic Order has been to accelerate the obliteration of a separate national British economy.

Judgements about the desirability or otherwise of these processes plainly depend on the moral values and social beliefs of the observer. Defenders of the New Economic Order can picture what is happen-ing as a rational reallocation of resources. The power of the state is retreating before that of markets, especially world markets. The extent to which peripheral, depressed areas continue to experience recession depends on how well their populations respond to the demand of those world markets – either by providing wanted goods and services in the regions at the appropriate price, thus attracting demand, or by moving to areas where demand already exists.

These social arrangements will plainly appeal to some more than others. It is nevertheless plain that a state which substantially loses control of its economic fate to wider international forces faces crucial problems of power and legitimacy. To take the most elementary problem of all: while the economy is part of a wider whole, governments have to win elections among the national population. This need not be an insuperable problem, as the Conservatives showed in both 1983 and 1987. But as we saw in Chapter 3, territorial divisions within the electorate are growing under the differential impact of economic decline in the regions. The Conservatives have suffered a long-term loss of support among the electorate as a whole, and a particularly serious loss in the depressed regions of the country. Their victories in the 1980s, so conclusive in parliamentary terms, were due to their support in those parts of Britain benefiting from integration into the buoyant parts of the international economy, coupled with the way the electoral system exaggerated popular support at the Parliamentary level.

The problems of sustaining electoral support for the New Economic Order are compounded by the more general difficulty of sustaining the legitimacy of the state among the population. Can a state whose military and imperial might have vanished, and whose economic policy consists in the management of economic decline, continue to command the loyalty and obedience of its people, especially that considerable part of its people suffering the worst consequences of decline? The question is not rhetorical, because the outcome is truly uncertain. The tasks of building a United Kindgom and navigating it through the tensions of an industrial revolution were accomplished by skilful mixtures of coercion, economic sanctions and appeals to a common purpose. Skill and good fortune may also suffice in the future. But successful political management in the past was accomplished by confident, historically ascending elites working on a largely illiterate and ill-organised population. It remains to be seen how far it will be possible successfully to manage a literate, politically confident people experiencing economic decay and the end of the benefits and expectations conferred by Welfare Democracy. We have had just over a decade of the New Economic

Order. The social impact of its most striking consequence, mass unemployment, has been blunted by a number of short-term features: some of the unemployment benefits established by Welfare Democracy have been retained; a disproportionate number of those affected in the early stages have been older workers for whom redundancy faded into early retirement, and adolescents who were not yet fully involved in the obligations and ambitions of adult life.

It would be wrong to imply that there exist no alternatives to the New Economic Order. Decline has created a ferment of political argument in Britain. To simplify, the possible alternative solutions are threefold: the abandonment of the British state in favour of some supranational political arrangement; the break-up of the British state into its constituent national units; or the reassertion of the power of the state to regain control over the fate of the economy.

The first of these solutions is in many ways the appropriate functional response. The nation state developed in an era of national economic systems. The welding of national economies into larger units might be thought a suitable prelude to the welding of states into larger political units. Many of the biggest firms have already 'abandoned' Britain, treating it as a minor market in a wider international economy. Since 1973 the country has been part of a larger political unit, the European Economic Community. Some supporters of the Community have seen it as the prototype of a supranational state. Entry undoubtedly assisted the international integration of the British economy. Since 1979 there has been a directly elected European Parliament in which some efforts exist to organise parties along ideological lines that ignore national boundaries. There has occurred a substantial transfer of power to EEC institutions, and in response to this many powerful British pressure groups have begun to lobby at the EEC level.

Despite these hints of political formation at a supranational level, the ECC is an unconvincing candidate as a replacement for the British state. Some transfer of power has undoubtedly occurred, but there has been no corresponding transfer of loyalties. Though a small section of the British intelligentsia are enthusiastic 'Europeans', the population as a whole, on the evidence of surveys and of turnout in elections for the European Parliament, are less enthusiastic about the European 'idea' than are any other people in the EEC. Nor does the development of the Community since Britain's entry suggest that it is much more than an arena for bargaining on behalf of domestic client groups.

There seems little likelihood of the British state being absorbed into a bigger supranational institution, but for a time in the 1970s there seemed a distinct possibility, with the rise of Welsh and Scottish nationalism, that it would dissolve into its constituent national parts. As we saw in Chapter 3, this possibility has now receded, though without disappearing. Support for nationalist parties has been falling since the peak of the mid-1970s, and support for independence was never as great as readiness to cast a vote for a nationalist movement. Nor, leaving aside these electoral practicalities, was it clear what was involved in a nationalist solution to the problem of decline, for the nationalist campaigns necessarily involved postponing many key policy choices until after independence. In the case of Scotland, for instance, some seemed to see independence as an opportunity to use oil to tie the country to the most advanced parts of the world capitalist economy; for others, nationalism seemed an opportunity to establish an economically independent Scottish socialist state.

The failure of nationalism to build on its early successes is puzzling. The conditions which gave rise to nationalist support – the declining ability of the central state machinery to run the economy efficiently, the existence of significant territorial inequalities, the expansion of social groups committed to the culture of small nations in the UK – still exist. The hold over the popular mind exercised by the idea of the British state plainly still remains strong.

Nationalism's challenge to the sovereignty of central government has to some degree been superseded by defiance from individual local authorities, especially those controlled by radical socialist groups in big cities like Liverpool and London. Shrewd politicians, building on local political movements and claiming legitimacy from elected status, have been able periodically to outmanoeuvre those at the centre attempting to implement the New Economic Order. But these are tactics of evasion and defiance; they hardly constitute – and are not seriously intended as – an alternative political strategy in the manner of nationalism.

If attachment to the state remains durable, this strengthens the chances of a third set of solutions, those involving the reassertion of the power of the British state. Under these solutions, the New Economic Order would be swept away. Many of Britain's present economic links with the advanced world economy would be broken. Tariffs and quotas would be erected against foreign competition. Extensive state direction and public control would be introduced to try to revive home manufacturing industry. The country's ties with supranational institutions like the EEC would be broken. Multinational corporations would be expropriated or controlled and the financial institutions of the City of London brought under public ownership or tight regulation.

This strategy is offered in a number of political forms. One variant combines central direction and economic self-sufficiency with the preservation of private property. It stresses patriotism, attacks nonwhite citizens and is politically authoritarian. It is, in short, a Fascist solution to the problem of decline. As we saw in Chapter 4, potential support for Fascism in Britain is probably greater than its miserable electoral performance suggests, and it is possible that the support is growing among the young. It would nevertheless require a startling, though far from inconceivable, change in the political atmosphere to put a Fascist solution high on the political agenda.

An alternative political variant is Marxist authoritarianism, involving all the economic elements associated with Fascism, with the added ingredient of the wholesale abolition of private ownership of productive property. The examples of Eastern Europe suggest that Marxist dictatorships can be just as effective as Fascist regimes in arousing support on patriotic grounds (and almost as prone to sustain patriotism by attacking racial minorities).

There seems, however, little likelihood of the triumph of Marxist authoritarianism in Britain. The one party with some commitment to such a solution, the Communist Party of Great Britain, is in decline, and is attempting to abandon both authoritarianism and support for full public control of the economy as a way of halting that decline.

This leaves a third variant of the strategy of reasserting the power of the British state: that advocated by those in the Labour Party who support an 'alternative economic strategy'. The strategy retains competitive democratic policies, but erects tariff and quota barriers to protect home industry. It proposes greatly extended public ownership and public direction of remaining privately owned firms. It breaks or modifies ties with advanced economies, thus reversing Britain's integration into that wider international economy.

Fierce arguments surround the case for such a strategy. The

Labour Party is itself divided. Though many of those who supported the policies pursued between 1976 and 1979 have left the Party for the Social Democrats, or have retired from high office, only some elements of the 'alternative economic strategy' are apparently Party policy. Indeed after Labour's defeat in the 1987 General Election the Party leadership began a policy review designed, apparently, to come to terms with many of the economic changes introduced by Mrs Thatcher's administrations. The more general arguments about the strategy revive familiar differences between supporters and opponents of free market economics. Would the kind of economy envisaged under the alternative economic strategy allow the state to allocate resources according to some rational criteria, or would it succumb to shortages, rationing and black markets? Would a substantial extension of public control, especially if accompanied by more extensive union participation in management, amount to a significant increase in democratic control, or would it undermine the economic diversity and autonomy associated with liberty in Britain? Would a protected economy rebuild a sound base of manufacturing industry or would it be merely one where immunity from international competition perpetuated inefficiency? Would the attempt to curb the powers of multinationals and the City restore control of the country's economic fate to elected governments, or is Britain too deeply enmeshed in a wider international economic system to allow the British state an independent economic role? Could an alternative economic strategy be implemented within the limits of a parliamentary system?

*   *   *

Politics is not a very important human activity. Our really intense experiences come in more private ways: from love and friendship, the practice of religion, the consolation of pleasure, the excitement of sport. But governments can determine whether or not we have these experiences. They can destroy our lives by unemployment or end them by war. We thus cannot afford to give ourselves over completely to private life. Political judgements are demanded of us. Academic study encourages the calm evaluation of evidence as an aid to political judgement. But calm evaluation is only some help, for in politics our conclusions about action also involve moral choices and the attempt to make sense of the uncertain past and to guess an unknown future. In the end, no matter how careful our examination of the evidence, we will always have to take a leap into the dark. The future of the British state is enveloped in such darkness.

Recommended Reading

Chapter 1 The Changing Social Structure

The social origins of industrialism are traced in Perkin (1969). Hobsbawm (1969) remains a brief and information-packed account of the rise and fall of the industrial economy. Pollard (1983) is an encyclopaedic survey of twentieth-century changes in economic structure. Thompson, P. (1975) summarises the state of social inequality at the start of the century. Westergaard and Resler (1976) present a commited and fact-packed review of the development of social inequality. Halsey (1981) is more discursive but is strong on changing ideas. Reports of the Royal Commission on the Distribution of Income and Wealth (1979–80) are vital on changes in income, wealth and occupational structure. Routh (1980) is a standing study of the changing workforce. Goldthorpe *et al.* (1980) report the latest evidence on social mobility; Heath (1981) does the same job more briefly and sets the data in the context of the literature on social mobility. Noble (1981) contains a vast range of evidence on the social structure.

Anyone beginning the study of British Society should spend some hours browsing through two invaluable official publications which are published annually by Her Majesty's Stationery Office: *Social Trends* and *Regional Trends*.

Chapter 2: Political Culture and Political Instability

The great literary versions of the political culture can be read in Bagehot (1867, 1964) and Orwell (1941, and widely reprinted). Almond and Verba (1963, paperback 1965), though widely criticised, remains a classic study. Almond and Verba (eds) (1980) is a valuable reconsideration of the original argument and contains, in Kavanagh's paper, a careful examination of evidence about the changing culture. Kavanagh's original (1971) demolition of the deference thesis is still well worth reading. Hart (1978) is both a report on comparative US/UK research, and a useful discussion of a wide range of evidence on trust in government. Barnes and Kaase (1979) is valuable for linking the debate about change to the post-affluence model. Beer (1982) is the outstanding statement of the 'populist' model. and is a mine of information about the 1960s and 1970s. Anderson (1964) is in many ways still the best statement of a Gramscian 'hegemonic' model; Leys (1983) offers a similar view.

The large literature on Northern Ireland has produced two outstanding studies: Rose (1971) and Moxon-Browne (1983). Rose unites survey data and historical evidence in a striking way; Moxon-Browne traces the evolution of public attitudes, often using Rose's findings as a framework. For the beginner on Northern Ireland, Arthur (1980) is an excellently compressed survey of history and institutions; Norton's summary of recent events (1984) will supplement Arthur on more recent developments. Rowthorn (1981) examines the economic background to, and the economic consequences of, the Irish crisis.

Chapter 3: Elections and Electors

For the beginner, Harrop (1982) provides a brief and readable summary of recent changes. For a deeper understanding three works are essential: Butler and Stokes (1974) and Särlvik and Crewe (1983) which report the most important survey data on voting structure over nearly two decades and Heath *et al.*, (1985), who survey voting in the 1980s. Crewe (1982) brings out the particular implications of electoral change for Labour. Finer (1980) is a synthesis of a wide range of material. Pulzer (1967, 2nd edn, 1975), though now a little dated, for exactly that reason gives a good picture of the 'class' model of voting. Miller (1981) is detailed on Scottish nationalism; Balsom *et al.* (1983) are authoritative on Plaid Cymru. Curtice and Steed (1982) is an outstanding paper on both the workings of the electoral system and on territorial divisions in the electorate. Bogdanor (1981) is unusual in adding historical constitutional depth to a discussion of the working of the electoral system. Dunleavy (1979 and 1980a, b and c) and Dunleavy and Husbands (1985) are the best surveys of more unorthodox approaches to understanding voting behaviour.

Chapter 4: The Political Parties

McKenzie (1963), though now out of date, is the classic work on British parties and is still invaluable on historical development. Finer (1980) covers some of the modern ground more briefly and more polemically. The best general study of the Conservative Party is Gamble (1974), it is especially strong on history and ideology. Harris (1972) is the most original study of Conservative ideology, but is not easy reading. Beer (1969) has excellent chapters on the intellectual history of the Party. Norton and Aughey (1981) are especially good on party organisation. Layton-Henry (1980) is an uneven collection, but has good chapters on electoral support, factions, front-bench organisation and the social composition of leaders. Studies of the Thatcher years are as yet stronger on narrative than analysis. The collection edited by Hall and Jacques (1983) is highly polemical but contains

Gamble's excellent analysis. Leach's (1983) short paper is the best existing review of the debate about 'Thatcherism'.

Three works dominate the vast literature on the Labour Party: the historical chapters in McKenzie (1963) Howell's analytic history (1980), and Minkin's analysis of the Party Conference (1980), which is much wider in its illuminations than its title suggests. The best starting-point for the beginner is probably the collection edited by Kavanagh (1982). Miliband (2nd edn, 1973) is the outstanding example of a critical history of the Party's commitment to parliamentary institutions. Coates (1980) both applies and adapts Miliband's insights to Labour's most recent experience of office. Whiteley (1983) has good material on Labour's recent institutional and ideological problems. Forrester (1976) is still an excellent guide to the debate about Labour and the working class.

There exists no satisfactory book-length work on the Liberal Party and its Byzantine internal politics. Cyr (1977) still remains a useful introduction. Bogdanor (1983) has edited a more recent collection, in which Kavanagh's paper is the most illuminating. The best starting-point is historical, through Wilson (1968), and the best brief entry into the modern party is Steed's chapter in the collection edited by Drucker (1979). Bradley (1981) describes the origins of the Social Democrats. Haseler (1969), though published long before the formation of the new party, is illuminating on the strands in the Labour Party which helped create the SDP. Döring (1983) briefly and usefully sketches the social composition of SDP activists and compares them with those in other parties.

Drucker's collection (1979) is still a useful guide to minority parties. Miller (1981) is strong on the SNP. Nairn (1981) is required reading for any study of nationalism. Newton (1969) is the standard study of the sociology of British Communism. Husbands (1984) should be read on Fascism. Benewick (1969), a study of Fascism in the 1930s, provides an interesting point of comparison.

Chapter 5: Pressure Group Politics

Marsh's collection (1983) contains case studies of a wide range of both functional and preference groups. The general historical development of groups is sketched by Wooton (1975) in his introduction to a collection of historical documents. There is no single study of business as a whole in Britain, but there is a survey article by Marsh and Locksley in Marsh (1983), which connects the material to Lindblom (1977). Grant and Marsh (1977) is the standard study of the Confederation of British Industry. King's collection (1983) contains more up-to-date papers on the CBI, on the City of London and on business at local level. Saunders (1980) contains vivid material about business in one local community.

There is a large literature on the general place of unions in the political and social system, but surprisingly little in detail on their lobbying activities. This means that May (1975), though now dated, is still valuable for its description of institutional arrangements, while Martin (1980) is authoritative on the TUC. Taylor (1980) is a survey of the union world by a well-informed journalist. Finer (1973) and Brittan (1975) are provocative arguments that the powers of unions are destructively great. Literature cited above on the Labour Party (notably Howell, and Minkin) is rich in detail on unions. Material on professions in interest representation is scattered. Dunleavy (1980a) has some sections which are a beginning. Wilding (1982) examines professions and social welfare policy. Johnson (1972) is the outstanding introduction to professionalism. Medicine is the most widely studied example of professional representation: Eckstein (1960) is a study of the British Medical Association and an early classic in the pressure group literature; it should be read alongside Jones's paper in Marsh (1983).

Byrne and Lovenduski (1983) examine the newer movements. The literature on preference groups is thin, and many studies of the pure pressure groups are now dated. The powerful pro-abortion and pro-contraception lobbies are the best documented: see in particular Marsh and Chambers (1981), and Pym (1974) which deals with a wide range of so-called 'moral' groups.

On the general debate about the character of pressure group politics, Middlemas (1979) is highly original, but perhaps a bit elusive for the beginner. Cawson (1982) and Richardson and Jordan (1979) are more straightforward.

Chapter 6: Rulers and Representatives

Crewe (1974) and Stanworth and Giddens (1974) are collections containing a wide range of evidence: Crewe's collection is strongest on methodological problems, Stanworth and Giddens's on substantive studies. Guttsman (1963) remains the standard source on the historical evolution of political elites; Mellors (1978) and Johnson (1972) carry the evidence through to the 1970s. Scott (1982) summarises a wide range of historical and sociological data; Heath (1981) sets elite studies in their theoretical context. Aberach *et al* (1981) contain evidence on British elite attitudes, compared with those in some other Western democracies. Heclo and Wildavsky (1981) though couched as a study of public expenditure politics can also be read as a study of the political culture of the elite in Whitehall. Hewitt (1974) tries to test the applicability of elitist models to Britain and finds them wanting. Leys (1983) is a 'ruling class' interpretation. Parry (1969) is the standard study of elite theory; Lukes (1974) carries the debate forward.

Chapter 7: The Decline of the British State?

Two interpretations of decline stand out: Gamble (1981) and Nairn (1981). Works cited earlier – Beer (1982) and Middlemas (1979) – can also be read on this theme. Rose (1982) and Birch (1977) are both illuminating on territory, as is Sharpe's paper (1982). King (1976) and Rose and Peters (1978) are the standard texts in a large literature on 'ungovernability'. In the polemical literature on decline and its causes, Barnett (1972) and Pollard (1982) stand out. Coates (1980) is a chronicle and an interpretation of the shift in policy which heralded the New Economic Order. The literature on 'Thatcherism' cited in reading for Chapter 4 – especially Leach (1983) and Hall and Jacques (1983) – is also relevant. Hood and Wright (1981) contains studies of the impact on government of the end of the welfare democratic consensus.

References

Official Publications

Atkinson, Sir A., *Selection of Fast Stream Graduate Entrants to the Home Civil Service* (London: Management and Personnel Office, 1983).

Black, Sir D., *Inequalities in Health* (London: DHSS, 1980).

Central Statistical Office, *Regional Trends 1983* (London: HMSO, 1983).

Central Statistical Office, *Regional Trends 1984* (London: HMSO, 1984a).

Central Statistical Office, *Monthly Digest of Statistics* (London: HMSO, February, 1984b).

Central Statistical Office, *Social Trends 1984* (London: HMSO, 1984c).

Central Statistical Office, *Annual Abstract of Statistics* (London: HMSO, 1988a).

Central Statistical Office, *Regional Trends 1988* (London: HMSO, 1988b).

Central Statistical Office, *Social Trends 1988* (London: HMSO, 1988c).

Civil Service Commission, *Annual Reports* (Basingstoke: Civil Service Commission, 1981–3).

Electoral Register Working Party, *Report* (London: HMSO, 1978).

Houghton, D. (Chairman): *Report of the Committee on Financial Aid to Political Parties*, Cmnd 6601 (London: HMSO, 1976).

House of Commons, Expenditure Committee, *Eleventh Report: the Civil Service* (HC. 535-I, 1976–77).

Office of Population Censuses and Surveys, *Labour Force Survey 1981* (London: HMSO, 1982).

Office of Population Censuses and Surveys, *1980 Mortality Statistics perinatal and infant: social and biological factors* (London: HMSO, 1983).

Royal Commission on the Distribution of Income and Wealth, *Report No. 7*, Cmnd 7595 (London: HMSO, 1979–80).

Royal Commission on the Distribution of Income and Wealth, *Report No. 8*, Cmnd 7679 (London: HMSO, 1979–80).

Other Sources

Aberach, J., Putnam, R., Rockman, B., *Bureaucrats and Politicians in Western Democracies* (Cambridge, Mass.: Harvard University Press, 1981).

Abrams, M., Rose, R., Hinden, R., *Must Labour Lose?* (Harmondsworth: Penguin, 1960).
Alexander, K. and Hobbs, A., 'What Influences Labour M.P.'s?', in Rose, R., (ed.), *Studies in British Politics* (London: Macmillan, 1966) pp. 110–21.
Almond, G. and Verba, S., *The Civic Culture* (Princeton: Princeton University Press, 1963; paperback, Boston: Little Brown, 1965).
Almond, G. and Verba, S. (eds), *The Civic Culture Revisited* (Boston: Little Brown, 1980).
Anderson, P., 'Origins of the Present Crisis', *New Left Review* (1964) pp. 26–53.
Arthur, P., *Government and Politics of Northern Ireland* (London: Longman, 1980).
Atkinson, A. B., *Unequal Shares* (Harmondsworth: Penquin 1974).
Atkinson, A. B. and Harrison, A. J., *Distribution of Personal Wealth in Britain* (Cambridge: Cambridge University Press, 1978).
Attlee, C., *The Labour Party in Perspective* (London: Gollancz, 1937).
Bagehot, W., *The English Constitution* (London: Watts, 1964, original publication 1867).
Balsom, D., Madgwick, P., Van Mechelen, D., 'The Red and the Green: Patterns of Partisan Choice in Wales', *British Journal of Political Science* (1983) pp. 299–325.
Barker, A. (ed.), *Quangos in Britain* (London: Macmillan, 1982).
Barnes, S. and Kaase, M. (eds), *Political Action: Mass Participation in Five Western Democracies* (London: Sage, 1979).
Barnett, C., *The Collapse of British Power* (London: Eyre Methuen, 1972).
Beer, S., *Modern British Politics* (London: Faber, 1969).
Beer, S., *Britain Against Itself* (London: Faber, 1982).
Beer, S. and Ulam, A., *Patterns of Government* (New York: Random House, 1962).
Benewick, R., *Political Violence and Public Order* (London: Allen Lane, 1969).
Birch, A. H., *Political Integration and Disintegration in the British Isles* (London: Allen & Unwin, 1977).
Blank, S., 'Britain: the Politics of Foreign Economic Policy, the Domestic Economy, and the Problems of Pluralistic Stagnation', in Katzenstein, P. (ed.), *Between Power and Plenty* (Wisconsin: University of Wisconsin Press, 1979).
Blewett, N., 'The Franchise in the United Kingdom, 1885–1918', *Past and Present* (1965) pp. 27–56.
Blondel, J., *Voters, Parties and Leaders: The Social Fabric of British Politics* (Harmondsworth: Penguin, 1963).
Blumler, J. and McQuail, D., *Television in Politics: its Uses and Influence* (London: Faber, 1968).
Bogdanor, V., *The People and the Party System* (Cambridge: Cambridge University Press, 1981).
Bogdanor, V. (ed.), *Liberal Party Politics* (Oxford: Clarendon Press, 1983).
Borthwick, R. L. and Spence, J. E. (eds), *British Politics in Perspective* (Leicester: Leicester University Press, 1984).

Boyd, D., *Elites and their Education* (Windsor: NFER, 1973).

Bradley, I., *Breaking the Mould* (Oxford: Martin Robertson, 1981).

Briggs, A., *The Age of Improvement* (London: Longman, 1960).

Brittan, S., 'The Economic Contradictions of Democracy', *British Journal of Political Science* (1975) pp. 129–59.

Budge, I. and O'Leary, C., *Belfast: Approach to Crisis* (London: Macmillan, 1973).

Burch, M., 'Mrs Thatcher's Approach to Leadership in Government: 1979–June 1983', *Parliamentary Affairs* (1983) pp. 399–416.

Burch, M. and Moran, M., 'The Changing British Parliamentary Elite', *Parliamentary Affairs* (1985) pp. 1–15.

Burch, M. and Wood, B., *Public Policy in Britain* (Oxford: Martin Robertson, 1983).

Butler, D. and Stokes, D., *Political Change in Britain*, 2nd edn (London: Macmillan, 1974).

Butler, D. and Kavanagh, D., *The British General Election of 1979* (London: Macmillan, 1980).

Butler, D. and Kavanagh, D., *The British General Election of 1987* (London: Macmillan, 1988).

Butler, D. and Sloman, A., *British Political Facts 1900–1979* (London: Macmillan, 1980).

Butler, D. and Pinto-Duschinsky, M., 'The Conservative Elite 1918–78: Does Unrepresentativeness Matter?', in Layton-Henry, Z. (ed.), *Conservative Party Politics* (London: Macmillan, 1980).

Butt, R., *The Power of Parliament* (London: Constable, 1967).

Byrne, P. and Lovenduski, J., 'Two New Protest Groups: The Peace and Women's Movements', in Drucker, H., Dunleavy, P., Gamble, A., Peele, G. (eds), *Developments in British Politics* (London: Macmillan, 1983).

Cawson, A., *Corporation and Welfare: Social Policy and State Intervention in Britain* (London: Heinemann, 1982).

Churchill, R., *The Fight for the Tory Leadership* (London: Heinemann, 1964).

Coates, D., *Labour in Power?* (London: Longman, 1980).

Cocks, Sir B. (ed), *Erskine May's Treatise on the Law, Privileges, Proceedings and Usage of Parliament*, 18th edn (London: Butterworth, 1971).

Cook, C. and Stevenson, J., *The Longman Handbook of Modern British History 1714–1980* (London: Longman, 1983).

Cotgrove, S., *Catastrophe or Cornucopia: The Environment, Politics and the Future* (Chichester: Wiley, 1982).

Crewe, I. (ed.), *British Political Sociology Yearbook, Volume I: Elites in Western Democracy* (London: Croom Helm, 1974).

Crewe, I., 'The Labour Party and the Electorate', in Kavanagh, D. (ed.), *The Politics of the Labour Party* (London: Allen & Unwin, 1982) pp. 9–49.

Crewe, I., 'The Disturbing Truth Behind Labour's Rout'; *and* 'How Labour Was Trounced All Round', *Guardian* (13/14 June 1983a).

Crewe, I., 'Representation and the Ethnic Minorities', in Glazer, N. and Young, K. (eds), *Ethnic Pluralism and Public Policy* (London: Heinemann, 1983b).

Crewe, I., 'On the death and resurrection of class voting: some comments on How Britain Votes', *Political Studies* (1986) pp. 620–38.

Crewe, I., 'A new class of politics', *Guardian* (15 June 1987).

Crewe, I., Fox, T., Alt, J., 'Non-Voting in British General Elections 1966–October 1974', in Crouch, C. (ed.), *British Political Sociology Yearbook* (London: Croom Helm, 1977) pp. 38–109.

Crouch, C., *Class Conflict and the Industrial Relations Crisis* (London: Heinemann, 1977).

Crouch, C., 'The Peculiar Relationship: the Party and the Unions', in Kavanagh, D. (ed.), *The Politics of the Labour Party* (London: Allen & Unwin, 1982) pp. 171–90.

Curtice, J. and Steed, M., 'Electoral Choice and the Production of Government: The Changing Operation of the Electoral System in the United Kingdom since 1955', *British Journal of Political Science* (1982) pp. 249–98.

Curtice, J. and Steed, M. 'Proportionality and Exaggeration in the British Electoral System', *Electoral Studies* (1986) pp. 209–28.

Cyr, A., *Liberal Party Politics in Britain* (London: Calder, 1977).

Dangerfield, G., *The Strange Death of Liberal England* (London: MacGibbon & Kee, 1966).

Daniel, W. W., *The PEP Survey on Inflation* (London: PEP, 1975).

Dearlove, J., *The Politics of Policy in Local Government* (London: Cambridge University Press, 1973).

Devlin, L. J., *Report of the Commission of Inquiry into Industrial and Commercial Representation* (London: ABCC/CBI, 1972).

Döring, H., 'Who are the Social Democrats?', *New Society,* 8 September (1983) pp. 351–2.

Dowse, R. and Hughes, J., 'Sporadic Interventionists', *Political Studies,* (1977) pp. 84–92.

Drucker, H. M. (ed.), *Multi-Party Britain* (London: Macmillan, 1979).

Dudley, G., 'The Road Lobby: A Declining Force', in Marsh, D. (ed.), *Pressure Politics: Interest Groups in Britain* (London: Junction Books, 1983) pp. 104–28.

Dunleavy, P., 'The Urban Basis of Political Alignment', *British Journal of Political Science* (1979) pp. 409–43.

Dunleavy, P., *Urban Political Analysis* (London: Macmillan, 1980a).

Dunleavy, P., 'The Political Implications of Sectoral Clevage and The Growth of State Employment: Part I, The Analysis of Production Cleavages', *Political Studies* (1980b) pp. 364–83.

Dunleavy, P., 'The Political Implications of Sectoral Cleavages and the Growth of State Employment, Part 2: Cleavage Structures and Political Alignment', *Political Studies* (1980c) pp. 527–49.

Dunleavy, P., *The Politics of Mass Housing 1945–75* (Oxford: Clarendon Press, 1981).

Dunleavy, P., 'Fleet Street: its bite on the ballot', *New Socialist* (January 1985) pp. 24–6.

Dunleavy, P., and Husbands, C., *British Democracy at the Crossroads: Voting and Party Competition in the 1980s* (London: Allen and Unwin 1985)

References   215

Dunleavy, P., and O'Leary, B., *Theories of the State* (Basingstoke: Macmillan, 1987).
Dyson, K. and Wilks, S. (eds), *Industrial Crisis: A Comparative Study of the State and Industry* (Oxford: Martin Robertson, 1983).
Eckstein, H., *Pressure Group Politics: The Case of the British Medical Association* (London: Allen & Unwin, 1960).
Finer, S. E., 'The Political Power of Organised Labour', *Government and Opposition* (1973) pp. 391–406.
Finer, S. E. (ed.), *Adversary Politics* (London: Wigram, 1975).
Finer, S. E., *The Changing British Party System 1945–1979* (Washington: American Enterprise Institute, 1980).
Forrester, T., *The Labour Party and the Working Class* (London: Heinemann, 1976).
Foster, J., *Class Struggle and the Industrial Revolution* (London: Methuen, 1979).
Gamble, A., *The Conservative Nation* (London: Routledge, 1974).
Gamble, A., *Britain in Decline* (London: Macmillan, 1981).
Gamble, A., 'Thatcherism and Conservative Politics', in Hall, S. and Jacques, M. (eds), *The Politics of Thatcherism* (London: Lawrence & Wishart, 1983a) pp. 109–31.
Gamble, A., 'Liberals and the Economy', in Bogdanor, V. (ed.), *Liberal Party Politics* (Oxford: Clarendon Press, 1983b) pp. 191–216.
Gilmour, I., *Inside Right: A study of Conservatism* (London: Hutchinson, 1977).
Glasgow University Media Group, *Bad News* (London: Routledge, 1976).
Glasgow University Media Group, *More Bad News* (London: Routledge, 1980).
Glass, D. V., (ed.), *Social Mobility in Britain* (London: Routledge & Kegan Paul, 1954).
Goldthorpe, J. H., Lockwood, D., Bechofer, F. and Platt, J., *The Affluent Worker: Political Attitudes and Behaviour* (Cambridge: Cambridge University Press, 1968).
Goldthorpe, J. H. *et al., Social Mobility and Class Structure in Modern Britain* (Oxford: Clarendon Press, 1980).
Goldthorpe, J., and Payne, C., 'Trends in intergenerational class mobility in England and Wales, 1972–83' *Sociology* (1986) pp. 1–24.
Gough, I., *The Political Economy of The Welfare State* (London: Macmillan, 1979).
Gramsci, A., *The Modern Prince and other writings* (New York: International Publishers, 1972).
Grant, W., 'The Government Relations Function in Large Firms Based in the United Kingdom: A Preliminary Study', *British Journal of Political Science* (1982) pp. 513–16.
Grant, W., 'Representing Capital', in King, R. (ed.), *Capital and Politics* (London; Routledge, 1983), pp. 69–84.
Grant, W., 'The Role And Power of Pressure Groups', in Borthwick, R. L. and Spence, J. E. (eds), *British Politics in Perspective* (Leicester: Leicester University Press, 1984) pp. 133–44.

Grant, W. and Marsh, D., 'The Representation of Retail Interests in Britain', *Political Studies* (1974) pp. 168–177.

Grant, W. and Marsh, D., *The Confederation of British Industry* (London: Hodder & Stoughton, 1977).

Griffith, J. A. G., *The Politics of the Judiciary* (London: Fontana, 1977).

Guttsman, W. L., *The British Political Elite* (London: MacGibbon & Kee, 1963).

Gyford, J., *The New Urban Left: Origins, Style and Strategy* (London: Town Planning Discussion Paper, No. 38, University College, 1983).

Hall, S. and Jacques, M. (eds), *The Politics of Thatcherism* (London: Lawrence & Wishart, 1983).

Halsey, A. H., *Change in British Society* (Oxford: Oxford University Press, 1981).

Harris, N., *Competition and the Corporate Society: British Conservatives, the State and Industry 1945–1964* (London: Methuen, 1972).

Harrop, M., England, J. and Husbands, C., 'The Bases of National Front Support', *Political Studies* (1980) pp. 271–83.

Harrop, M., 'The Changing British Electorate', *Political Quarterly* (1982) pp. 385–402.

Hart, V., *Distrust and Democracy* (Cambridge: Cambridge University Press, 1978).

Haseler, S., *The Gaitskellites* (London: Macmillan, 1969).

Haxey, S., *Tory M.P.* (London: Gollancz, 1942).

Heath, A., *Social Mobility* (London: Fontana, 1981).

Heath, A., Jowell, R. and Curtice, J., *How Britain Votes* (Oxford: Pergamon, 1985).

Heath, A., Jowell, R. and Curtice, J., 'Trendless fluctuation: a reply to Crewe', *Political Studies* (1987) pp. 256–77.

Heclo, H. and Wildavsky, A., *The Private Government of Public Money*, 2nd edn (London: Macmillan, 1981).

Hewitt, C., 'Policy-Making in Postwar Britain: a Nation-Level Test of Elitist and Pluralist Hypotheses', *British Journal of Political Science* (1974) pp. 187–216.

Hewitt, C., 'Catholic Grievances, Catholic Nationalism and Violence in Northern Ireland During the Civil Rights Period: A Reconsideration', *British Journal of Sociology* (1981) pp. 362–80.

Hills, J., 'Britain', in Lovenduski, J. and Hills J. (eds), *The Politics of the Second Electorate: Women and Public Participation* (London: Routledge, 1981) pp. 8–32.

Hindess, B., *The Decline of Working-Class Politics* (London: Paladin, 1971).

Hobsbawm, E. J., *Industry and Empire* (Harmondsworth: Penquin: 1969).

Hollis, P. (ed.), *Pressure From Without* (London: Edward Arnold, 1974).

Hood, C. and Wright, M. (eds), *Big Government in Hard Times* (Oxford: Martin Robertson, 1981).

Howell, D., *British Social Democracy* (London: Croom Helm, 1980).

Husbands, C., *Racial Exclusiveness and the City: the Urban Support of the National Front* (London: Allen & Unwin, 1984).

Inglehart, R., *The Silent Revolution: Changing Values and Political Styles Among Western Publics* (Princeton: Princeton University Press, 1977).

Jay, P., *Inflation, Employment and Politics* (London: IEA, 1976).

Jessop, R. D., 'Civility and Traditionalism in English Political Culture', *British Journal of Political Science* (1971) pp. 1–24.

Johnson, R. W., 'The British Political Elite, 1955–72', *European Journal of Sociology* (1973) pp. 35–77.

Johnson, T., *Professions and Power* (London: Macmillan, 1972).

Jones, P., 'The British Medical Association: Public Good or Private Interest?', in Marsh, D. (ed.), *Pressure Politics: Interest Groups in Britain* (London: Junction Books, 1983) pp. 83–103.

Joyce, P., *Work, Society and Politics: The Culture of the Factory in Later Victorian England* (Brighton: Harvester, 1980).

Kavanagh, D., 'The Deferential English: A Comparative Critique', *Goverment and Opposition* (1971) pp. 333–66.

Kavanagh, D., 'Political Culture in Great Britain: The Decline of the Civic Culture', in Almond, G. and Verba, S. (eds), *The Civic Culture Revisited* (Boston: Little Brown, 1980).

Kavanagh, D. (ed.), *The Politics of the Labour Party* (London: Allen & Unwin, 1982).

Kavanagh, D., 'Organisation and Power in the Liberal Party', in Bogdanor, V. (ed.), *Liberal Party Politics* (Oxford: Clarendon Press, 1983).

Kelsall, R. K., 'Recruitment to the Higher Civil Service: How Has the Pattern Changed?', in Stanworth, P. and Giddens, A. (eds), *Elites and Power in British Society* (Cambridge: Cambridge University Press, 1974) pp. 170–84.

King, A. (ed.), *Why is Britain Becoming Harder to Govern?* (London: British Broadcasting Corporation, 1976).

King, R. (ed.), *Capital and Politics* (London: Routledge, 1983).

King, R. and Raynor, J., *The Middle Class* (London: Longman, 1981).

Klapper, J., *The Effects of Mass Communication* (New York: Free Press, 1960).

Layton-Henry, Z. (ed.), *Conservative Party Politics* (London: Macmillan, 1980).

Leach, R., 'Thatcherism, Liberalism, and Tory Collectivism', *Politics 3* (1983) pp. 9–14.

Lee, J. M., *Social Leaders and Public Persons* (Oxford: Clarendon Press, 1963).

Le Grand, J., *The Strategy of Equality: Redistribution and the Social Services* (London: Allen & Unwin, 1982).

Leys, C., *Politics in Britain* (London: Heinemann, 1983).

Lindblom, C., *Politics and Markets* (New York: Basic Books, 1977).

Lukes, S., *Power: A Radical View* (London: Macmillan, 1974).

Marsh, A., *Protest and Political Consciousness* (London: Sage, 1977).

Marsh, D., 'Political Socialisation: the Implicit Assumptions Questioned', *British Journal of Political Science* (1971) pp. 354–65.

Marsh, D. (ed.), *Pressure Politics: Interest Groups in Britain* (London: Junction Books, 1983).

Marsh, D. and Chambers, J., *Abortion Politics* (London: Junction Books, 1981).

Marsh, D. and Locksley, G., 'Labour: The Dominant Force in British Politics?', in Marsh, D. (ed.) (1983).

Marshall, T. H., *Sociology at the Crossroads* (London: Heinemann, 1963).

Martin, R. M., *TUC: The Growth of a Pressure Group 1868–1976* (Oxford: Clarendon Press, 1980).

Martin, R. M., 'Pluralism and the New Corporatism', *Political Studies* (1983) pp. 86–102.

Mathias, P., *The First Industrial Nation: An Economic History of Britain 1700–1914* (London: Methuen, 1969).

May, T., *Trade Unions and Pressure Group Politics* (Farnborough: Saxon House, 1975).

McKenzie, R. T., *British Political Parties*, 2nd edn (London: Heinemann, 1963).

McKenzie, R. T. and Silver, A., *Angels in Marble* (London: Heinemann, 1968).

McMahon, P., 'The sale of local authority houses in Britain', *Geography* (1987) pp. 169–71.

McQuail, D. *et al.*, 'Elite Education and Political Values', *Political Studies* (1968) pp. 257–66.

Middlemas, K., *Politics in Industrial Society: The Experience of the British System Since 1911* (London: André Deutsch, 1979).

Miles, R. and Phizacklea, A., 'Class, Race, Ethnicity And Political Action', *Political Studies* (1977) pp. 491–507.

Miliband, R., *Parliamentary Socialism*, 2nd edn (London: Merlin, 1973).

Miller, W. L., *The End of British Politics? Scots and English Political Behaviour in the Seventies* (Oxford: Clarendon Press, 1981).

Mellors, C., *The British MP: A Socio-economic Study of the House of Commons* (Farnborough: Saxon House, 1978).

Minkin, L., *The Labour Party Conference: A Study in the Politics of Intra-Party Democracy* (Manchester: Manchester University Press, 1980).

Minns, R., *Pension Funds and British Capitalism* (London: Heinemann, 1980).

Moore, B., *Social Origins of Dictatorship and Democracy* (Harmondsworth: Penguin, 1969).

Moran, M., 'Finance Capital and Pressure-Group Politics in Britain', *British Journal of Political Science* (1981) pp. 381–404.

Morrison, H., *Government and Parliament: A Survey From the Inside* (London: Oxford University Press, 1954).

Moxon-Browne, E., *Nation, Class and Creed in Northern Ireland* (Aldershot: Gower, 1983).

Nairn, T., *The Break-Up of Britain*, 2nd edn (London: Verso, 1981).

Newton, K., *The Sociology of British Communism* (London: Allen Lane, 1969).

Newton, K., *Second City Politics* (Oxford: Clarendon Press, 1976).

Noble, T., *Modern Britain: Structure and Change* (London: Batsford, 1975).

Noble, T., *Structure and Change in Modern Britain* (London: Batsford, 1981).

Norton, P., *The British Polity* (London: Longman, 1984).

Norton, P. and Aughey, A., *Conservatives and Conservatism* (London: Temple Smith, 1981).

O'Connor, J., *The Fiscal Crisis of the State* (New York: St Martin's Press, 1973).

O'Hearn, D., 'Catholic Grievances, Catholic Nationalism: A Comment', *British Journal of Sociology* (1983) pp. 438–45.

Orwell, G., *The Lion and the Unicorn: Socialism and the English Genius* (London: Secker & Warburg, 1941).

Owen, D., *Face the Future* (Oxford: Oxford University Press, 1981).

Pahl, R. and Winkler, J., 'The Coming Corporatism', *New Society*, 10 October (1974) pp. 13–15.

Panitch, L., 'Recent Theorisations of Corporatism: Reflections on a Growth Industry', *British Journal of Sociology* (1980) pp. 161–87.

Parkin, F., 'Working-Class Conservatives: A Theory of Political Deviance', *British Journal of Sociology* (1967) pp. 278–90.

Parry, G., *Political Elites* (London: Allen & Unwin, 1969).

Peacock, A. T. and Wiseman, J., *The Growth of Public Expenditure in the United Kingdom*, 2nd edn (London: Allen & Unwin, 1967).

Pelling, H., *Social Geography of British Elections 1885–1910* (London: Macmillan, 1967).

Perkin, H., *The Origins of Modern English Society 1780–1880* (London: Routledge & Kegan Paul, 1969).

Pinto-Duschinsky, M., 'Central Office and Power in the Conservative Party', *Political Studies* (1972) pp. 1–16.

Pinto-Duschinsky, M., *British Political Finance 1830–1980* (Washington: American Enterprise Institute, 1981).

Pinto-Duschinsky, M., 'Why Big Money is a Mixed Blessing', *The Times*, 26 February (1982).

Pollard, S., *The Wasting of the British Economy* (London: Croom Helm, 1982).

Pollard, S., *The Development of the British Economy, 1914–80* (London: Edward Arnold, 1983).

Pulzer, P., *Political Representation and Elections in Britain* (London: Allen & Unwin, 1967; 2nd edn 1975).

Pym, B., *Pressure Groups and the Permissive Society* (Newton Abbott: David & Charles, 1974).

Rasmussen, J., 'David Steel's Liberals: Too Old to Cry, Too Hurt to Laugh', in Penniman, H. (ed.), *Britain at the Polls 1979* (London: American Enterprise Institute, 1981) pp. 159–76.

Reid, I., *Social Class Differences in Britain*, 2nd edn (London: Grant McIntyre, 1981).

Rex, J. and Moore, R., *Race, Community and Conflict* (London: Oxford University Press, 1967).

Richardson, J. and Jordan, A. G., *Governing Under Pressure* (Oxford: Martin Robertson, 1979).

Roberts, K., Cook, F. G., Clark, S. C., Semeonoff, E., *The Fragmentary Class Structure* (London: Heinemann, 1977).

Robertson, D., 'Judicial Ideology in the House of Lords: A Jurimetric Analysis', *British Journal of Political Science* (1982) pp. 1–25.

Rose, R., 'The Political Ideas of English Party Activists', *American Political Science Review* (1962) pp. 360–71.

Rose, R., 'Parties, Factions and Tendencies in Britain', *Political Studies* (1964) pp. 33–46.

Rose, R., *Governing Without Consensus: An Irish Perspective* (London: Faber, 1971).

Rose, R., *Understanding the United Kingdom: The Territorial Dimension in Government* (London: Longman, 1982).

Rose, R. and Peters, B. G., *Can Government Go Bankrupt?* (New York: Basic Books, 1978).

Roth, A., *The MP's Chart* (London: Parliamentary Profiles, 1979).

Routh, G., *Occupation and Pay in Great Britain 1906–79* (London: Macmillan, 1980).

Rowthorn, B., 'Northern Ireland: An Economy in Crisis', *Cambridge Journal of Economics* (1981) pp. 1–31.

Rubinstein, W. D., 'Men of Property: Some Aspects of Occupation, Inheritance, and Power Among Top British Wealthholders', in Stanworth, P. and Giddens, A. (eds). *Elites and Power in British Society* (Cambridge: Cambridge University Press, 1974).

Runciman, W. G., *Relative Deprivation and Social Justice* (Harmondsworth: Penguin, 1966).

Sampson, A., *The Changing Anatomy of Britain* (London: Coronet, 1983).

Särlvik, B. and Crewe, I., *Decade of Dealignment: The Conservative Victory of 1979 and Electoral Trends in the 1970s* (Cambridge University Press, 1983).

Saunders, P., *Urban Politics: A Sociological Interpretation* (Harmondsworth: Penguin, 1980).

Schmitter, P., 'Still the Century of Corporatism?', in Schmitter, P. and Lehmbruch, G. (eds) *Trends Toward Corporatist Intermediation* (London: Sage, 1979) pp. 7–52.

Scott, J., *The Upper Class: Property and Privilege in Britain* (London: Macmillan, 1982).

Seyd, P., 'Factionalism in the 1970s', in Layton-Henry, Z. (ed.), *Conservative Party Politics* (London: Macmillan, 1980) pp. 231–43.

Seyd, P. and Minkin, L., 'The Labour Party and its Members', *New Society*, 20th September (1979).

Sharpe, L. J., 'The Labour Party and the Geography of Inequality: A Puzzle' in Kavanagh, D. (ed.), *The Politics of the Labour Party* (London: Allen & Unwin, 1982) pp. 135–70.

Shonfield, A., *Modern Capitalism* (Oxford University Press, 1965).

Stanworth, P. and Giddens, A., *Elites and Power in British Society* (Cambridge: Cambridge University Press, 1974).

Steed, M., 'The Liberal Party', in Drucker, H. M. (ed.), *Multi-Party Britain* (London: Macmillan, 1979) pp. 76–106.

Strange, S., *Sterling and British Policy* (Oxford University Press, 1971).

Taylor, R., *The Fifth Estate* (London: Pan, 1980).
Thomas, J. A., *The House of Commons 1906–1911* (Cardiff: University of Wales Press, 1958).
Thompson, E. P., *The Making of the English Working Class* (London: Gollancz, 1963).
Thompson, E. P., *Whigs and Hunters* (London: Allen Lane, 1975).
Thompson, P., *The Edwardians: The Remaking of British Society* (London: Weidenfeld & Nicolson, 1975).
Times Newspapers, *The Times Guide to the House of Commons June 1983* (London: Times Books, 1983).
Turner, M. (ed.), *The Parlour Song Book* (London: Pan Books, 1972).
Ward, H., 'The Anti-Nuclear Lobby: An Unequal Struggle?', in Marsh, D. (ed.), *Pressure Politics: Interest Groups in Britain* (London: Junction Books, 1983) pp. 182–210.
Westergaard, J. and Resler, H., *Class in a Capitalist Society: A Study of Contemporary Britain* (Harmondsworth: Penguin, 1976).
Whiteley, P., 'The Structure of Democratic Socialist Ideology In Britain', *Political Studies* (1978) pp. 209–31.
Whiteley, P., 'The National Front Vote in the 1977 GLC Elections: An Aggregate Data Analysis', *British Journal of Political Science* (1979) pp. 370–81.
Whiteley, P., 'The Decline of Labour's Local Party Membership and Electoral Base, 1945–79', in Kavanagh, D. (ed.), *The Politics of the Labour Party* (London: Allen & Unwin, 1982) pp. 111–34.
Whiteley, P., *The Labour Party In Crisis* (London: Methuen, 1983).
Whitley, R., 'The City and Industry: The Directors of Large Companies, Their Characteristics and Connections', in Stanworth, P. and Giddens, A. (eds), *Elites and Power in British Society* (Cambridge: Cambridge University Press, 1974)
Wiener, M., *English Culture and the Decline of the Industrial Spirit 1850–1980* (Cambridge: Cambridge University Press, 1981).
Wilding P., *Professional Power and Social Welfare* (London: Routledge, 1982).
Williams, P., *Hugh Gaitskell* (London: Jonathan Cape, 1979).
Wilson, C. S. and Lupton, T., 'The Social Background and Connections of "Top Decision-Makers"', *The Manchester School* (1959) pp. 39–51.
Wilson, D., *Power and Party Bureaucracy in Britain* (Farnborough: Saxon House, 1975).
Wilson, M., 'Grass Roots Conservatism: Motions to the Party Conference', in Nugent, N. and King, R. (eds), *The British Right* (Farnborough: Saxon House, 1977) pp. 64–98.
Wilson, T., *The Downfall of the Liberal Party* (London: Fontana, 1968).
Winkler, J., 'Corporatism', *European Journal of Sociology* (1976) pp. 100–36.
Wooton, G., *Pressure Groups in Britain 1720–1970* (London: Allen Lane, 1975).

Index

Aberach, J. 179, 209
Abortion Law Reform
    Association 124
Abrams, M. 69
Advisory, Conciliation and
    Arbitration Service 132
agriculture 2, 5, 8
Alliance *see* Liberal Party, Social
    Democratic Party
Almond, G. 33, 34, 35, 36, 37, 41,
    48, 206
alternative economic strategy
    203–4
ambassadors, recruitment of 165–7
Anderson, P. 206
Anglicanism 6–7, 8, 46, 68, 73, 149
Anti-Nazi League 142
aristocracy 2, 36, 159–60
Arthur, P. 50, 207
Arts Council 139, 148, 197
Atkinson, Sir A. 162
Atkinson, A. B. 18, 19
Attlee, C. 93
Aughey, A. 89, 98, 106, 207

Bagehot, W. 34, 36, 43, 206
Balsom, D. 68, 85, 207
Bank of England 128–9, 174
Barker, A. 139
Barnes, S. 39, 41, 206
Barnett, C. 184, 185, 210
Beer, S. 35, 40, 41, 99, 187, 206,
    207, 209
Benewick, R. 208
Bevin, E. 132, 194

Birch, A. H. 5, 210
Birmingham 2, 43
Black Report 15, 16
Blank, S. 185
Blondel, J. 35
Blumler, J. 47
Bogdanor, V. 207, 208
bombings 33, 41
    see also Northern Ireland,
        political culture, riots
Boyd, D. 165, 166
Bradley, I. 112, 208
Briggs, A. 38
British economy
    concentration in 7–11
    decline of 183–6
    rise of 2–7
British Empire 2–3, 5, 183–4
British Medical Association 136–7
British Roads Federation 127
British state
    decline of 5, 182–3, 193–4
    in international society xiv, 2
    see also nationalism, Northern
        Ireland
Brittan, S. 41, 133, 189, 209
Budge, I. 50
Burch, M. 145, 155, 159
business community
    leaders of 167–9, 171–2
    and pressure group politics 11–
        12, 125–31
    see also Conservative Party
Butler, D. 59, 60, 64, 66, 67, 68,
    69, 75, 78, 80, 106, 155, 207

Butler, R. 89
Butt, R. 125
Byrne, P. 124, 141, 209

Callaghan Government 134
Campaign for Nuclear
    Disarmament 39–40, 124, 141
Catholicism 50–7, 68, 78
Cawson, A. 123, 145, 148, 209
Citrine, W. 132
Chambers, J. 140, 208
charities, as pressure groups 139
churches, as pressure groups 138–9
Churchill, R. 90
Churchill, Sir W. 183, 194
City of London 125, 128–9, 168–9,
    185, 194–5
Civil Service Commission 164, 165
civil service recruitment 161–7
civility 35–8, 45
    see also political culture
Clarendon Schools 152, 162, 165,
    168, 170
class
    consciousness 30, 64–6
    and industrialism 3–4, 7–12
    and inequality 12–26
    theories of 28–32
    and voting 63–9, 72–3, 81–5
closure theory 170
Coates, D. 133, 208, 210
Cocks, Sir B. 178
Communist Party of Great
    Britain 116–7, 203
    see also Marxism
Confederation of British
    Industry 127, 130, 147
    see also business community
Congregationalists 7
consensus 35–8
Conservative Party
    business interests in 3, 118, 156–
    7, 175
    electoral support for 63–76
    factions in 90–1
    historical evolution of 3, 7, 89–
    90
    ideology 97–100, 191–2

leadership and power in 88–92,
    154–7, 159–61
membership of 104–7
Young Conservatives 105, 117
consumption classes 31, 83–4
Cook, C. 27
corporatism 145–9, 176, 186
Cotgrove, S. 143
Crewe, I. 60, 61, 65, 67, 72, 73, 75,
    77, 78, 83, 151, 207, 209
Crouch, C. 107, 186
Curtice, J. 75–6, 81, 207
Cyr, A. 208

Dangerfield, G. 4
Daniel, W. 42
deference 36, 38, 40–4
    see also political culture
Democratic Unionist Party 56
Devlin, L. J. 126, 130
Döring, H. 112, 114, 208
Dowse, R. 122
Drucker, H. 208
Dudley, G. 127
Dunleavy, P. 31, 47, 84, 135,
    137–8, 144, 207, 209
Dyson, K. 193

Eckstein, H. 209
Edwardian Britain 4–7, 12–14
electorate
    composition 60–3
    turnover 76–9
elites
    political culture of 177–80
    power of 175–7
    social composition of 153–69
    study of 150–3
embourgeoisement 67–8
employers associations 126
Engineering Employers
    Federation 12, 126
England
    civil war in 35
    economic development of 4–5
    in British state 184
Establishment the 175

Eton College 35, 152, 155–6, 159–
60, 165, 168–9, 170, 174
European Economic
Community 201

Falklands War 74
Family Planning Association 141
Fascism 35, 36, 117–18, 203
Finer, S. 111, 133, 207, 209
Forrester, T. 109, 208
Foster, J. 48
France 186
Friedman, M. 188

Gamble, A. 100, 113, 184, 195,
207, 209
generals, recruitment of 165–6,
170–1
Germany 10, 183, 184, 193
giant firms 10–11, 125–6
Giddens, A. 157, 168, 209
Gilmour, Sir I. 99
Glasgow Media Group 46
Glass, D. 22, 23
Goldthorpe, J. 23, 29, 44, 69, 206
Gough, I. 21
Gramsci, A. 45–6
Grant, W. 123, 126, 127, 208
Griffith, J. 137
Guttsman, W. 155, 159, 209
Gyford, J. 109

Hall, S. 192, 207
Halsey, A. H. 21, 206
Harris, N. 98, 207
Harrison, A. J. 19
Harrop, M. 73, 117, 207
Hart, V. 43, 206
Heseler, S. 102, 208
Hattersley, R. 160
Haxey, S. 125
Hayek, F. 188
Health and Safety Executive 132
Health Education Council 140
Heath, A. 23, 83, 170, 206, 207,
209
Heath, E. 90, 99–100, 159
Heath Government 134, 187

Heclo, H. 209
hegemonic value system 44–7
Hewitt, C. 53, 177, 209
Hills, J. 67
Hindess, B. 109
Hindus 7
Hobsbawm, E. 2, 206
Hobson, J. A. 5–6
Hollis, P. 140, 141
Home Office 11
homogeneity 35, 37
    see also political culture
Hood, C. 192, 210
Houghton Report 104–5, 108
housing
    changes in tenure 26–7, 192
    classes 31
Howell, D. 208, 209
Hughes, J. 122
Husbands, C. 84, 117, 207, 208

immigrants
    in labour force 25–6
    in society 37
    as voters 62–3, 77
industrialism in Britain
    development 4–5, 24–5, 28
    origins 2–3
    see also British economy
industrial concentration 10
inequality
    attitudes towards 41–2
    of class 12–26, 28–9, 82, 195–6
    of gender 18, 172
    of income 16–18
    of opportunity 22–3, 153–75
    of territory 4–9, 24, 32, 196
Inglehart, R. 39, 43
International Monetary Fund 191
Ireland
    economic development 4–5, 55
    'Irish question' 4, 6, 42–3
    see also Northern Ireland
Irish Republican Army 50–2

Jacques, M. 192, 207, 210
Japan 184, 186, 193, 199
Jay, P. 187

Jenkins, R. 112
Jessop, R. 36
Jews 7, 37, 62
Johnson, R. 157, 170, 209
Johnson, T. 135, 209
Jones, P. 137, 209
Jordan, A. G. 209
Joyce, P. 48
judges, recruitment of 165–6, 170–1

Kaase, M. 39, 41, 206
Kavanagh, D. 38, 41, 48, 108, 111,
    155, 206, 208
Kelsall, R. 162, 163
King, A. 189, 190, 210
King, R. 13, 208
Kinnock, N. 94, 96, 160
Klapper, J. 47

Labour Party
  block vote in 91–3
  candidate selection 95
  electoral support for 63–76
  federal nature of 92–6
  historical evolution of 6, 92–3
  ideology of 101–3
  leadership and power in 92–6,
    157–60
  membership of 107–10
  money in 118–20
law profession, power of 136
Layton-Henry, Z. 207
Le Grand, J. 21
Leach, R. 100, 208, 210
Lee, J. 106
Leys, C. 45, 176, 207, 209
Liberal party
  electoral support for 71, 74, 78,
    80
  history of 6
  ideology of 113–14
  leadership and power in 111–12
  membership of 111–12
  death of 110
Lindblom, C. 123, 130, 208
Lobby, the 177, 179
local government, decline of 10,
    197–8, 202

Locksley, G. 134, 208
Lockwood, D. 44, 69
Lord's Day Observance
    Society 140
Lovenduski, J. 124, 141, 209
Luddites 49
Lukes, S. 180, 209
Lupton, T. 128

McKenzie, R. 44, 69, 89, 207, 208
McQuail, D. 47
McMahon, P. 27
Macmillan, H. 89
Manchester 2
Marsh, A. 39
Marsh, D. 48, 127, 134, 140, 208,
    209
Marshall, T. 21
Martin, R. 147, 209
Marxism 21, 36, 44–7, 103, 116–
    17, 176, 203
  see also Communist Party of
    Great Britain
mass media 8, 46–7
Mathias, P. 4
May, T. 131, 133, 208
Mellors, C. 155, 209
meritocracy 153, 161–2, 165,
    167–8, 172–4
middle class
  evolution of 13–14
  modern structure of 30–2
  pressure groups 140–4
  voting 63–76
Middlemas, K. 133, 147, 148, 149,
    178, 209
Miles, R. 26
Miliband, R. 102, 133, 208
Miller, W. 84, 115, 207, 208
millionaires 14, 153
ministerial responsibility 177, 179
Minkin, L. 95, 108, 208, 209
Minns, R. 20
Mond, Sir A. 157
monetarism 188, 191–2
Moore, B. 48
Moore, R. 31
Morrison, H. 178

mortality rates 15, 16
Mosca, G. 176
Moxon-Browne, E. 54, 56, 207
multinational corporations 194–5,
    202
Muslims 7

Nairn, T. 6, 32, 46, 84, 208, 209
National Association for the Care
    and Resettlement of
    Offenders 139
National Economic Development
    Council 132
National Front see Fascism
nationalism 46, 48, 49–57, 75, 78,
    84–5, 114–6, 202–3
    see also Plaid Cymru, Scottish
        National Party
New Economic Order
    alternatives to 199–205
    impact 193–9
    implementation 190–2
    origins 188–90
Newton, K. 139, 208
Noble, T. 23, 206
Nonconformists 6, 8, 68
Northern Ireland
    causes of troubles 52–5
    development of troubles 55–8
    historical origins of troubles
        50–2
Norton, P. 41, 89, 98, 106, 207
Nottingham High School 174

O'Connor, J. 31
Official Unionist Party 56, 80
O'Hearn, D. 53
O'Leary, C. 50
O'Neill, T. 51, 54
Orwell, G. 35, 48, 206
overload thesis 189–90
Owen, D. 111, 112, 113
Oxbridge, 155, 158, 159, 161–5,
    168–9, 171, 173

Pahl, R. 147
Panitch, L. 147

Pareto, V. 176
Parkin, F. 46
parliament
    politics of 49, 103, 177–9
    social composition of 153–8
Parry, G. 150, 209
party identification 71–2
patricians 171, 173
Peacock, A. 10
peak associations 126–7
peasants 37, 49
Peel, Sir R. 97
Pelling, H. 7
Perkin, H. 3, 43, 206
Peters, G. 190, 210
Phizacklea, A. 26
Pinto-Duschinsky, M. 90, 106, 119
Plaid Cymru 84–5, 115–16
    see also nationalism
pluralism 145, 148–9, 175–6, 180,
    189
political culture
    definitions 34–5, 47
    of elites 175–81
    models of 35–49
    and violence 47–9
political funds 107–8, 119
political movements 124, 141–4
Pollard, S. 11, 183, 185, 206, 210
populism 40–4
post-affluent policies 39–40, 142–3
power
    of business 125–31
    competing views of 180
    in Conservative Party 87–92
    in Labour Party 92–7
    of professions 135–8
    of trade unions 131–5
    and study of elites 175ff
pressure group politics
    classified 121–5
    defined 121–2
    preference groups in 124, 138–
        44
    functional groups in 125–38
    theories of 144–9
privatisation 191–2
production sectors 31, 83–4, 143–4

professions
  earnings 17–18
  as pressure groups 124, 135–8
Protestant Unionism 50–7
public sector
  size of 10–11, 24–5
  and voting 69
public schools 13, 152, 154–60
Pulzer, P. 35, 63, 207
Putamn, R. 179
Pym, B. 209

Rasmussen, J. 74
Raynor, J. 13
Reid, I. 107
Representation of the People
  Act 62
Resler, H. 22, 28, 29, 31, 206
Retail Consortium 127
Rex, J. 31
Richardson, J. 209
riots 33, 38, 40, 42
  see also bombings, political
    culture
Rockman, B. 179
Roberts, K. 30
Robertson, D. 137
Rodgers, W. 112
Rose, R. 37, 52, 56, 85, 92, 106,
  115, 190, 206, 210
Roth, A. 158
Routh, G. 8, 17, 18, 25, 206
Rowthorn, B. 55, 207
Royal Air Force Marshals,
  recruitment of 165, 166
Royal Commission on Distribution
  of Income and Wealth 19, 206
Royal Society for the Prevention
  of Cruelty to Animals 123
Rubinstein, W. 14, 156–7
ruling-class model 176–7
ruling-elite model 176–7
Runciman, W. G. 41–2

Sampson, A. 174
Särlvik, B. 61, 65, 72, 75, 78, 84,
  207
Saunders, P. 31, 208

Schmitter, P. 146
Scotland 4–5, 8, 9, 37, 48, 74, 202
  see also nationalism
Scottish National party 84–5, 114–
  15
  see also nationalism
Second World War 183–4, 187,
  191
Seyd, P. 92, 108
Scott, J. 209
secrecy 175–80
self-made men 171, 173
self-regulation 128, 136
share ownership 20
Sharpe, L. J. 210
Shipping Federation 12
Shonfield, A. 186
Sillars, J. 115
Silver, A. 44, 69
Sloman, A. 80
Social and Liberal Democrats 87,
  111
Social Contract 190
Social Democratic Party
  electoral support 74, 78, 80, 82
  ideology 113
  leadership and power 112
  membership 114
  after 1987 General
    Election 110–11
socialisation 45–7
social mobility 14, 22–3, 29
Society for the Protection of the
  Unborn Child 139
Sports Council 139, 148
Stanworth, P. 157, 168, 209
Steed, M. 75–6, 81, 113–14, 207,
  208
Stevenson, J. 26
Stokes, D. 60, 64, 66, 67, 68, 69,
  75, 207
Strange, S. 184
strikes 42, 45, 134–5

Taylor, R. 209
Thatcher, M. 90, 100, 105, 147,
  159, 191
Thatcherism 100

Thomas, J. 155
Thompson, E. P. 48
Thompson, P. 2, 5, 13, 14, 206
Thorpe, J. 111
trade association 126, 130
trade unions
  industrial development 3–4, 11–12
  in Labour Party 92–6, 101–2, 131–3
  in pressure-group politics 131–5, 194
  origins of leaders 167–8

Trades Union Congress 11, 120, 131–4, 147
Turner, M. 142

Ulam, A. 35
unemployed 25–6, 29, 31, 40, 193
United States 10, 37, 183, 184, 193
universities, 10, 13, 22, 155, 197

Verba, S. 33, 34, 35, 36, 37, 41, 48, 208
voting
  and class 63–6
  decline of class 72–3
  and election results 76–81
  modifiers of class 66–9
  and new influences on 69–76
  theories of change 81–5

Wales 4–5, 8, 9, 68, 75, 202
  see also nationalism

Ward, H. 144
Welfare Democracy
  decline of 187–8, 191
  nature of 186–7
Welfare State 20–1, 186–7
Westergaard, J. 22, 28, 29, 31, 206
Whiteley, P. 108, 110, 117, 151, 208
Whitley, R. 168
Wiener, M. 185
Wildavsky, A. 209
Wilding, P. 137, 209
Wilks, S. 193
Williams, P. 92
Williams, S. 112
Wilson, M. 106
Wilson, S. 128
Wilson, T. 208
Winkler, J. 147
Wiseman, J. 10
women
  in elite groups 172
  in labour force 25
  in Parliament 156
  and voting 67
Wood, B. 145
Wooton, G. 125, 208
working class
  affluence in 44
  changing structure of 24–5, 30–1
  and inequality 14–24, 153–75
  as voters 63–9, 72–3, 81–5
Wright, M. 192, 210